He Will Lead Me: A Spiritual Biography of Oscar M. Knutson

He Will Lead Me: A Spiritual Biography of Oscar M. Knutson

Pentecostal Minister, Evangelist, and Gospel Publisher

ALEX M. FERGUS

WIPF & STOCK · Eugene, Oregon

HE WILL LEAD ME: A SPIRITUAL BIOGRAPHY OF OSCAR M. KNUTSON
Pentecostal Minister, Evangelist, and Gospel Publisher

Copyright © 2025 Alex M. Fergus. All rights reserved. Except for brief quotations in critical publications or reviews, no part of this book may be reproduced in any manner without prior written permission from the publisher. Write: Permissions, Wipf and Stock Publishers, 199 W. 8th Ave., Suite 3, Eugene, OR 97401.

Wipf & Stock
An Imprint of Wipf and Stock Publishers
199 W. 8th Ave., Suite 3
Eugene, OR 97401

www.wipfandstock.com

PAPERBACK ISBN: 979-8-3852-5850-5
HARDCOVER ISBN: 979-8-3852-5851-2
EBOOK ISBN: 979-8-3852-5852-9

12/02/25

Scripture quotations marked NIV taken from The Holy Bible, New International Version®, NIV®. Copyright © 1973, 1978, 1984, 2011 by Biblica, Inc. Used with permission of Zondervan. All rights reserved worldwide. www.zondervan.com.

Scripture quotations marked HCSB are taken from the Holman Christian Standard Bible®, Copyright © 1999, 2000, 2002, 2003 by Holman Bible Publishers. Used by permission. Holman Christian Standard Bible®, Holman CSB®, and HCSB® are federally registered trademarks of Holman Bible Publishers.

Scripture quotations marked RSV are taken from the Revised Standard Version of the Bible, copyright © 1946, 1952, and 1971 National Council of the Churches of Christ in the United States of America. Used by permission. All rights reserved worldwide.

Scripture quotations marked KJV are taken from The Authorized (King James) Version. Rights in the Authorized Version in the United Kingdom are vested in the Crown. Reproduced by permission of the Crown's patentee, Cambridge University Press.

To Rachel, Felicity, and Benedict

To the Knutson family

Thou dost show me the path of life;
in thy presence there is fulness of joy,
in thy right hand are pleasures for evermore.

PSALM 16:11

Contents

Acknowledgments		ix
Introduction		xi
1	"Down Came the Fire"	1
2	"There's a Drawing From on High"	18
3	"I've Found the Way"	42
4	"He Will Lead Me"	58
5	"Thou Art My All"	77
6	"Praise the Lord"	93
7	"Pilot Me Home"	121
Conclusion		143
Appendix: Photographs		163
Bibliography		191
Index		207

Acknowledgments

This book presents a spiritual biography of my great-grandfather, Oscar M. Knutson, for the purpose of telling his story as a contribution to Pentecostal church history in the Pacific Northwest and beyond, and to offer reflection on spiritual biography as a literary genre within the field of Christian theology. The book is a slight revision of my graduate thesis, written in 2024.

This book was not an individual effort. I have received tremendous help with it, and I want to recognize those who have contributed to it. For any errors which have unknowingly made their way into this spiritual biography, I take responsibility. I have only gratitude to offer to those who have helped make this book what it is.

First, many thanks to the Theology and History Departments of Whitworth University, especially to Professor Anthony E. Clark, who served as my thesis advisor, and to Professor Matthew T. Bell, who offered his expertise in the field of historical theology as external reader. Thanks also to Whitworth University for helping cover the cost of publishing expenses, and to the university Archives in particular for accessioning, preserving, and making accessible for research the Oscar M. Knutson archival collection.

Second, thank you to many people in various archives, libraries, and historical societies, who have assisted in my research process, providing access to primary (and secondary) sources that were absolutely vital to the writing of Oscar Knutson's story. Thank you especially to the Flower Pentecostal Heritage Center, the official archives and research center of the Assemblies of God denomination, and its amazing archival staff—especially Reference Archivist Glenn Gohr. Thank you also to Barry I. George, volunteer at the Okanogan County Historical Society.

Acknowledgments

Third, thank you to the grandchildren of Oscar Knutson, specifically the children of Oscar's son Lloyd, whose familial support for this project has been so helpful. This book would not be possible without them. Thanks also to all my friends and fellow parishioners who have been so supportive of this book.

Fourth, thank you to Matt Wimer and the editing and typesetting team at Wipf and Stock. I am very grateful for all of your support in making publication possible.

Fifth, words cannot express my gratitude to my wife Rachel. She, like Oscar Knutson's beloved Marie, is an amazing partner in the gospel. Here I also recognize my children, who are a great joy and blessing from the Lord.

Although they died before I was born, I must acknowledge the subject of this spiritual biography, Oscar Knutson, and his wife, Marie. I am deeply grateful for, and inspired by, their faithful ministry work and their robust example of trust in Jesus Christ. I suspect that as my great-grandparents, they also prayed for me years before I came into the world. I also believe that even now, in heaven, they continue to pray for me and my family.

Finally, all glory, laud, honor, and thanksgiving to our great God—Father, Son, and Holy Spirit—now and forever. Praise God from whom all blessings flow! His loving care is more than we can ask or imagine. To him, all glory is due! More than anything else, may this spiritual biography be an offering of worship to our triune God.

Introduction

SPIRITUAL BIOGRAPHY IS SOMETHING of an elusive genre.[1] While numerous formal monographs address the genre of biography, the more particular genre of spiritual biography has been largely untouched on the monograph level.[2] The genre of spiritual biography occasionally enters academic conversations about other forms of Christian literature, such as *hagiography* ("lives of saints"), *narrative theology*, and *conversion literature*, but remains generally undefined and undeveloped in its own right.

The lack of academic engagement with the genre of spiritual biography in no way lessens the significance of this genre to the Christian tradition. Christianity has almost always been at the forefront of efforts to collect, preserve, and provide access to history. Christianity has also been highly involved in the work of telling and engaging with people's stories, both in formal capacities and in informal, more organic contexts. History and biography, it seems, are just as important to the Christian faith as theology, spirituality, and even ecclesiology. This is because within the Christian tradition, history and biography are vehicles of theology, spirituality, and ecclesiology. Exploring and interpreting human experience through the past—the act of doing history—is not limited to geography, ethnicity, culture, economics, technology, politics, and war. Engaging with the lives of people—the act of doing biography—is not limited to a person's place of origin, race, gender, major life experiences, work history,

---

1. Although the genre of spiritual biography may be understood and observed in various religious traditions, this book is exclusively concerned with spiritual biography within the Christian religious tradition.

2. Thomas Heffernan's *Sacred Biography: Saints and Their Biographers in the Middle Ages* is something of a possible exception to this statement. However, Heffernan does not primarily focus on the genre of spiritual biography. Rather, Heffernan focuses on the related yet distinct medieval literature concerning saints, often called *hagiography*, which he dubs *sacred biography*.

Introduction

hardships, organizational affiliations, and family relationships. History and biography necessarily also include spirituality, theology, religion, and faith. As a unique genre of literature, spiritual biography is significant because it brings together history, theology, and spirituality.

Spiritual biography is, in one sense, the intersection of history, theology, and spirituality. In another sense, for author, subject, and (hopefully) reader, it is primarily a spiritual or even liturgical venture—an act of pursuing greater relationship with God—by way of doing a particular mode of theology, that of prayerful historical exploration and engagement, contextualized by biblical interpretation, doctrinal understanding, and ecclesial participation.

A working definition of spiritual biography should be attempted here: *Spiritual biography, within the Christian context, is a form of literature that articulates the lives of faithful followers of Jesus by way of extensive historical research and robust theological analysis, for the purpose of deep spiritual engagement.* Each detail of this working definition matters. Beyond the biographical aspect, three elements are particularly significant—history, theology, and spirituality.

Spiritual biography is deeply historical, in that it is rooted in extensive empirical research and engagement with available primary source materials and also contextualizes findings within a larger framework. In this way, spiritual biography has a grounding effect—its historical element offers something real, concrete, and substantive.

Spiritual biography is also deeply theological, in that it is rooted in Scripture and in historic Christian doctrine and seeks to faithfully place these in meaningful conversation with personal convictions and experiences. In this way, spiritual biography seeks to uphold the dignity of both received tradition and personal experience, with Truth as its trajectory and target.

Finally, spiritual biography is deeply spiritual, in that its definite and ultimate purpose is to draw people into deeper life and relationship with the triune God—Father, Son, and Holy Spirit. In this way, spiritual biography is intended to support and strengthen true faith and facilitate true worship of the living God.

The Christian tradition embraces and engages in the genre of spiritual biography because it recognizes its inherent value to the Christian faith. First,

Introduction

spiritual biography tells the story of a person's relationship to God and how that relationship was worked out concretely. This is significant, because as with nearly everything in life—take swimming, reading, or cooking, for example—relationship with God must be learned from faithful examples set by other people. We must learn to be people of faith—how to pray, how to worship as a community, how to trust God in good times and in hard times, and how to care for one another and our world. Spiritual biography provides a roadmap for fellow brothers and sisters in Christ, and even for people exploring the possibility of embracing the Christian faith. Spiritual biography does not necessitate agreement with every conviction or decision of the person in question, nor does it require exact imitation of their actions, behaviors, and judgments. But as the story of how a person related to God over the course of their life, it offers others an opportunity to reflect and determine how they themselves might relate to God over the course of their own lives.

Second, spiritual biography is, in its own way, a work of church history. It is a record of God's people and where and how they have been active in the world. Or, perhaps more accurately, it is a record of the activity of the triune God in and through his people. Church history has always been important for documenting past experiences—both good and bad—and for making sense of where the church is in the present time, and where it ought to be going. The holy Scriptures are replete with affirmations of the importance of history and especially the heritage of faith. Even in the present, the past is never fully gone. The experiences and impact of the past carry forward into the present, which means that historical exploration is vital in order for the church to make sense of its own being, its missional purpose, and the needs of the world to which it has been sent. No more acutely is church history observed than in the tangible experiences of real Christians living and ministering in the world.

Third, spiritual biography provides ample opportunity for extensive theological reflection. Admittedly, for lay folk, theology is sometimes disregarded as a stodgy, academic endeavor devoid of God. While this dismissal is at times understandable, it is nonetheless tragic. Theology exists to lead people closer to God, not further away from him. Properly understood, theology is the ongoing work of coming to know and understand the triune God whom we serve and to whom we belong. Theology is thus paramount for the life and worship of the church. Furthermore, spiritual biography is crucial to the act of doing theology because God is most known in tangible experiences of him. This includes personal and ongoing encounters with God which transform the lives of real people experiencing his presence in their lives. It also includes redeemed people going out into the world to participate in God's redemptive mission to save it, and God working in and through them to impact and transform others.

Fourth, related to the previous points, spiritual biography is itself an act of worship of the triune God. Setting forth an example of faith that encourages others to "go and do likewise,"[3] offering a record of God's redeeming and life-giving activities in and through the church, and inviting robust theological reflection on who God is and what he is up to in the world are all intended to lead people to a deeper relationship with God and, hence, greater worship of him. To draw on the Westminster Shorter Catechism, the "chief end of man" is to "glorify God, and to enjoy him forever."[4] Indeed, all created things exist to serve God and give him glory. All of life is liturgical—a great dance between call and response. God calls, and his creatures respond to his voice. Spiritual biography is, then, something that God uses to call us to himself. It is a means of repentance, faith, and worship, both personally and within the life of the church, the assembly of the faithful.

The theological value of history and biography is worth further exploration, as it has bearing on spiritual biography. History and biography are important for all people, but especially for Christians. The Christian faith is rooted in history, and more particularly, in biography—the life, experience, and impact—of one specific person in history: Jesus of Nazareth. Everything about the Christian faith flows into and out from the Person and work of Jesus. Jesus is himself the perfect image of the invisible God—the True Human Being. He redeems us from sin and shows us what it means to be truly human, like him.

Jesus' redemption also brings us into the family of God. His exhortation is for us to participate in God's family such that we bear a family resemblance. Each has his or her own specific stories and experiences which are bound up together in God's greater story, the narrative of all that is. Although every person is unique—fearfully and wonderfully made by God—God's ultimate desire for all is life and flourishing in relationship with him for all eternity. God desires for people to not only do life with

---

3. Luke 10:37, NIV.

4. Pelikan and Hotchkiss, "Westminster Shorter Catechism," 652.

him, but also to live and flourish together as a family. This loving familial desire flows out of the relationality and community that everlastingly exists within the Godhead between the Father, the Son, and the Holy Spirit—the Persons of the Holy Trinity. Through union with Christ, human beings find themselves wrapped up into the divine life of the triune God and, as such, intimately related to other members of God's family. As God Incarnate, Jesus is himself the point at which heaven and earth come together. By virtue of our union with Christ, we as Christians are also united to the rest of God's family. Jesus connects us to God and to one another, and as God's family, we relate to one another across time and space. As fellow humans and fellow Christians, our stories and experiences are inherently meaningful to one another. They knit us together into the family that we are and move us deeper into relationship with God.

Jesus reveals who we are meant to be as human beings, serving as a mirror for us, a picture of what we ought to be. We are called to imitate Jesus—to be like him. The apostle Paul exhorted the church at Corinth: "Imitate me, as I also imitate Christ."[5] Paul's words are true for all of God's family, especially those saints of old, who have paved the way of faith before us. The saints—our fellow family members in God's household—are icons of Jesus. They show us how to follow God. They point to Jesus by imaging him. As icons of Jesus, the saints share in Jesus and in turn become for us a picture of our own destiny in Christ.

In the sermon to the Hebrews, the author makes this very point. He calls his congregation to remember the saints of old who trusted in God and paved the way of faith. The author calls his congregation to imitate these faithful people from the past, framing his exhortation with the language of an athletic contest: a great race to run. Not only do the saints of old offer an example of how to run with endurance and reach the end, the author also tells his congregation that these historic people actually surround them and urge them forward toward Jesus, who is waiting at the finish. "Therefore, since we also have such a large cloud of witnesses surrounding us, let us lay aside every weight and sin that so easily ensnares us. Let us run with endurance the race that lies before us, keeping on our eyes on Jesus, the source and perfecter of our faith."[6] This point about the saints invisibly surrounding the congregation is significant. The church has long held that when the faithful gather together for worship, the liturgy becomes a point

---

5. 1 Cor 11:1, HCSB.
6. Heb 12:1–2, HCSB.

Introduction

of intersection between heaven and earth, in which time does not exist and worshipers in heaven and on earth come together to offer praises to God for a moment in eternity. The author of Hebrews corroborates this concept later in his sermon: "For you have not come to what may be touched . . . . But you have come to Mount Zion and to the city of the living God, the heavenly Jerusalem, and to innumerable angels in festal gathering, and to the assembly of the first-born who are enrolled in heaven, and to a judge who is God of all, and to the spirits of just men made perfect, and to Jesus, the mediator of a new covenant, and to the sprinkled blood that speaks more graciously than the blood of Abel."[7]

The sermon to the Hebrews affirms that Christians engage with Jesus and with God's family throughout space and time, and thus Christians must engage with history. This is the basis for spiritual biography—the intersection of history, theology, and spirituality. As followers of Jesus, Christianity compels us to acknowledge and cherish history and to view it as an opportunity to better understand and relate to God by becoming more aware of God's Self-revelatory actions within and across space and time. Additionally, Christianity invites us to view history, and specifically biography, as an opportunity to connect with the lives and experiences of real men and women—our brothers and sisters in Christ—and imitate them in faith insofar as they imitated Jesus. As we participate in the communion of the saints, we are invited to engage in the stories of these historic people of faith. Engaging with their stories allows us to engage with and make sense of our own. Spiritual biography allows us to walk with the saints of old, learn from their mistakes, and follow their faithful example. Through spiritual biography we do not simply learn more historical information. Instead, we find ourselves drawn deeper into relationship with God and changed through the same grace of God which the saints experienced themselves. By coming to know the saints, we come to know ourselves. In turn, we come to know God.

Drawing on an understanding of the value of spiritual biography for Christian faith and life, this book explores and examines the life and ministry of Oscar Marius Knutson (1900–1993), a Pentecostal pastor, evangelist, and gospel publisher who ministered in various communities in Washington, Montana, South Dakota, Michigan, Iowa, Illinois, and other states, mostly

---

7. Heb 12:18, 24, RSV.

Introduction

between the 1920s and 1950s. This spiritual biography of Oscar Knutson is based on extensive research and analysis of historical materials, including Knutson's writings and songbooks, newspaper clippings, correspondence, scrapbooks, and other available sources. It also incorporates significant scriptural engagement and theological reflection. Knutson's life-story is contextualized both historically and theologically within the broader Pentecostal movement, making this spiritual biography also a story of Pentecostal church history, mostly between the Pacific Northwest and the Midwest. Music was central to Knutson's ministry work—in evangelistic and pastoral ministry, as well as in publishing Pentecostal songbooks—and as such, each chapter title features the name of a song written and composed by Knutson himself, along with an epigraph containing excerpts of song lyrics. In addition to historical and theological considerations, the primary purpose of this spiritual biography is to connect others to Oscar Knutson's story, encourage them in their faith, and draw them deeper into relationship with our triune God.

On a personal level, Oscar Knutson is relevant for three reasons. First, I am a student of both history and theology, and as mentioned above, I believe theological and spiritual truths are often best grasped and conveyed through peoples' stories. Second, I was raised in the Pentecostal tradition. While I presently worship within the Anglican tradition, rather than a classical Pentecostal fellowship, I continue to be fascinated by the work of the Holy Spirit in the world, including within Pentecostalism. Third, Oscar Knutson was my maternal great-grandfather. I am compelled and inspired by his spiritual legacy within my own family, and I consider my own ministry work to follow after his.

As Jesus has brought together all his followers into the family of God, I encourage those reading this spiritual biography of Oscar Knutson to discern the activity of the Lord within the life of this particular Pentecostal brother in Christ and to seek to share in the same grace of God in which he walked. Marked by deep faith in Jesus, daily attunement to the Holy Spirit, and an incarnated vision of ministry on the local level, the life and work of Reverend Knutson provide an important roadmap for Christians of any tradition. His life of faith exemplifies concretely what it means to "work out your salvation with fear and trembling," to trust wholly in God's loving care, and to serve the Lord with one's entire life.[8]

---

8. Phil 2:12, NIV.

1

"Down Came the Fire"

Today the Lord is giving the Comforter to men,
Enduing them with power from on high;
The fountain still is open, you'll get your portion yet:
Just call on Him, for He'll not pass you by.

Then down came the fire, down came the fire,
Down came the fire from on high,
O hallelujah! For the Holy Ghost will enter your life and take control;
Down came the fire, praise the Lord!
—O. M. Knutson, "Down Came the Fire"

Oscar Marius Knutson[1] (Oskar Marelius Knudsen) was born May 16, 1900, in Sortland, a town located in the northern part of Norway within the Arctic Circle. The second of what would become ten children, Oscar Knutson was the son of Andrew and Elvina Knutson, a Lutheran couple

---

1. *Knutson* is pronounced "kuh-noot-sun."

of humble means with Norwegian heritage stretching back to at least the 1760s.[2]

Andrew Knutson—twenty-seven years old at Oscar's birth—was a fisherman, having inherited this occupation from his father and other forebears. Andrew was also the neighborhood shoemaker and tanner, was considered a man "ahead of the times," and was a leader in the Sortland community.[3] A man with an active Christian faith since his youth, Andrew Knutson had a robust spiritual heritage. His parents, Knut Johannessen and Inger Knutsdat, were both active Christians with a deep spiritual life. Additionally, various church records of marriages, baptisms, and confirmations from the eighteenth and nineteenth centuries indicate church participation by the family in earlier generations.[4]

Elvina (née Kibsgaard) Knutson—twenty-four years old at Oscar's birth—was evidently the first in her family line to join the Christian faith. Converted as a teenager, Elvina's early spirituality and church attendance seem to have been largely influenced by the man who became her husband. Elvina's conversion to Christianity and subsequent marriage to an active Christian provoked great bitterness and opposition from her mother. By contrast, Elvina's father—a ship captain—was apparently unconcerned about her conversion. Instead, he was pleased that his daughter had married a man who captained his own fishing boat. Elvina's mother's disapproval of her newfound faith made for a difficult relationship that was never reconciled. Even so, Elvina remained active in her faith throughout the rest of her life, and two of her sisters followed her to become Christians themselves.[5]

When Oscar was born, Andrew and Elvina Knutson were members of the Evangelical Free Lutheran Church in Norway, that is, not the state Lutheran Church. As per their Lutheran tradition, Oscar Knutson was baptized as an infant at Sortland Evangelical Church on July 1, 1900.[6] There is little documentary evidence that Oscar talked much about his infant water

---

2. Oscar Knutson, "Knutson Family Tree, 1766–1983," 1–2, Oscar M. Knutson archival collection, box 2, folder 7.

3. Oscar Knutson, "Knutson Family Tree, 1766–1983," 1–2, Oscar M. Knutson archival collection, box 2, folder 7.

4. Oscar Knutson, "Knutson Family Tree, 1766–1983," 1–2, Oscar M. Knutson archival collection, box 2, folder 7.

5. Oscar Knutson, "Knutson Family Tree, 1766–1983," 1–2, Oscar M. Knutson archival collection, box 2, folder 7.

6. Oscar Knutson baptismal certificate, Oscar M. Knutson archival collection, box 2, folder 1.

baptism, but he did seem to hold his parents' faith—as well as their church in Norway—in high regard. Later in life, Oscar described his parents as "born again" and wrote that "their lives provided a shining example for us to follow as we grew up."[7] Recollecting his spiritual upbringing, Oscar fondly remembered that when he was three or four years old, his father would gather him and his siblings around and tell them Bible stories. These experiences "planted a love and respect for God's Word in my young heart," Oscar wrote.[8] Some undated personal notes, probably penned by Oscar's wife, indicate that Oscar had been "saved at his father's knee" in Norway at six years old.[9] In an oral history interview in 1983, Oscar said of his parents' church in Norway: "They preach salvation, you have to be born again, they pray for the sick like we do in Pentecost, and they believe in the soon-coming of the Lord and preach the soon-coming of the Lord."[10] Evidently, Knutson saw continuity between his parents' faith in Norway and that of the early Pentecostal movement in the United States of America, to which he would later belong.[11]

---

7. Oscar Knutson, "Knutson Family Tree, 1766–1983," 2, Oscar M. Knutson archival collection, box 2, folder 7; Knutson, *His Loving Care*, 7.

8. Knutson, *His Loving Care*, 7.

9. Notecard with biographical information regarding Oscar and Marie Knutson, probably written by Marie, Oscar M. Knutson archival collection, unprocessed box.

10. Oscar and Marie Knutson, oral history interview with Wayne Warner, Sept. 5, 1983, audio recording, Flower Pentecostal Heritage Center. By the "soon-coming of the Lord," Oscar Knutson is referring to an eschatological viewpoint that emphasizes the *parousia*, that is, the "Glorious Appearing" or "Second Coming" of Jesus Christ (Titus 2:13, KJV) in which he will come to "judge the living and the dead," to use creedal parlance. In this particular eschatological framework, the *parousia* is expected to happen "soon." It could happen any time as far as people are concerned, and thus people must with urgency attend to their spiritual condition and relationship with God so as to be prepared for this event. Christians, who presumably are always preparing themselves for this event—sometimes referred to as "Judgment Day," or as "the Day of the Lord" in the holy Scriptures—also look forward to Jesus' *parousia* with eager anticipation and hope.

11. The Norwegian Free Lutheranism of Oscar Knutson's early years and the American Pentecostalism to which he would belong for most of his life were, arguably, similar in their theological convictions and spiritual impulses. Norway's Free Lutheran tradition was heavily influenced by German Pietism as well as revivalist folk preachers like Hans Nielsen Hauge (1771–1824), who emphasized true conversion, personal salvation, active faith, holy living, spiritual vigilance, and evangelism. Lee, *New Springtime*, 11–22.

In 1907, economic conditions in Norway were poor, and Andrew and Elvina Knutson determined to leave their little Sortland community and move their family to the United States. Andrew Knutson immigrated to America first, intending to get a job and establish a home for the family before they joined him. Although America had been described as a "land of abundance and great opportunities," Andrew arrived shortly before the Panic of 1907, a devastating financial crisis that resulted in widespread bankruptcy and suspension of operations for banks and businesses throughout the United States.[12] Andrew, who had initially settled in Wisconsin, found himself unable to cash paychecks. As such, he was unable to establish a robust home for his family in a timely fashion and was also unable to send money back to Norway to support their emigration. The family had to wait and, in that waiting, wait upon the Lord. It was a difficult time. In spring 1908, Andrew relocated to the booming Great Falls, Montana, and began working as a carpenter. By mid-1909, he built a cabin for the family and saved enough money that, together with the sale of the house in Norway, would cover the cost of emigration for them.[13]

On Oscar's ninth birthday, May 16, 1909, Elvina Knutson and her five children boarded a ship bound for the United States.[14] After a stormy voyage, they arrived at Ellis Island in New York in early June, only to have American immigration officials promptly separate Oscar's younger sister Ragna from the rest of the family for medical examination, believing she was deaf and mute.[15] Meanwhile, Oscar, his siblings, and his mother spent ten days in an immigration detention cell with shoddy rations and little communication. When Oscar's father, Andrew, contacted the immigration department to inquire about his family, he received no response. Finally, after ten days, Oscar's sister Ragna was discharged, and the Knutson family

---

12. Oscar Knutson, "Knutson Family Tree, 1766–1983," 4, Oscar M. Knutson archival collection, box 2, folder 7; Knight, *Panic, Prosperity, and Progress*, 113.

13. Oscar Knutson, "Knutson Family Tree, 1766–1983," 3–5, Oscar M. Knutson archival collection, box 2, folder 7.

14. Elvina Knutson gave birth to five more children after settling in the United States. Handwritten notes featuring Knutson family genealogical information, courtesy of Bernice M. Fergus.

15. Oscar Knutson, "Knutson Family Tree, 1766–1983," 5–6, Oscar M. Knutson archival collection, box 2, folder 7; "Record of Aliens Held for Special Inquiry," New York, US, featuring Knutson family (spelled Knudsen), June 2, 1909, Ancestry.com.

was released from detention. With thankfulness, they reunited with Andrew in Montana not long afterward.[16]

The new home in Great Falls, Montana, was temporary, as Andrew Knutson had acquired from the US government 160 acres of free land some twenty to forty miles from the town.[17] The intention was to move onto the land and begin homesteading soon after the family reunited, but the move was halted when Oscar fell deathly ill with "malaria fever." It was a brutal sickness, so much so that on the tenth day after the illness struck, a local doctor told Andrew that Oscar would not live through the night. Oscar overheard the conversation. Although he could not speak, he said in his mind, "I *will not* die."[18] Although it took about a year, Oscar eventually recovered. The Knutson family then moved and began homesteading in summer 1910.[19]

The Knutson family's homesteading years in Montana were quite a pioneering experience. They lived miles away from the nearest town, and the only form of transportation other than walking was horseback. Admittedly, this lack of proximity to town also meant a lack of proximity to a local church community. For several years the Knutson family did not attend church, although they did make regular worship and prayer at home a priority. The family loved to sing hymns together, and their home was often filled with sounds of worship.[20]

Around 1915 or 1916, about two miles from the Knutson homestead, the town of Fairfield, Montana, was established as a station for the Milwaukee Railroad. With some of their neighbors from the new town, the Knutson family helped establish Fairfield's first church. Although a humble

---

16. Oscar Knutson, "Knutson Family Tree, 1766–1983," 5–6, Oscar M. Knutson archival collection, box 2, folder 7.

17. The discrepancy in the distance between Great Falls and the Knutsons' land comes from Oscar Knutson's own handwritten reflections. Handwritten reflections on Oscar Knutson's early life, Oscar M. Knutson archival collection, box 2, folder 12.

18. Handwritten reflections on Oscar Knutson's early life, Oscar M. Knutson archival collection, box 2, folder 12.

19. Oscar Knutson, "Knutson Family Tree, 1766–1983," 7, Oscar M. Knutson archival collection, box 2, folder 7.

20. Reflections on Oscar Knutson's early life, Oscar M. Knutson archival collection, box 2, folders 8–12; Oscar Knutson, "Knutson Family Tree, 1766–1983," 11–12, 13–14, Oscar M. Knutson archival collection, box 2, folder 7.

little fellowship, Fairfield Community Church was nonetheless an important part of the spiritual life of the Knutson family.²¹

Homesteading in Montana was a trying time. Concerning these experiences, Oscar Knutson later wrote: "Faith, and confidence in God, and a willingness to stand the tests brought our parents through."²² Despite the challenges of Montana pioneering life in the 1910s, these years were not insignificant to Oscar's life and spiritual journey. It was during this time that he learned to speak English, received a more or less "formal" education up to the sixth-grade level, and learned what it meant to work hard, think creatively, and persist in the faith through hard times.²³

In fall 1919, Andrew and Elvina Knutson decided to move their family to Seattle. Andrew had been corresponding with Rev. Abraham Vereide, pastor of the First Norwegian Methodist Church of Seattle, and the move seemed promising.²⁴ Among other things, they had plans for Oscar to attend college the following year.²⁵ In the snowy Montana winter, the Knutson family boarded a train for their new home. "What a sight met our eyes

---

21. Oscar Knutson, "Knutson Family Tree, 1766–1983," 13–14, Oscar M. Knutson archival collection, box 2, folder 7.

22. Oscar Knutson, "Knutson Family Tree, 1766–1983," 14, Oscar M. Knutson archival collection, box 2, folder 7.

23. Reflections on Oscar Knutson's early life, Oscar M. Knutson archival collection, box 2, folders 9, 12.

24. *Daily Herald*, "Church News" (May 16, 1917), 9. In subsequent decades, Rev. Abraham Vereide, himself a Norwegian immigrant, became a significant Christian leader and conservative social activist in the Pacific Northwest and beyond. In 1918, a year prior to the arrival of the Knutson family in Seattle, Vereide established a community organization for vocational training of "unwed mothers, unskilled men, and homeless children" on Puget Sound's Vashon Island (near Seattle). Soden, *Outsiders in a Promised Land*, 142. In 1923, Vereide was involved in the establishment of Seattle's first chapter of Goodwill Industries, and served as its superintendent for several years before resigning in 1931 to take on a greater leadership role of Goodwill Industries on the national level. During the 1930s and 1940s, among other activities, Vereide organized a series of prayer breakfast groups among businessmen and civic leaders in the Pacific Northwest, designed to unite said leaders in prayer for the proliferation of conservative community concerns—especially, resistance to socialism—in both the business and civic sectors. Vereide eventually brought this vision to the nation's capital, and in the 1950s established the annual event that later became known as the National Prayer Breakfast. Soden, *Outsiders in a Promised Land*, 142–45.

25. Handwritten reflections on Oscar Knutson's early life, Oscar M. Knutson archival collection, box 2, folder 12.

when we arrived in Seattle," Oscar wrote in later reminiscences. "Everything was green, and the weather was mild."[26]

Although the family had formally moved to Seattle, they kept their Montana farm. Oscar Knutson returned to the farm in spring 1920 and stayed through harvest that summer. In fall 1920, he rejoined his family in Seattle, and notably, at First Norwegian Methodist Church. Oscar was disappointed, however, to find that the Methodist church's standards had "fallen" to endorse social dancing. "This was more than I could take, so I left the church," Oscar wrote.[27]

Oscar Knutson subsequently "went from church to church," searching for a new "church home."[28] Sometime in late 1920, while walking down Third Avenue in Seattle one evening, he happened upon a large new concrete building with a sign that read "Bethel Temple." Oscar noted that a church service was about to begin, and, wondering what type of church it could be, decided to go in and find out. It was a life-changing experience. Although significantly different from the form of worship that he was familiar with back in Norway—or even in Montana—Bethel Temple made quite an impression on him. At first, Knutson thought he may have found something "wild," but his perception quickly changed.[29]

Inside the building was a large sanctuary space, and it was soon completely packed with people. Oscar Knutson noted that nearly half of them were young people—something that was unusual based on his previous church experiences. The choir loft was especially full of young people, all of whom were kneeling in prayer when Knutson arrived. Knutson also observed that as others arrived, "there was no talking or gossiping."[30] Instead, people repeatedly whispered expressions like "praise you Jesus," or "thank you Lord." The service commenced promptly at eight p.m. with several "old Gospel songs," which were familiar to Knutson.[31]

---

26. Oscar Knutson, "Knutson Family Tree, 1766–1983," 14–15, Oscar M. Knutson archival collection, box 2, folder 7.

27. Knutson, *His Loving Care*, 9.

28. Knutson, *His Loving Care*, 15.

29. Oscar and Marie Knutson, oral history interview with Wayne Warner, Sept. 5, 1983, audio recording, Flower Pentecostal Heritage Center.

30. Typewritten reflections, "How I Came into the Pentecost," Oscar M. Knutson archival collection, box 2, folder 13.

31. Typewritten reflections, "How I Came into the Pentecost," Oscar M. Knutson archival collection, box 2, folder 13. The Christian musical tradition includes many wonderful musical forms. *Gospel songs*, which could also be called *testimony-songs*, are

For Oscar Knutson, a striking moment in the service occurred when everyone got down on their knees and began praying out loud, all at the same time. Listening intently to those around him praying, Knutson was "convinced that these people were well acquainted with the One they prayed to—the Lord."[32] After the service concluded, Oscar went home that night and prayed about the experience:

> I told the Lord that if this which I had just seen and heard was from Him, then, I wanted it. Almost immediately a wonderful peace and blessing came over me such as I had never before experienced. All my fear melted away, and I was flooded with an assurance that what I had seen and heard indeed was truly of God.[33]

Bethel Temple, where Oscar Knutson was introduced to Pentecostalism, was none other than Seattle's first Pentecostal church. Originally known as the Pine Street Mission, it had in 1914 come under the pastoral leadership of William H. Offiler—an Englishman who had come to the United States some fifteen years earlier and who had been serving as a Pentecostal pastor in Spokane, Washington, from 1908 until his call to Seattle.[34] Although not affiliated with a broader network or denomination, the Pine Street congregation flourished under Reverend Offiler's leadership as an independent Pentecostal church. Between 1914 and 1922, it changed its

---

a staple of the Holiness and Pentecostal musical tradition. Gospel songs are generally evangelistic in nature, testifying to God's grace in action within people's lives and exhorting others to repentance or deeper faith. As such, gospel songs are often addressed to people, rather than God himself, and tend to be more enthusiastic and cheerful in timbre. *Hymns*, by comparison, are generally prayers set to music. As sung prayers, hymns are typically addressed to God (I say "typically," because within traditional Christian circles—especially Roman Catholicism and Eastern Orthodoxy—there are hymns which address the Blessed Virgin Mary and other saints, imploring their intercessions) and tend to be more reverential in timbre. Kerr, *Music in Evangelism*, 66–67.

32. Oscar and Marie Knutson, oral history interview with Wayne Warner, Sept. 5, 1983, audio recording, Flower Pentecostal Heritage Center; Knutson, *His Loving Care*, 10.

33. Knutson, *His Loving Care*, 11.

34. Reed, "From Bethel Temple, Seattle to Bethel Church, Indonesia," 93–94, 96. Every religious organization has its own parlance. In the Pentecostal context—and in several Christian denominational contexts, both historically and presently—the term *mission* refers to a small church or fellowship that is often called a *church plant* in contemporary parlance. The significance of the term *mission*, however, is that it connects the identity of the church plant directly to the missiological activity of the church at large, that is, the church's participation in the redemptive mission of the Lord Jesus by carrying the gospel throughout the world.

name a couple of times and moved locations to accommodate its growth. By 1922, it had established itself as "Bethel Temple" at the Third Avenue location in Seattle, which Knutson initially encountered in late 1920.[35] Relocating again in the 1940s, Bethel Temple eventually became the largest independent Pentecostal church in the Pacific Northwest. It was active until 2002, when it formally closed after a merger with City Church, an up-and-coming mega-church in nearby Kirkland, Washington.[36]

After Oscar Knutson's initial experience at the young people's Saturday evening service, he returned to Bethel Temple for Sunday worship the following morning and for subsequent regular worship services. As he began to make a home for himself in the Pentecostal context, Knutson began to seek the "baptism of the Holy Spirit"—the central doctrine and experience of the Pentecostal movement.

While the baptism of the Holy Spirit stood at the center of the early Pentecostal theological tradition, it was generally understood as distinct from water baptism. In the New Testament, the sacrament of (water) baptism finds its primary scriptural root within the Great Commission of Jesus, found at the end of the Gospel According to Matthew. Jesus commands his followers to "go, therefore, and make disciples of all nations, baptizing them in the Name of the Father and of the Son and of the Holy Spirit, teaching them to observe everything I have commanded you."[37] Water baptism is thus traditionally understood to be the sacramental rite of initiation into the church, the body of Christ.[38] In baptism, one is united to Christ—clothed with Christ. In baptism, one's sins are forgiven—washed

---

35. Pentecostal church names often had scriptural inspiration and carried important theological meaning. The term *temple*, found in the name of Bethel Temple and other Pentecostal churches with similar names, draws on biblical imagery of the temple in Jerusalem. The implication of *temple* in the name of a Pentecostal church is that that fellowship was a place where God was and is present and where people could come to meet with him. *Bethel*, meanwhile, means "house of God" and comes from the story of Jacob from the book of Genesis, who in a dream saw a glorious "ladder"—probably a ziggurat—bridging heaven and earth and then received God's covenant promise. "'How awesome is this place!' Jacob exclaimed when he awoke. 'This is none other than the house of God; this is the gate of heaven.' Jacob then named the place *Bethel*" (Gen 28:10–22, NIV).

36. Reed, "From Bethel Temple, Seattle to Bethel Church, Indonesia," 93–94, 96.

37. Matt 28:19–20, HCSB.

38. Here I use a broadly traditional understanding of the term *sacrament*—a physical material and/or rite through which God's grace is manifestly bestowed upon a person.

away—and one is identified with Christ through participation in his death, burial, and resurrection.[39]

Scripturally, there is just one baptism. The apostle Paul writes: "There is one body and one Spirit, just as you were called to one hope when you were called; one Lord, one faith, *one baptism*; one God and Father of all."[40] If there is just "one baptism"—and that is the sacrament of (water) baptism—it begs the question, what is the baptism of the Holy Spirit?

In all four Gospel accounts in the New Testament, John the Baptist describes Jesus as the One who "baptizes with the Holy Spirit." Matthew and Luke specifically add, "and with fire."[41] In the Acts of the Apostles, Jesus himself instructs his disciples to "wait for the promise of the Father," for they would "be baptized with the Holy Spirit not many days from now."[42] This statement from Jesus anticipates the great outpouring of the Holy Spirit at Pentecost, recorded in Acts 2, in which the presence of the Holy Spirit upon Jesus' disciples in the upper room in Jerusalem was marked by "tongues of fire."[43]

Some traditional Christian interpretations have understood the baptism of the Holy Spirit to be connected to water baptism and thus hold to the doctrine of baptismal regeneration—the idea that God uses the sacrament of (water) baptism to convey his saving grace. Pentecostal, charismatic, and other revivalist traditions, however, tend to understand water baptism not as a sacrament but as an *ordinance*—a rite or ceremony ordained or commanded by God to symbolize his saving work, but not carrying any salvific implications itself.[44] This theology of water baptism as an ordinance means that Pentecostals and the like tend to understand water baptism and the baptism of the Holy Spirit as distinct, although sometimes related, experiences.[45] In making this distinction between water baptism and the baptism of the Holy Spirit—also referred to as baptism *in* the Holy Spirit or baptism *with* the Holy Spirit—Pentecostals and related traditions do not intend to

---

39. Rom 6:5; Gal 3:27; Rom 6:3–11; Col 2:12–13; Acts 2:38; 1 Pet 3:21.
40. Eph 4:4–5, NIV. Emphasis mine.
41. Matt 3:11; Mark 1:8; Luke 3:16; John 1:33.
42. Acts 1:4, KJV; Acts 1:5, HCSB.
43. Acts 2:3–4, NIV.
44. J. Rodman Williams, "Baptism in the Holy Spirit," in Burgess and van der Maas, *New International Dictionary*, 360–61.
45. J. Rodman Williams, "Baptism in the Holy Spirit," in Burgess and van der Maas, *New International Dictionary*, 360–61.

contradict the apostle Paul's statement that there is "one baptism." As noted above, these are seen as two distinct experiences. This theological position is often scripturally defended by pointing to the experience of the centurion Cornelius in Acts 10, upon whom the Holy Spirit "fell" before he had been baptized in water. The apostle Peter, witnessing the event, declared, "Can anyone withhold water and prevent these people from being baptized, who have received the Holy Spirit just as we have?"[46]

Contextually, Cornelius's experience had continuity with the great outpouring of the Holy Spirit on the 120 disciples of Jesus in the upper room in Jerusalem at Pentecost, as recorded in Acts 2. Cornelius's experience was, in some sense, a continuation of what had happened in Jerusalem at Pentecost. In the first decade of the twentieth century, in the early years of the Pentecostal movement—and even at various moments of revival or spiritual awakening in decades or centuries prior to it—many people had extraordinary spiritual experiences which they sought to make sense of.[47] Often, they came to understand these experiences as, likewise, having continuity with Acts 2. The spiritual experiences of these early Pentecostals—and those involved in even earlier revivalist traditions—often included profound physical manifestations that were out of the ordinary for typical Christian experience. However, they generally brought about deep inner renewal. Particularly when these spiritual experiences included "speaking in tongues," they were identified as the baptism of the Holy Spirit—especially as the initial evidence of this experience.[48] After all, in the Acts of the Apostles, speaking in tongues was the tangible sign that the Holy Spirit had fallen upon Jesus' followers. Why would it be any different for Christians in the twentieth century?

The early history of the Pentecostal movement was marked by theological debates seeking to sort out the nature and experience of baptism in the Holy Spirit, "tongues," and how it all related to the gospel. As Pentecostalism was largely rooted in the Wesleyan-Holiness tradition of the nineteenth century, its theological articulations of the baptism of the Holy Spirit were contextualized within preexisting conversations about the relationship between that tradition's theological concepts of *justification*

---

46. Acts 10:47, HCSB.
47. Jacobsen, *Thinking in the Spirit*, 1–3.
48. Roger J. Stronstad, "Initial Evidence," in Stewart, *Handbook of Pentecostal Christianity*, 125–27.

and *sanctification*.[49] Largely disconnected from a traditional, sacramental understanding of salvation, classical Holiness preachers generally understood justification as *conversion*, a distinct, one-time, salvific work of God in a person's life, in which God granted forgiveness—that is, pardon from guilt—to those who confessed their sins and placed their trust in him. Theologically, it was understood that at a person's conversion—when a person was justified—one was made fit for heaven and would go there upon death.[50]

If forgiveness was central to justification for the nineteenth-century Holiness tradition, purification was central to its theology of sanctification. Likewise disconnected from a traditional sacramental theology, the Holiness tradition's understanding of sanctification was that of another mighty act of God, although this time in the form of cleansing from sin—especially one's "sin nature" or impulse or disposition toward sinning. Within the Holiness tradition, however, there was some dispute about whether sanctification (a) occurred immediately and totally at the time of justification by virtue of one's union with Christ; (b) occurred as a distinct event sometime after one's justification, as a second great, one-time work of God; or (c) was a process of growth in holiness over the course of a faithful life, which may be reached at a person's death or, possibly, may be even attained sometime beforehand.[51]

The early Pentecostal experience complicated Holiness conversations of justification and sanctification by inquiring how the baptism of the Holy Spirit should be rightly understood in relation to these Holiness theological categories. Is a person baptized in the Holy Spirit at the moment of their justification, and is this event the same thing as sanctification? Is the baptism of the Holy Spirit something that follows justification, and should it be identified as a distinct, one-time event of total sanctification? Are justification and sanctification two distinct works of God in the life of the believer, and is Holy Spirit baptism a third great work of the Lord? Is the baptism of the Holy Spirit something that can be experienced before full sanctification has occurred, or must a person be completely holy (that is, sanctified)

---

49. Adam Stewart, "Holiness Movement," in Stewart, *Handbook of Pentecostal Christianity*, 117, 119–21.

50. Jacobsen, *Thinking in the Spirit*, 69.

51. Adam Stewart, "Holiness Movement," in Stewart, *Handbook of Pentecostal Christianity*, 117–21.

before receiving Holy Spirit baptism?[52] Far from being playful theological jaunts, these questions had serious implications for people. These were significant points that had nothing less than the nature of one's salvation and relationship with God at stake.

Oscar Knutson, like many people, had to navigate these consequential questions for himself. He also had to navigate them with close family members, and likely others as well. Reminiscing on this part of his spiritual journey, Knutson noted that he had more or less embraced the view that a person could not receive the baptism of the Holy Spirit if they were not completely holy.[53] After all, if God and sin cannot dwell together, how can the Holy Spirit dwell in a heart that is filled with sin? With this mindset, Knutson began to seek the baptism of the Holy Spirit that his Pentecostal brothers and sisters proclaimed. Weeks turned into months as Knutson attended church prayer meetings and worship services, and petitioned the Lord in prayer day after day, to no avail. Reflecting on this experience, Knutson later wrote: "when I, after tarrying for some time[,] came to the conclusion that possibly my life was not holy enough, I began to search myself, and anything that I thought could possibly displease the Lord had to go."[54] It became an exhausting endeavor of self-examination and, apparently, self-chastisement. "Finally I reached the place that I could find nothing more I thought might be displeasing to the Lord," Knutson wrote. "I was now desperately hungry and dry. All my efforts had been in vain."[55]

For about a month in early 1921, a family of Pentecostal evangelists from Canada held a series of daily services at Bethel Temple, Seattle. Rev. A. H. Argue—who had received the baptism of the Holy Spirit in Chicago in 1906 and subsequently founded Calvary Temple, Winnipeg, one of Canada's largest Pentecostal churches—led most of the evangelistic meetings. Occasionally, his children, Zelma Argue and Watson Argue Sr., preached too, although they mostly led musical worship with slide trombones. According to newspaper accounts, the revival services drew large crowds.

---

52. Adam Stewart, "Holiness Movement," in Stewart, *Handbook of Pentecostal Christianity*, 117–21.

53. Knutson, *His Loving Care*, 11.

54. Knutson, *His Loving Care*, 11.

55. Knutson, *His Loving Care*, 11.

Rev. A. H. Argue "exhorted the people to prayer and said great things are continually being wrought by prayer," especially "remarkable healings."[56]

Oscar Knutson was present for the Argue trio's evangelistic services at Bethel Temple, and he sought the baptism of the Holy Spirit during their revival meetings. The more he strained for it, however, the emptier he felt. "I was very discouraged," Knutson remembered. "I had been seeking the baptism in the Holy Spirit for quite a long while and not receiving what I desperately wanted. What was wrong with me?"[57]

On February 6, 1921, about three months after his introduction to the Pentecostal movement, Knutson attended the Sunday evening revival service at Bethel Temple. Watson Argue Sr. preached that night, and Knutson sat with the other young people in the choir loft. "I was so discouraged I hardly heard his message," Knutson recounted. In desperation, Knutson turned to God in silent prayer: "I'm through, I give up. I surrender to your will, Lord, whatever it is. I will not beg any longer, but I will serve you any way. I'm not going to try to make myself perfect. You can do with me what you want to. You make me what *You* want me to be."[58] It was, for Knutson, a pivotal moment in his spiritual journey. With this "complete surrender to the Lord," an immediate, "unspeakable peace" flooded over Knutson. He felt that "an immens[e]ly heavy load was then lifted," and received "an assurance that 'tonight' I would receive what I had so desperately wanted."[59]

At the altar call, Knutson went forward. He knelt between the platform and the first row of seats, next to a pillar that supported the roof of the building. An altar worker, an Italian man, knelt down next to him. According to Knutson:

---

56. *Seattle Star*, "Crowd Again Attends Evangelistic Service," 13; *Seattle Star*, "Canadian Evangelist Service Draws Crowds," 11.

57. Typewritten reflections, "How I Came into the Pentecost," Oscar M. Knutson archival collection, box 2, folder 13.

58. Knutson later recounted this experience in various writings. The quotation provided here is not a selection of just one of the ways that Knutson remembered this significant prayer, but rather compiles into one the three or four different ways that Knutson recorded the prayer, all of which say essentially the same thing, but with slightly different wording. This compilation is for narrative purpose but is also done to convey Knutson's theological and spiritual disposition at this significant point in his spiritual journey, as well as the way in which this prayer is cherished in his own memory. Knutson, *His Loving Care*, 11–12; typewritten reflections, "How I Came into the Pentecost," Oscar M. Knutson archival collection, box 2, folder 13.

59. Knutson, *His Loving Care*, 11–12; typewritten reflections, "How I Came into the Pentecost," Oscar M. Knutson archival collection, box 2, folder 13.

I did not beg the Lord for the baptism in the Holy Spirit, I just praised Him, and waited. I had not waited very long before suddenly, without any eff[o]rt on my part[,] I began to speak in tongues. The words were distinct and clear, but I did not understand them. This continued for ten or fifteen minutes, then it stopped, but only for a minute or so, then I began to speak again, but in a different language . . . . When this happened I noticed that the alt[a]r worker next to me began to get excited. After I had spoken for three or four minutes, I noticed a Fin[n]ish sister, who spoke broken [E]nglish, came walking toward me with her eyes closed. At the same time that my speaking stopped, she began to speak in fluent [E]nglish. She was interpreting what I had spoken in tongues. By this time the alt[a]r worker was almost h[y]sterical. After the Fin[n]ish sister had finished the interpretation, the alt[a]r worker told us that I had spoken in fluent Italian, and that the Fin[n]ish sister had interpreted what I had said correctly. You can be sure that there was quit[e] a group around rejoicing together with us. And you can be sure that I was doing my share of rejoicing.[60]

Knutson's particular recounting of his baptism in the Holy Spirit brings up some interesting theological points. First, Knutson understood his experience to be completely from God. There was no effort on his part. If anything, his own efforts were desperate and futile. Second, as Knutson spoke "in tongues," the words were "distinct and clear."[61] It was not indiscernible babbling, nor a chaotic trance of sorts. Other people around him could understand the words, and Knutson himself could consciously remember the experience. Third, the words that Knutson was speaking were not some kind of "heavenly prayer language," a spiritual phenomenon described by later Pentecostals and charismatics. Instead, Knutson was speaking in Italian, a human language. Fourth, the experience happened in the context of corporate worship, and other people were present to witness it and validate it. It was a deeply personal experience, but not a private one.

In the early years of the Pentecostal movement—shortly after the Azusa Street Revival that began in California in 1906—Christians who had

---

60. Typewritten reflections, "How I Came into the Pentecost," Oscar M. Knutson archival collection, box 2, folder 13.

61. Typewritten reflections, "How I Came into the Pentecost," Oscar M. Knutson archival collection, box 2, folder 13.

experienced "speaking in tongues" were often rejected from their existing church homes and affiliations.[62] Various ecclesial bodies, mostly within the Holiness tradition, did not know how to make sense of the Pentecostal experiences that were beginning to propagate, and they did not want to be too closely associated with them. They could be rather wild, after all. What if these experiences were not of God, but of the devil? As Pentecostals experienced resistance or criticism from their former church homes, they found it necessary to defend themselves theologically to try to retain or regain membership within their former communities of worship. For those who organized their own Pentecostal fellowships separate from other formal ecclesial bodies, such theological defenses served as attempts to gain recognition by other Christians as legitimate, orthodox, and part of the family of God. To those ends, early Pentecostals argued that the "baptism of the Holy Spirit" which they had experienced was none other than a continuation of, and participation in, the same thing that God had done at Pentecost, as recorded in the New Testament in the second chapter of the Acts of the Apostles.

In Acts 2, the 120 disciples in the upper room experienced a great outpouring of the Holy Spirit and began speaking in other languages—specifically, other *human* languages—which were understood by their fellow Jews from different lands who were gathered in Jerusalem for the festival of Pentecost.[63] Traditionally understood as a reversal of the Tower of Babel story from the Book of Genesis, these Jews who had been scattered to different lands after the exile heard the gospel proclaimed in their own languages, all for the purpose of uniting them under the Lordship of the Messiah, Jesus of Nazareth.[64] In this way, *speaking in tongues*—according to the New Testament—was essentially a gift of God that was primarily purposed for evangelism to people of other nations or who spoke other languages.[65]

Early Pentecostals thus defended themselves, explaining that their experience was nothing less than apostolic. Although within a few years, early Pentecostals began to explore the possibility that at their baptism in the Holy Spirit they were speaking in "heavenly" or "angelic" tongues, the earliest Pentecostals understood their speaking in tongues experience to be a divine

---

62. Dwight J. Wilson, "Ecclesiastical Polity," in Burgess and van der Maas, *New International Dictionary*, 596.

63. Acts 1:15; 2:1–13.

64. Gen 11:1–9.

65. McGee, "Early Pentecostal Missionaries," 32.

gift of speaking in other human languages, in continuity with Acts 2. The prevalence of this particular understanding of the Pentecostal experience is evidenced by the sheer number of global Pentecostal missions launched in the early part of the twentieth century. Pentecostals—who were also driven by the urgency of their (largely dispensational) eschatology—believed that with this divine ability to speak in other human languages, God had called and equipped them for mission to diverse peoples and nations.[66]

Although Oscar Knutson did not rush toward global evangelization—that initial wave of Pentecostal foreign missions mostly happened in years prior to his own introduction to the Pentecostal movement—he too shared in the understanding that when he had spoken "in tongues," it was in another human language. In this way, Knutson seems to have found some solidarity with the early, classical Pentecostals, despite "coming into the Pentecost" after the Pentecostal movement had already experienced expansion and development for nearly two decades.[67] Moreover, Knutson's own commitment to evangelism was not lacking. Knutson largely agreed with the eschatology and evangelistic urgency of his new-found fellows in the Pentecostal movement and was committed to serving the Lord in whatever capacity God called him.

---

66. McGee, "Early Pentecostal Missionaries," 32.

67. Every theological tradition has its own parlance. "Coming into the Pentecost" refers to Knutson's baptism in the Holy Spirit experience, in which he understood himself to have come to share in the outpouring of the Holy Spirit experienced at Pentecost.

2

"There's a Drawing From on High"

Glory, glory hallelujah,
There's a drawing from on high,
'Tis the heav'nly gravitation of our Lord.
—O. M. KNUTSON, "THERE'S A DRAWING FROM ON HIGH"

OSCAR KNUTSON'S EXPERIENCES AT Bethel Temple in Seattle, Washington, led his father, mother, and siblings to leave the Methodist church and join him in the Pentecostal tradition. At first, Oscar's involvement at Bethel Temple caused some theological discord between Oscar and a couple of his sisters who, after leaving the Methodist church themselves, had become involved with the Apostolic Faith Mission based in Portland, Oregon. Apparently, the Apostolic Faith Mission and Bethel Temple held different theological positions concerning the relationship between sanctification and the baptism of the Holy Spirit.[1]

Founded in 1908, the Apostolic Faith Mission in Portland was established by Florence Crawford, a former leader at Rev. William J. Seymour's Azusa Street Mission in Los Angeles, California. Crawford had left the Azusa Street Mission due to personal and theological disagreements, specifically due to a lack of confidence in Reverend Seymour's commitment to

---

1. Oscar and Marie Knutson, oral history interview with Wayne Warner, Sept. 5, 1983, audio recording, Flower Pentecostal Heritage Center.

the Holiness doctrine of sanctification. As such, her Apostolic Faith Mission in Portland seems to have been a kind of coup d'état of Seymour's leadership of the early Pentecostal movement.[2] Crawford not only assumed leadership of several daughter missions planted by Seymour's Azusa Street Mission, but she also took with her Seymour's paper *The Apostolic Faith*—along with its mailing lists—when she left the Azusa Street Mission and continued publishing it herself under the same name after establishing her own mission in Portland.[3]

Although it is unclear how much Oscar Knutson's sisters were involved in, or compelled by, Crawford's Apostolic Faith Mission, it is possible that they were influenced by *The Apostolic Faith* paper. Or, if not influenced by the paper itself, then at least the radical Pentecostal-Holiness theology of sanctification which it taught—namely, the belief that a person could not receive the baptism of the Holy Spirit without first being totally sanctified, that is, made completely holy and cleansed of sin.[4] Oscar Knutson was himself influenced by this theological position as he was seeking the baptism of the Holy Spirit, but he ultimately changed his view after his own experience testified that his personal efforts toward holiness did not yield that which was exclusively a work of God.[5] Ultimately, Oscar's own baptism of the Holy Spirit experience seems to have compelled his sisters' theological transition from the radical Holiness teaching of the Apostolic Faith Mission and, thus, the whole Knutson family's ecclesial move.[6]

Not long after Oscar Knutson's baptism in the Holy Spirit experience at Bethel Temple in February 1921, he and his father returned to the family homestead near Fairfield, Montana. Oscar's mother and younger siblings remained in Seattle for a few months to finish the school year, but they too joined Oscar and his father after school was out for the summer. As Oscar and his father traveled back to the family farm, they briefly stopped

---

2. Robeck, *Azusa Street Mission and Revival*, 299–301.

3. Robeck, *Azusa Street Mission and Revival*, 299–301.

4. Edith L. Blumhofer, "Apostolic Faith Mission (Portland, OR)," in Burgess and van der Maas, *New International Dictionary*, 327.

5. Knutson, *His Loving Care*, 11–12.

6. Oscar Knutson, "Knutson Family Tree, 1766–1983," 15, Oscar M. Knutson archival collection, box 2, folder 7; Oscar and Marie Knutson, oral history interview with Wayne Warner, Sept. 5, 1983, audio recording, Flower Pentecostal Heritage Center.

in Great Falls, Montana, to meet Rev. Joseph Lantz, the pastor of a local Pentecostal mission which had been planted just a few years prior, between 1916 and 1917.[7]

Born in Swanton, Ohio, in 1869, Joseph Lantz became a Christian in 1892.[8] In 1902, Lantz married Rosalina Schlatter of Greybill, Indiana, and although he only had an eighth-grade education, subsequently attended the Christian and Missionary Alliance Bible College in Nyach, New York, the first Bible college in the United States. In 1906, Lantz was ordained by the Missionary Church Association, a mission-focused denomination with roots in the Mennonite Church.[9] In 1910, Lantz and his wife moved to Alberta, Canada, and there received the baptism of the Holy Spirit.[10] In 1916, Lantz visited Great Falls, Montana, where he received a call to plant a local Pentecostal church. Originally having visited Great Falls selling Hurlbut Bible story books for children, Lantz met a group of women that had for the last several years been meeting in homes each week for Bible study and

---

7. Knutson, *His Loving Care*, 13; "Montana Assembly Sponsors Jail Ministry," 15; *Great Falls Leader*, "Rites Friday for Rev. Lantz," 15. Presently, the parlance of *church planting* is used to describe the process of establishing a new local church. In the early Pentecostal context, the parlance of *pioneering*, or specifically *pioneering a new work*, was used to describe this activity. In the American context, the language of *pioneering* carries some historical and cultural freight—particularly, that of the experience of white Euro-American settlers moving West during the nineteenth century, striking out into territory unknown to them (but long inhabited by various indigenous tribes), and forging a trail that had not yet been formally established. While recognizing that this contemporary parlance does not convey all of the same meaning as the old Pentecostal parlance, this spiritual biography of Oscar Knutson uses the language of *church planting* for the sake of contemporary understanding.

8. "Pioneer Montana Minister Passes," unidentified obituary clipping for Joseph Lantz, 1952, in "Deceased Ministers—Lantz, Joseph," archival record file, Flower Pentecostal Heritage Center.

9. "Pioneer Montana Minister Passes," unidentified obituary clipping for Joseph Lantz, 1952, in "Deceased Ministers—Lantz, Joseph," archival record file, Flower Pentecostal Heritage Center; *Great Falls Tribune*, "Rev. Lantz, Local Church Founder, Dies," 9; Justus H. Hunter, "Missionary Church," in Kurian and Lamport, *Encyclopedia of Christianity in the United States*, 1527–28; Day, *Dictionary of Christian Denominations*, 313. On his application for an ordination certificate with the Assemblies of God denomination, Rev. Joseph Lantz noted that he had been ordained on March 8, 1906, by J. E. Ramseyer, the founder of the Missionary Church Association. Ordination documents, in "Deceased Ministers—Lantz, Joseph," archival record file, Flower Pentecostal Heritage Center.

10. "Pioneer Montana Minister Passes," unidentified obituary clipping, 1952, in "Deceased Ministers—Lantz, Joseph," archival record file, Flower Pentecostal Heritage Center; Oscar and Marie Knutson, oral history interview with Wayne Warner, Sept. 5, 1983, audio recording, Flower Pentecostal Heritage Center.

"There's a Drawing From on High"

prayer, but who desired a formal church community and more robust spiritual leadership.[11] Accompanied by Charles Simmonett, an English-born Pentecostal evangelist who had been pastoring a small church in the city of Lethbridge, in Alberta, Canada, Lantz arrived in Great Falls in July 1916 and began holding revival meetings.[12]

By February 1917, a humble Pentecostal mission had been established in Great Falls, with Lantz as pastor and Simmonett remaining in a temporary capacity as evangelist. After Simmonett moved on to other ministry work, Lantz's Pentecostal mission continued to hold regular worship and prayer services and even engaged in a local prison ministry.[13] Admittedly, although the Pentecostal mission was active in the Great Falls community between 1918 and 1921, it was little more than a modest fellowship in its early years. Church services were mostly held in the private home of Reverend Lantz and his family, attendance was low, and Lantz had very little time to evangelize or attend to pastoral work, as he was also employed by the Great Northern Railroad, trying to support his family of six.[14] Despite the Pentecostal mission's humble beginnings, Reverend Lantz and his family remained faithful to their ministry work and sought to keep a positive outlook. In the May 4, 1918, issue of *The Weekly Evangel*, a weekly publication of the Assemblies of God denomination later titled *The Pentecostal Evangel*, Reverend Lantz's wife wrote: "The Lord is blessing the work here. Pray much for this place that many may be saved and made ready for the coming of Jesus."[15]

When Oscar Knutson and his father arrived in Great Falls in spring 1921, they found the Pentecostal mission frail but full of potential. Although they were committed to their responsibilities on the family homestead, Oscar and his father traveled back to Great Falls "as often as possible that

---

11. Roset et al., *Assemblies of God in Montana*, 40.

12. *Great Falls Tribune*, "Will Open a Two Weeks' Mission," 7; *Times Leader*, "Charles Simmonett," 6; "Need a Pastor," 15.

13. *Great Falls Leader*, "Pentecostal Assembly," 7; *Great Falls Tribune*, "Pentecostal Mission" (Dec. 15, 1918), 21; *Great Falls Leader*, "Pentecostal Tent Meetings," 5; *Great Falls Leader*, "Pentecostal Mission," 7; "Montana Assembly Sponsors Jail Ministry," 15.

14. Handwritten and typewritten reflections on Oscar Knutson's early life, Oscar M. Knutson archival collection, box 2, folder 14; Knutson, *His Loving Care*, 13–14.

15. Lantz, "Reports from the Field," 14.

summer" to participate in the Pentecostal services held by Rev. Joseph Lantz.[16] In June 1921, two Pentecostal evangelists and pastors—Rev. A. D. Guth of Sterling, Kansas, and Rev. J. Feuk of Minneapolis, Minnesota—visited the Pentecostal mission in Great Falls and held a series of evangelistic services.[17] Although these revival services did little to raise the profile of Reverend Lantz's modest Pentecostal mission, they were not totally in vain. Reverend Guth—who according to some of Oscar's unpublished notes was one of the first to receive the baptism of the Holy Spirit at the Azusa Street Mission in Los Angeles—had previously published a Pentecostal songbook called *Selected Gospel Songs*. Before leaving Great Falls for other evangelistic work, Reverend Guth gave fifty copies of the songbook to Reverend Lantz, to be used for regular church services.[18]

The Knutson farm yielded a good crop in 1921, and after harvest the Knutson family moved to a rental house in Great Falls to participate regularly in the life and worship of Reverend Lantz's Pentecostal mission and to assist in its growth.[19] Twenty-one-year-old Oscar Knutson noted that worshiping in the Lantz family's private home might have been inhibiting church growth and suggested that the church find another meeting location to hold services.[20] Reverend Lantz, almost fifty-two years old, "heartily agreed" with Oscar's suggestion but was himself financially limited and unable to support the cost of renting a more formal meeting location.[21] To meet this need, Oscar searched for an available space, found one above a local grocery store, and rented it out for twenty dollars a month.[22] He also

16. Knutson, *His Loving Care*, 13.

17. *Great Falls Tribune*, "Pentecostal Mission Holds Its Services," 9; *Great Falls Leader*, "In the Churches" (June 30, 1921), 5. This was not the first visit to Great Falls for either A. D. Guth or J. Feuk (whose name is often misprinted as "Fenk"). Guth had previously held some services with Reverend Lantz in Great Falls in March 1920, while Feuk and another Pentecostal evangelist—"Rev. Douglas of Washington"—had previously held services with Reverend Lantz in Great Falls in January 1921. *Great Falls Tribune*, "Pentecostal Assembly," 21; *Great Falls Leader*, "South Side S. S. Chapel," 13.

18. Handwritten and typewritten reflections on Oscar Knutson's early life, Oscar M. Knutson archival collection, box 2, folder 14; Guth, *Selected Gospel Songs*.

19. Knutson, *His Loving Care*, 13; handwritten reflections on Oscar Knutson's early life, Oscar M. Knutson archival collection, box 2, folder 14.

20. Knutson, *His Loving Care*, 13; handwritten reflections on Oscar Knutson's early life, Oscar M. Knutson archival collection, box 2, folder 14.

21. Knutson, *His Loving Care*, 13; handwritten reflections on Oscar Knutson's early life, Oscar M. Knutson archival collection, box 2, folder 14.

22. Knutson, *His Loving Care*, 13; handwritten reflections on Oscar Knutson's early

purchased about 150 used chairs and a used piano for a "reasonable price," moved them into the space, and put up a sign that read "Full Gospel Assembly," along with church meeting times.²³

In the nineteenth century, much of the theology of the Wesleyan-Holiness tradition came to be formulated as the *Fourfold Gospel*, which identified Jesus Christ as "Savior, Sanctifier, Healer, and Coming King."²⁴ According to the Fourfold Gospel, Jesus was responsible for saving souls from hell, cleansing people from sin, divinely healing their physical maladies, and coming "soon" to judge the world and lead the faithful into eternal life with God in heaven. The Pentecostal movement, based largely in the Holiness tradition, affirmed the Fourfold Gospel but added a crucial and distinctly "Pentecostal" element to it—the baptism of the Holy Spirit. For Pentecostals, the Fourfold Gospel thus became the *Full Gospel*, with Jesus Christ as "Savior, Sanctifier, Baptizer with the Holy Spirit, Healer, and Coming King."²⁵ The shift in terms from *Fourfold Gospel* to *Full Gospel* is noteworthy, because from a Pentecostal standpoint, the gospel was only "full" when it included the baptism of the Holy Spirit. It is for this reason that, especially in the early decades of the Pentecostal movement, the term "Full Gospel" appears in the names of innumerable Pentecostal churches and fellowships, including the Full Gospel Assembly in Great Falls, Montana, in 1921.

In addition to securing a meeting place, chairs, and a piano for Rev. Joseph Lantz's Full Gospel Assembly, Oscar Knutson also began working to secure people to attend church services. Having ordered some Pentecostal gospel tracts covering a variety of "scripture subjects—such as salvation, the new

---

life, Oscar M. Knutson archival collection, box 2, folder 14. Twenty dollars in 1921 dollars is the equivalent of approximately 350 dollars in 2024 dollars.

23. Handwritten reflections on early life, Oscar M. Knutson archival collection, box 2, folder 14.

24. A. B. Simpson, founder of the Christian and Missionary Alliance, was responsible for this precise articulation.

25. Kenneth J. Archer, "Full Gospel," in Stewart, *Handbook of Pentecostal Christianity*, 89–90. Some Pentecostals, who understood sanctification and the baptism of the Holy Spirit to be the same event, simply changed the articulation to Jesus as "Savior, Healer, Baptizer in the Holy Spirit, and Soon-Coming King." Archer, "Full Gospel," in Stewart, *Handbook of Pentecostal Christianity*, 90.

birth, Atoning Blood, healing, the baptism of the Holy Spirit, [and] the soon coming of Jesus," Knutson went house to house through Great Falls during the winter of 1921, sharing the gospel and inviting locals to come to church services at the newly relocated Full Gospel Assembly.[26] In later reflections, Knutson described Great Falls as "a strongly Catholic town of 30,000 to 35,000 population in those days."[27] Nevertheless, he deemed his door-to-door evangelism important. Concerning these experiences, Knutson remembered:

> When someone would answer the door, I would ask as pleasantly as I could, "Are you a Christian?" [t]hen take note of the various responses I would get. A few would say ["]no.["] Others would look surprised, hesitate, then finally say ["]yes.["] Even though they perhaps were church members, they probably weren't really born again. Catholics would almost always say, "No, we are Catholic." And although true Christians might look a little surprised, they would answer with a smile, "Yes!"[28]

Knutson noted that as he went house to house, people "often invited me into their homes to talk," and when they did, he gave them whichever gospel tract "felt appropriate" and discussed it with them.[29] Ultimately, because of Knutson's door-to-door evangelism, church attendance for Reverend Lantz's Full Gospel Assembly increased, and Knutson noted that many people "were saved" and "began to receive the baptism in the Holy Spirit."[30]

As 1922 commenced, the Full Gospel Assembly in Great Falls—still called the "Pentecostal Mission" in local newspapers—experienced great growth. Under the pastoral leadership of Reverend Lantz, the church continued holding Sunday services, prayer meetings, and Bible studies.[31] Oscar

---

26. Knutson, *His Loving Care*, 14.

27. The federal census of 1920 indicates that Great Falls, Montana, had a population of 26,040. "Fourteenth Census of the United States: 1920: Bulletin, Population: Montana," Department of Commerce, prepared under the supervision of Wm. C. Hunt, 1920, 7.

28. Knutson, *His Loving Care*, 14–15.

29. Knutson, *His Loving Care*, 14–15.

30. Knutson, *His Loving Care*, 14–15; handwritten reflections on Oscar Knutson's early life, Oscar M. Knutson archival collection, box 2, folder 14; Oscar and Marie Knutson, oral history interview with Wayne Warner, Sept. 5, 1983, audio recording, Flower Pentecostal Heritage Center.

31. *Great Falls Leader*, "In the Churches: Pentecostal Mission" (Jan. 22, 1922), 6; *Great Falls Leader*, "In the Churches: Pentecostal Mission" (Feb. 5, 1922), 7; *Great Falls Tribune*, "Church Services Today," 5; *Great Falls Leader*, "In the Churches: Pentecostal

"There's a Drawing From on High"

Knutson was pleased to see the Lord at work in Great Falls. As spring arrived, however, responsibility called, and he and his father left to return to work on the family homestead just outside Fairfield, Montana. Meanwhile, Oscar's mother and his younger siblings returned to Seattle for school.[32]

Responsibility was not all that called Oscar Knutson that spring of 1922. One day, while operating a "noisy tractor" on a "rough field" on the Knutson family farm, Oscar heard a soft but clear voice speaking to him: "*I want you in My field.*"[33] Oscar knew it was the Lord speaking to him, calling him "to preach the Gospel."[34] Knutson told God that "I would gladly go after harvest," as "I had promised to help my father till after harvest."[35] After all, "it would not be right to leave papa with more work than he could do."[36] Oscar's response "seemed to please the Lord."[37] God then told Knutson that "when I went to Seattle I would meet a brother that I should work with."[38] Oscar wondered how he would recognize this partner in ministry.[39] The Lord's voice came again: "a man will ap[p]ro[a]ch you, work with him."[40]

Mission" (May 28, 1922), 6.

32. Handwritten reflections on Oscar Knutson's early life, Oscar M. Knutson archival collection, box 2, folder 14.

33. Handwritten and typewritten reflections on Oscar Knutson's early life and call to ministry, Oscar M. Knutson archival collection, box 2, folders 14, 15, 16.

34. Handwritten reflections on Oscar Knutson's early life and call to ministry, Oscar M. Knutson archival collection, box 2, folders 14, 16. Oscar Knutson's call to ministry in a farming context is fitting, given that in the New Testament, ministry work is often spoken of in agricultural terms. The apostle Paul even described ministry as a "field" in his First Epistle to the Corinthians: "For we are God's coworkers. You are God's field" (1 Cor 3:9, HCSB).

35. Handwritten reflections on Oscar Knutson's early life and call to ministry, Oscar M. Knutson archival collection, box 2, folders 14, 16.

36. Handwritten reflections on Oscar Knutson's early life and call to ministry, Oscar M. Knutson archival collection, box 2, folders 14, 16.

37. Handwritten reflections on Oscar Knutson's early life and call to ministry, Oscar M. Knutson archival collection, box 2, folders 14, 16.

38. Handwritten reflections on Oscar Knutson's early life and call to ministry, Oscar M. Knutson archival collection, box 2, folders 14, 16.

39. Handwritten reflections on Oscar Knutson's early life and call to ministry, Oscar M. Knutson archival collection, box 2, folders 14, 16.

40. Typewritten reflections on Oscar Knutson's early life and call to ministry, Oscar M. Knutson archival collection, box 2, folder 15.

He Will Lead Me

That evening at supper, Oscar Knutson told his father about the call to ministry and his promise to the Lord that he would pursue gospel work after harvest was over. "I am not surprised," his father replied, likely thinking of Oscar's previous experiences at Bethel Temple in Seattle and his zeal for ministry in Great Falls.[41] Oscar's news also seemed to confirm a decision that his father had been deliberating for some time, namely, to sell the family farm and move back to Seattle.[42] Thus, when harvest concluded, Oscar visited the local newspaper publisher in Fairfield—a man he knew well, having started a Sunday school with him some years prior—and inquired if he knew of someone who might be interested in buying the Knutson family farm.[43] The newspaper publisher pondered the question for a few minutes and then replied, "I'll buy it."[44] The next morning, Oscar's father met with the newspaper publisher. By noon, they had closed the deal and sold the farm.[45] Oscar's later reflections on these events reveal that he interpreted the sale of the farm as God's provision for the Knutson family and his confirmation of Oscar's call to ministry.

It was not long before Oscar Knutson arrived back in Seattle. The first evening back he attended Bethel Temple, expecting to meet the man whom the Lord had promised would disciple him and become his partner in ministry. Knutson did not meet anyone that night, however, so the following evening he attended a service at a Pentecostal rescue mission in Seattle which had recently opened.[46] A local evangelist preached that night,

---

41. Handwritten reflections on Oscar Knutson's early life and call to ministry, Oscar M. Knutson archival collection, box 2, folder 14.

42. Handwritten reflections on Oscar Knutson's early life and call to ministry, Oscar M. Knutson archival collection, box 2, folder 14.

43. Handwritten reflections on Oscar Knutson's early life and call to ministry, Oscar M. Knutson archival collection, box 2, folder 14.

44. Handwritten reflections on Oscar Knutson's early life and the sale of the Knutson homestead and farm in Montana, Oscar M. Knutson archival collection, box 2, folder 12.

45. Handwritten reflections on Oscar Knutson's early life and the sale of the Knutson homestead and farm in Montana, Oscar M. Knutson archival collection, box 2, folder 12.

46. Handwritten reflections on Oscar Knutson's early life and call to ministry, Oscar M. Knutson archival collection, box 2, folders 12, 14, 16. In the Pentecostal context, the term *mission* often refers to a church plant. See chapter 1, n34. Relatedly, the term *rescue mission* may refer to a church plant or another formal or informal religious organization with a particular emphasis on, and definite purpose toward, aiding persons in the local community who are vulnerable or impoverished. This focus is inherently missiological and understands the interconnectedness of spiritual needs and realities with physical needs and realities.

"There's a Drawing From on High"

and as he did, Knutson thought: "that is him."⁴⁷ After the service was over, the evangelist approached Knutson and promptly invited him to join him in Auburn, Washington, the following evening for an evangelistic service. Knutson agreed and offered his own car to drive them. It was the beginning of a fruitful ministry partnership that, along with his experiences in Great Falls, were deeply formative for Knutson's own ministry work.⁴⁸

The evangelist's name was Jacob Charley Nelson, although in ministry he was better known as Jack C. Nelson, or "Brother Jack."⁴⁹ Born in Ishpeming, Michigan, in 1887, Nelson was the son of Anton and Cecilia Nelson, both originally of Denmark. Formerly a Baptist-turned-Salvation Army officer, Jack Nelson became a Pentecostal evangelist after receiving the baptism of the Holy Spirit at the summer 1919 camp meeting at Green Lake in Seattle, held by the Pine Street Mission (later, Bethel Temple).⁵⁰ Nelson supported himself by working as a cook but spent a great deal of time holding

---

47. Handwritten reflections on Oscar Knutson's early life and ministry, Oscar M. Knutson archival collection, box 2, folders 12, 14, 16.

48. Handwritten reflections on Oscar Knutson's early life and ministry, Oscar M. Knutson archival collection, box 2, folders 12, 14, 16.

49. Knutson, *His Loving Care*, 15; Jacob Charley Nelson, World War II Draft Registration Card, 1942, Ancestry.com.

50. Jack C. Nelson, Certificate of Death, 1963, Washington State Digital Archives; Oscar and Marie Knutson, oral history interview with Wayne Warner, Sept. 5, 1983, audio recording, Flower Pentecostal Heritage Center; *Seattle Union Record*, "Building Permits: Tent" (June 30, 1919), 17; *Seattle Union Record*, "Building Permits: Tent" (July 1, 1919), 7; Knutson, *His Loving Care*, 15; Peterson, "Bethel Temple Heritage Part 2." Admittedly, the precise timeline for Jack Nelson's baptism of the Holy Spirit experience is a bit unclear. In the oral history interview noted above, Marie Knutson recalled knowing Brother Jack Nelson for a "few years" prior to being introduced to Oscar. Marie told the interviewer that she knew Nelson the day he received the baptism of the Holy Spirit and indicated that this experience happened at Green Lake Camp Meeting. Evidently, there was a Green Lake Camp Meeting in summer 1919. However, there was another Green Lake Camp Meeting in summer 1921 that featured the Argue family and which received more press coverage. *Seattle Union Record*, "Healing Services Held at North Green Lake Tent," 9; Argue, *Contending for the Faith*, 47. It is possible that this 1921 meeting was the occasion of Nelson's Pentecostal experience, not 1919; 1921 is plausible, given that it was apparently more historically significant and that reports of Nelson's evangelistic ministry do not begin until 1922. Even so, 1919 to 1922 makes more sense of the "few years" time interval between Nelson's baptism of the Holy Spirit and Marie and Oscar's introduction, so 1919 is the date given in this biographical sketch of Nelson.

Pentecostal evangelistic services in the Seattle vicinity.[51] Newspaper reports indicate that rather than operate as an independent evangelist, Nelson preferred to have others accompany him in his ministry work, following the pattern set by Jesus himself in sending out apostles to minister together.[52] Newspaper articles from early 1922 indicate that Nelson and other ministry companions—"workers from Seattle"—visited the Pentecostal Christian Assembly in Tacoma, Washington, to hold evangelistic meetings on numerous occasions.[53] "Are you ill?" one newspaper notice inquired. "Come and be prayed for, and expect God to fulfill His Word."[54] Another beckoned: "Those who are sick in body or soul, come and be prayed for and let the Lord heal and save you."[55] Still another invited all to "Come and enjoy the service with us. Let God's holy spirit have His way with you."[56]

Early Pentecostal revival meetings and evangelistic services centered on the might and movement of the Holy Spirit to bring salvation, empowerment for ministry, and, often, divine healing of physical ailments. Although at times the Pentecostal tradition became marked by serious abuse regarding divine healing, it is nonetheless an important doctrinal tenet that saw great expression in the concrete experiences of real people within the Pentecostal context.[57] The theological emphasis on divine healing was, not surprisingly, rooted in the Fourfold Gospel of the Holiness tradition

---

51. Knutson, *His Loving Care*, 15; Jacob Nelson, "Thirteenth Census of the United States 1910—Population," Ancestry.com; Jack Nelson, "Fourteenth Census of the United States 1920—Population," Ancestry.com.

52. *Tacoma Daily Ledger*, "Pentecostal Christian Assembly" (Jan. 8, 1922), 13; *Tacoma Daily Ledger*, "Pentecostal Christian Assembly" (Feb. 19, 1922), 38; *Tacoma Daily Ledger*, "Pentecostal Christian Assembly" (Apr. 2, 1922), 43; Mark 6:7; Luke 10:1.

53. *Tacoma Daily Ledger*, "Pentecostal Christian Assembly" (Jan. 8, 1922), 13; *Tacoma Daily Ledger*, "Pentecostal Christian Assembly" (Feb. 19, 1922), 38; *Tacoma Daily Ledger*, "Pentecostal Christian Assembly" (Apr. 2, 1922), 43.

54. *Tacoma Daily Ledger*, "Pentecostal Christian Assembly" (Feb. 19, 1922), 38.

55. *Tacoma Daily Ledger*, "Pentecostal Christian Assembly" (Jan. 8, 1922), 13.

56. *Tacoma Daily Ledger*, "Pentecostal Christian Assembly" (Apr. 2, 1922), 43.

57. Candy Gunther Brown, "Healing," in Wilkinson, *Brill's Encyclopedia of Global Pentecostalism*, 279–82. Unfortunately, in many cases both historically and presently, persons claiming to be Christian ministers (Pentecostal or otherwise) have used the matter of divine healing for their own means—generally to get money or gain fame—and have caused egregious psychological, emotional, theological, and spiritual harm as a result. Such examples of hurt do not negate the reality of divine healing, but instead underscore the necessity of teaching and understanding divine healing properly, while also revealing the importance of engaging the matter with the utmost sensitivity and care.

which identified Jesus Christ as "Healer."[58] Indeed, the life of Jesus reflects that healing was of significant concern to him. The Gospel accounts are replete with instances of Jesus healing people's physical maladies—blindness, deafness, skin diseases, paraplegia, life-threatening fevers, and other serious sicknesses and medical conditions. The Gospels According to Mark and Luke even record an instance of a woman with a severe, twelve-year menstrual condition being healed by simply touching the edge of Jesus' garment.[59]

The New Testament indicates that Jesus also expected his followers to care about the healing of physical ailments, because for Jesus, divine healing and preaching the gospel were inherently linked. When commissioning his apostles to preach the gospel, Jesus sent them with power to heal physical maladies.[60] Luke records that after Jesus commissioned his apostles, "they went out and traveled from village to village, proclaiming the good news and healing everywhere."[61] Mark's account goes further, noting that after Jesus commissioned his apostles, "they went out and preached that people should repent. They drove out many demons and anointed many sick people with oil and healed them."[62]

In the Gospel According to John, Jesus told his disciples that "whoever believes in me will do the works I have been doing, and they will do even greater things than these, because I am going to the Father."[63] This statement from Jesus anticipates his ascension into heaven, after which would come the great outpouring of the Holy Spirit, the *Paraclete* whom Jesus promised to send to his disciples.[64] The Acts of the Apostles records that, in accordance with Jesus' promise, God worked many great miracles of divine healing through the apostles after the great outpouring of the Holy Spirit at Pentecost. Like with the woman who was healed by simply touching the edge of Jesus' garment, great healing was experienced by many people who merely touched handkerchiefs and aprons that the apostle Paul

---

58. Robins, *Pentecostalism in America*, 6–7.
59. Mark 5:24–34; Luke 8:42–48.
60. Matt 10:1, 8; Mark 6:7, 13; Luke 9:1–2, 6.
61. Luke 9:6, HCSB.
62. Mark 6:13, NIV.
63. John 14:12, NIV.
64. John 14:16–17, 25–26; 16:7–14. While Jesus spoke Aramaic, the Gospel According to John was written in Greek. *Paraclete* is an anglicization of the Greek term used to refer to the Holy Spirit in the passages listed. In English translations of the Scriptures, the term is translated into English in various ways: Helper, Comforter, Counselor, Advocate.

himself had touched.[65] Many people were also healed by simply having the shadow of the apostle Peter fall on them as he walked by.[66]

The early Pentecostals, along with earlier revivalist traditions, believed in the scriptural witness to divine healing, as well as Jesus' promise that "whoever believes in Me will do the works that I have been doing, and they will do even greater things than these."[67] If Jesus worked miracles, and if the Holy Spirit worked miracles through Jesus' apostles, why not expect miracles to happen today? Divine healing was thus a central component of the Pentecostal message.[68] In practice, it was usually connected to the instruction and exhortation from the Epistle of James in the New Testament: "Is anyone among you suffering? He should pray . . . . Is anyone among you sick? He should call for the elders of the church, and they should pray over him after anointing him with olive oil in the name of the Lord. The prayer of faith will save the sick person, and the Lord will restore him to health."[69] Frequently in Pentecostal circles, anointing with oil and the laying on of hands accompanied prayers for divine healing.[70]

Unfortunately, some Pentecostal evangelists—or rather, charlatans claiming to be Pentecostal evangelists—manipulated and abused the biblical message of divine healing for their own ends. Some claimed to "specialize" in healing certain types of physical maladies (which could be easily faked), or claimed that miracles were not happening within their healing services because God himself was withholding healing from people, perhaps due to sin in their lives or because of a lack of faith.[71] Such abuses hurt the Pentecostal witness. Over the course of his life and ministry, Oscar Knutson witnessed, and objected to, plenty of such abuses by so-called Pentecostal evangelists and faith healers. In a 1983 oral history interview,

---

65. Acts 9:12.

66. Acts 5:15–16.

67. John 14:12, NIV.

68. Candy Gunther Brown, "Healing," in Wilkinson, *Brill's Encyclopedia of Global Pentecostalism*, 279.

69. Jas 5:13–15, HCSB. Although restoration of health is certainly intended here, other translations take this word from James a step further, framing divine healing as a picture of resurrection: "And the prayer of faith shall save the sick, and the Lord shall raise him up" (Jas 5:15, KJV).

70. Keith Warrington, "Healing," in Stewart, *Handbook of Pentecostal Christianity*, 100–102.

71. Keith Warrington, "Healing, Gifts of," in Burgess, *Encyclopedia of Pentecostal and Charismatic Christianity*, 232.

Knutson noted that frauds were often identified by simply following up on the fruit of their "healing ministries" as they moved from town to town. If the "specializations" were easy to fake, if the sick were not really healed, and especially if the so-called evangelist did not pay their bills in each town—generally to rent space or get a street permit for a religious assembly—it was a sure sign that they were "fakes."[72]

Despite the abuses, testimonies of true divine healing and radical life-transformation abounded within the Pentecostal movement and certainly within the ministry experiences of Jack Nelson and Oscar Knutson in the early to mid 1920s. Knutson began working with Nelson in late 1922, primarily in a musical capacity. While Brother Jack preached, Oscar played guitar and sang.[73] Following Nelson's example of working to support himself and his ministry, Knutson worked during the day as a carpenter and then joined Nelson in the evenings for evangelistic services at various places in the Seattle area. Often assisting with opening new missions and aiding floundering churches, Nelson and Knutson visited and ministered in the cities of Auburn, Everett, Algona, and Black Diamond, along with other towns and neighborhoods around or near Seattle.[74] During their ministry together, they brought many people to Christ, witnessed several people receive the baptism of the Holy Spirit, and saw lots of people divinely healed. They also witnessed the Lord convict and redeem a man named Clarence W. Hart, an abusive husband who repented, reconciled with his wife and family, and later became a Pentecostal pastor with whom both Knutson and Nelson did ministry work on occasion in subsequent decades.[75]

Admittedly, while Oscar Knutson's ministry with Brother Jack Nelson was successful on many fronts, it was not without resistance, especially in the town of Black Diamond. "Satan got busy," Knutson noted.[76] Knutson recalled how his guitar was stolen out of his car, his car tires were slashed with a knife, and some ministry partners had the lug nuts on their car

---

72. Oscar and Marie Knutson, oral history interview with Wayne Warner, Sept. 5, 1983, audio recording, Flower Pentecostal Heritage Center.

73. Oscar and Marie Knutson, oral history interview with Wayne Warner, Sept. 5, 1983, audio recording, Flower Pentecostal Heritage Center.

74. Knutson, *His Loving Care*, 15.

75. Knutson, *His Loving Care*, 24–25, 71–72.

76. Knutson, *His Loving Care*, 22.

tires loosened by would-be saboteurs.[77] Knutson, Nelson, and their ministry associates also experienced intimidation on multiple occasions. One Sunday, a small boy tipped off Knutson about a box of dynamite that had been planted under the foundation of the church building in which he and Nelson were holding services. While Brother Jack conducted the service, Knutson crawled under the building and disarmed the dynamite.[78] Not long afterward, Knutson and Nelson welcomed some non-white Pentecostal ministry associates from Seattle to come and assist with services. Unfortunately, their lively and enjoyable time of worship together turned ominous and nearly fatal when, after the Sunday afternoon service, a racist mob gathered outside and threatened the visiting "colored folk."[79] Knutson remembered that the mob "finally let them get in their car, threatening them that if they ever came back again, they would lynch them."[80] Knutson lamented this experience of racism and near-violence as an expression of the sinister reality of the activity of the devil in trying to hinder the gospel.

Although the early Pentecostal movement saw a diversity of explanations concerning demonic activities in the world, it was generally agreed that cosmic powers of darkness were real and could be expected to resist the furthering of God's kingdom, ever seeking to reverse and undo the work of the gospel. Spiritual forces of darkness were behind the evil in the world, and God's people were to understand themselves to be engaged in an ongoing battle against them.[81] "Be strong in the Lord, and in the power of his might," the apostle Paul wrote in his Epistle to the Ephesians. "Put on the full armor of God so that you can stand against the tactics of the devil. For our battle is not against flesh and blood, but against the rulers, against the authorities, against the world powers of this darkness, against the spiritual forces of evil in the heavens."[82] Although there was spiritual warfare to be waged, victory was assured in Jesus Christ, who had already dealt a fatal blow to demonic powers through his incarnation, life, death, and resurrection. "The Son of God was revealed for this purpose: to destroy the devil's works," affirmed the apostle John in his First Epistle.[83] "The God

---

77. Knutson, *His Loving Care*, 25–26.
78. Knutson, *His Loving Care*, 22–23.
79. Knutson, *His Loving Care*, 23.
80. Knutson, *His Loving Care*, 23.
81. Wacker, *Heaven Below*, 91–92; Robins, *Pentecostalism in America*, 81–82.
82. Eph 6:10–12, KJV, HCSB.
83. 1 John 3:8, HCSB.

of peace will soon crush Satan under your feet," wrote the apostle Paul to the first-century church at Rome.[84]

Oscar Knutson understood his own ministry work to be an act of war upon the kingdom of darkness. The resistance to the gospel which Knutson encountered was not unexpected but also not something to be trifled with, especially in the case of the would-be lynch mob. What Knutson experienced in Black Diamond was a local expression of a greater reality. No sooner would the broader Pentecostal movement experience great victory in powerful movements of God, then it would encounter great devastations and setbacks due to the activities of Satan. Racism was a particularly destructive and pernicious example.

In his Great Commission, Jesus had sent his followers to go forth into the world and "make disciples of all nations."[85] At the great outpouring of the Holy Spirit at Pentecost, Jesus' disciples were equipped with the supernatural ability to speak different human languages to accomplish that very charge. The Pharisee Saul of Tarsus, later known as the apostle Paul, received a special commission from Jesus to be an apostle to the nations and wrote to the first-century church at Colossae that, in Christ, "there is not Gentile or Jew, circumcised or uncircumcised, barbarian, Scythian, slave or free, but Christ is all, and is in all."[86] Finally, in the Revelation to John, God's plan for the new creation includes a robust vision of ethnic diversity, namely, "a great multitude that no one could count, from every nation, tribe, people and language, standing before the throne and before the Lamb," united together in holy and glorious worship.[87]

In its origins, the Pentecostal movement in many ways reflected this heavenly vision of ethnic diversity. North American Pentecostalism was deeply rooted in the African American Christian experience and tradition.[88] The Azusa Street Revival in Los Angeles, California—born out of the radical spiritual experiences of a handful of African American Christians and largely representative of the broader Pentecostal movement—was originally an excellent example of a multiethnic community flourishing and thriving in its work of worship and mission. It was not long, however, before the

84. Rom 16:20, HCSB.
85. Matt 28:19, NIV.
86. Col 3:11, NIV.
87. Rev 7:9–10, NIV.
88. Lewis Brogdon, "African American Pentecostalism," in Stewart, *Handbook of Pentecostal Christianity*, 20.

Azusa Street Mission and the broader early Pentecostal movement split apart, with congregational and denominational divisions largely drawn on racial lines.[89] In this way, Pentecostalism in America came to reflect racist cultural attitudes and practices within the United States as a whole. From a theological standpoint, it was a devastating example of the cosmic powers of darkness gaining some spiritual ground back from the gospel.

Despite the spiritual warfare—racism and otherwise—that Oscar Knutson and Jack Nelson encountered in Black Diamond, they continued to labor for the sake of Christ. Satan's deeds were by no means insignificant, but as Knutson later wrote, "the Devil is no match for the Lord! . . . [I]n spite of the Devil and his servants' efforts to hinder, [t]he Lord gave us some precious victories! Praise His Name."[90] Even after their regular ministry partnership concluded in 1924, both Knutson and Nelson pursued gospel work and witnessed great victories of God against the forces of evil. Moreover, as they ministered according to God's call, they often did so with other ministry associates of color—for example, Nelson with Rev. Mary Sanders, a black female Pentecostal pastor from Los Angeles who ministered for multiple years in Everett, Washington, and Knutson with Rev. Lee Henson, a black Pentecostal minister who supported him powerfully in prayer and also assisted him in evangelistic work.

Oscar Knutson's early years in ministry with Jack Nelson were deeply formative for his own gospel work in later decades. Ministering with Nelson was also personally significant for Knutson, as it was Nelson who introduced him to the woman who ultimately became his wife and lifelong ministry companion. In fall 1922, just a week after their first evangelistic service together, Nelson and Knutson visited Rev. Carl G. Carlson's Pentecostal mission in Everett, Washington.[91] Entering the church building just ahead of them was a young woman by the name of Marie Baldwin. Brother Jack, who had met Marie previously, introduced her to Oscar in the foyer. "I decided right then and there I wanted to get better acquainted with her," Oscar later remembered.[92]

---

89. Knutson, *His Loving Care*, 24–25.
90. Knutson, *His Loving Care*, 24, 26.
91. Knutson, *His Loving Care*, 15–16.
92. Oscar and Marie Knutson, oral history interview with Wayne Warner, Sept. 5, 1983, audio recording, Flower Pentecostal Heritage Center; handwritten reflections on

"There's a Drawing From on High"

Born in Alma, Michigan, on October 25, 1905, Marie Bell Baldwin was the daughter of Jay and Cora May Baldwin, the third of what would become nine children. When Marie was four years old, the Baldwin family left the Midwest and moved to Yacolt, Washington, where they moved in with Marie's maternal grandparents. At the time of the move, Marie and her family were Christians, but only marginally so. A spiritual awakening for the whole family came at Yacolt in the summer of 1910. The family was threatened by a dangerous local forest fire, and Marie's father, Jay, left the house "to help fight the fire."[93] Meanwhile, the rest of the family prepared themselves for the worst. As time dragged on, there was no word from Marie's father. According to Marie's reflections on the experience:

> I went into the house to get a drink of water, and I heard Mother in the bedroom crying and on her knees praying. She told the Lord if He would spare all of us and send Papa home she would serve Him the rest of her life. A short time later Papa came home. He told us all about the fire . . . [God] was faithful to His promise . . . and the family was saved.[94]

Shortly after the forest fire, the Baldwin family moved to White Bluffs, Washington, and became involved in the local Union church, pastored by Rev. William Milnes Faux.[95] In early 1912, Reverend Faux visited the Azusa Street Mission in Los Angeles, California, to investigate reports of amazing experiences happening within the nascent Pentecostal movement. When

---

Oscar Knutson's ministry with Jack Nelson, Oscar M. Knutson archival collection, box 2, folder 16.

93. Handwritten reflections on Marie Baldwin's early life, Oscar M. Knutson archival collection, unprocessed box.

94. Marie Knutson recounted this experience on multiple occasions. This quotation is not a selection of just one of these recollections, but rather compiles together two recollections of the same event, one from archival documents and another in an oral history interview. This is done for narrative purpose as well as to convey Marie's theological and spiritual disposition regarding this event. Handwritten reflections on Marie Baldwin's early life, Oscar M. Knutson archival collection, unprocessed box; Oscar and Marie Knutson, oral history interview with Wayne Warner, Sept. 5, 1983, audio recording, Flower Pentecostal Heritage Center.

95. Handwritten reflections on Marie Baldwin's early life, Oscar M. Knutson archival collection, unprocessed box; Phyliss Ann Hart, Illinois, US, Deaths and Stillbirths Index, 1916–1947, Ancestry.com; Parker, *Tales of Richland, White Bluffs and Hanford*, 136; *Spokesman-Review*, "White Bluffs," 8. The "Union church" at White Bluffs, Washington, was "a Christian organization by the affiliation of the Methodist, Presbyterian, and other denominations in the valley," according to a local newspaper clipping. *Spokesman-Review*, "Church Members of White Bluffs Work Week in Pastor's Orchard," 9.

Reverend Faux returned to White Bluffs he was thoroughly Pentecostal, preaching about the baptism of the Holy Spirit, having received "the baptism" himself in California.[96] Under Reverend Faux's pastoral guidance, Marie's parents began seeking "more of God" in the baptism of the Holy Spirit. Marie reflected later:

> On February 17, 1912, [a]fter we children had gone to bed[,] Papa was reading the Bible to Mother[;] then they had prayer . . . . Soon Mother came in and woke us up[.] [S]he said ["]come and hear Papa. He is talking funny.["] So we went where Papa was in the kitchen[,] laying on the floor[,] . . . slain under the power . . . [,] talking in a language we did not know[, a]nd [p]raising the Lord . . . . The next night Mother received the Bapt[i]sm.[97]

If the forest fire experience in Yacolt marked the Baldwin family's spiritual awakening, their entrance into the Pentecostal movement in White Bluffs established their flourishing in the Christian faith. For the next several years, the family remained at Rev. William Faux's church in White Bluffs, where they worshiped in an old schoolhouse building.[98] "We had real good meetings," Marie remembered.[99] When Marie was nine years old, she and her older siblings, Vera and Wesley, "were saved during these meetings."[100] Between 1914 and 1915, Reverend Faux moved to Butler, New Jersey, where he pursued other ministry work.[101] The Baldwin

---

96. Oscar and Marie Knutson, oral history interview with Wayne Warner, Sept. 5, 1983, audio recording, Flower Pentecostal Heritage Center. Pentecostals often referred to their baptism in the Holy Spirit experience as simply "the baptism."

97. Handwritten reflections on Marie Baldwin's early life, Oscar M. Knutson archival collection, unprocessed box.

98. Handwritten reflections on Marie Baldwin's early life, Oscar M. Knutson archival collection, unprocessed box.

99. Handwritten reflections on Marie Baldwin's early life, Oscar M. Knutson archival collection, unprocessed box.

100. Handwritten reflections on Marie Baldwin's early life, Oscar M. Knutson archival collection, unprocessed box.

101. *White Bluffs Spokesman*, "Word has been received," 4. This 1917 newspaper clipping notes Rev. William Faux's move to Butler, New Jersey. Admittedly, this clipping also reports the death of Reverend Faux, but that part of the report is plainly inaccurate, based on misinformation. A New Jersey newspaper report from 1918 notes that Reverend Faux was active in the local community in Butler, New Jersey, and actively pastoring the First Baptist Church. *Morning Call*, "Butler," 7. Although Reverend Faux pastored a Baptist church in Butler, New Jersey, he also had membership in the Assemblies of God denomination. While in New Jersey, Reverend Faux became the principal of Beulah Heights Bible and Missionary Training School, located in the city of North Bergen. Reverend

"There's a Drawing From on High"

family, meanwhile, moved onto property in White Bluffs formerly owned by the Faux family, and Marie's father, Jay, began holding "Gospel Services" in their home on Sunday afternoons.[102] Beginning in December 1915, according to the local newspaper, these Pentecostal meetings continued until at least May 1916.[103] At eleven years old, Marie received water baptism, marking her own commitment to the faith in which her family had become well established.[104]

The year 1917 was difficult for the Baldwin family. Marie's older brother Wesley—her parent's eldest son—died suddenly in March due to illness, while Marie's younger brother Jay was born in April.[105] Marie's father had already begun looking for a new job and a new home for the family back in August 1916, and the mixed emotions of grief and joy concerning the two boys pushed the family to move again.[106] Marie's father took a job at a saw mill in Everett, Washington, and found a good church community for the family at the local Pentecostal Mission on Rockefeller Avenue, pastored

---

Faux was highly regarded at the institution. In 1923, he left New Jersey to move to Springfield, Missouri, and serve as missionary secretary for the Assemblies of God Foreign Missions Department. Reverend Faux served in this capacity until December 1926, when he was removed from the position on charges of "misappropriation of funds for personal use." During his time as missionary secretary, Reverend Faux had undertaken several overseas missionary trips, which were rather expensive for the Foreign Missions Department. Questions arose about the use of department funds on these trips, and although Reverend Faux denied wrongdoing, evidence to the contrary mounted. Reverend Faux was thus dismissed from the Assemblies of God, although there is evidence that denominational leaders clearly sought to deal with his case discreetly and with a great deal of pastoral care. Reverend Faux subsequently joined the Disciples of Christ denomination and continued doing ministry in the Midwest until his death in July 1943. McGee, "*This Gospel . . . Shall Be Preached*," 114–16; McKnight, *Empowering Spirit, Empowering Structures*, 96–97; "Non-Council Files—Faux, William M. (A/G Terminated)," archival record file, Flower Pentecostal Heritage Center; *Times*, "Calumet City Church of Christ," n.p.; *Chicago Tribune*, "Retired Villa Park Cleric Dies of Train Injuries," 12.

102. *White Bluffs Spokesman*, "Jay Baldwin," 4; *White Bluffs Spokesman*, "Gospel Services" (Dec. 17, 1915), 4.

103. *White Bluffs Spokesman*, "Gospel Services" (Dec. 17, 1915), 4; *White Bluffs Spokesman*, "Gospel Services" (May 5, 1916), 4.

104. Oscar and Marie Knutson, oral history interview with Wayne Warner, Sept. 5, 1983, audio recording, Flower Pentecostal Heritage Center.

105. *White Bluffs Spokesman*, "Wesley Baldwin," 1; *White Bluffs Spokesman*, "Town and Valley News" (Apr. 20, 1917), 4.

106. *White Bluffs Spokesman*, "Town and Valley News" (Aug. 18, 1916), 4; handwritten reflections on Marie Baldwin's early life, Oscar M. Knutson archival collection, unprocessed box.

by Rev. Beulah M. Palmer, a female Pentecostal minister.[107] The Baldwins moved shortly thereafter, in November 1917.

The Pentecostal community in Everett, Washington, was not quite a decade old when the Baldwin family arrived. The city's first resident Pentecostal preacher was Rev. Carl Gustaf Carlson, who arrived in Everett around 1909.[108] Born in 1873, Carlson was a Swedish immigrant who emigrated to the United States and spent a few years on the East Coast and then in the Great Lakes region before settling in Aberdeen, Washington, around the turn of the century.[109] Carlson became a Christian in 1903, got married in 1905, and received the baptism of the Holy Spirit at his home in Aberdeen in 1906, having sought this experience after receiving reports of amazing happenings at the Azusa Street Revival in California.[110] Over the next few years, Carlson began pursuing ministry and helped establish a Swedish-language Pentecostal mission in Aberdeen. Carlson then moved to Everett, where he first preached from church to church and then helped establish a handful of Pentecostal missions in the city, including the Pentecostal Mission on Rockefeller Avenue which the Baldwins joined in 1917.[111]

Joining the Pentecostal community in Everett was spiritually significant for the Baldwin family, as it gave them a robust community of faith for the next several years and provided an important context for their own active participation in local ministry. Jay Baldwin, Marie's father, ministered regularly at the Everett City Jail. Marie, although a mere twelve years old, helped her father in the local jail ministry and remembered several inmates receiving the gospel and converting to Christ.[112]

During their time in Everett, the Baldwin family occasionally visited Seattle and other cities for special Pentecostal prayer meetings and church

---

107. Handwritten reflections on Marie Baldwin's early life, Oscar M. Knutson archival collection, unprocessed box; *Daily Herald*, "Pentecostal Mission" (Feb. 16, 1918), 12. Reverend Palmer's first name is sometimes misprinted as "Veulah" instead of "Beulah," in newspaper clippings. *Daily Herald*, "Pentecostal Mission" (Sept. 14, 1918), 11.

108. Tannenberg, *Let Light Shine Out*, 11.

109. Tannenberg, *Let Light Shine Out*, 9.

110. Tannenberg, *Let Light Shine Out*, 9–10; Carl Gustaf Carlson and Marie Helmire Sand, Certificate of Marriage, 1905, Washington State Digital Archives.

111. Rev. Carl G. Carlson ministered in various Pentecostal communities throughout the Pacific Northwest over the next few decades. He often worked with his son, Rev. Reuben J. Carlson, who became an Assemblies of God minister and later the district superintendent of the Northwest District. Rev. Carl G. Carlson died in Spokane in July 1964. Tannenberg, *Let Light Shine Out*, 11–12, 184–85.

112. Knutson, *His Loving Care*, 16.

services. One such service was especially significant to Marie. On September 15, 1918, while visiting Seattle and participating in a special Pentecostal service conducted by Canadian pastor and evangelist A. H. Argue, Marie received the baptism of the Holy Spirit:

> We were at the altar praying, and we didn't seem to get anywhere. And [there was] this one girl that came with us . . . she was very up and down in her experience . . . and we seemed to have a burden for her, so we went into the pastor's office, and there we was praying for this girl that she would really straighten up for the Lord. And there I received the baptism of the Holy Ghost. And Brother Argue . . . was there praying with me, and they said between us, we were holding conversation in another language.[113]

Marie Baldwin's baptism in the Holy Spirit experience in Seattle, as with her family's previous experiences in Yacolt and White Bluffs, strengthened her faith and commitment to the Lord. Recalling these experiences decades later, Marie remembered a particular exhortation of Rev. A. H. Argue, who "told us to seek the Lord and wait upon Him."[114] Marie and her family sought to keep this charge and consequently remained active in the Pentecostal community in Everett, even as it experienced transition and change over the next few years. In early 1922, the handful of Pentecostal missions in Everett that had been over the past few years pastored at various times and in various locations by Rev. Carl G. Carlson, Rev. Beulah M. Palmer, Rev. Hans Hansen, and Rev. Mary Sanders consolidated into a single Pentecostal Mission.[115] Reverend Carlson took pastoral charge of

---

113. Oscar and Marie Knutson, oral history interview with Wayne Warner, Sept. 5, 1983, audio recording, Flower Pentecostal Heritage Center; note indicating significant events in Marie Knutson's spiritual journey, Oscar M. Knutson archival collection, unprocessed box. The specific timeline for Marie's baptism in the Holy Spirit experience is not exactly clear, admittedly. In the oral history interview, she said it happened in 1918 when she was thirteen years old. In a handwritten note, however, it says that the experience occurred on September 15, 1918, which was technically before Marie turned thirteen. To complicate matters, there are no newspaper clippings noting a visit by Rev. A. H. Argue to Seattle in fall 1918. Meanwhile, there are clippings that indicate a visit by Reverend Argue to Seattle in August 1919, and there is a newspaper advertisement for a special Pentecostal meeting held at the Pine Street Mission in Seattle on September 14, 1919, although it is only a brief clipping, and Reverend Argue is not mentioned. *Seattle Star*, "Strange Tongues Spoken by Cult," 7; *Seattle Star*, "Pine Street Pentecostal Mission," 8.

114. Oscar and Marie Knutson, oral history interview with Wayne Warner, Sept. 5, 1983, audio recording, Flower Pentecostal Heritage Center.

115. *Daily Herald*, "Missions" (Sept. 14, 1918), 11; *Daily Herald*, "City Charge Against

the consolidated fellowship, and it was here in October 1922 that Marie Baldwin and Oscar Knutson were introduced, just prior to one of Jack Nelson's evangelistic meetings.[116]

While he continued to pursue ministry with Brother Jack in 1923, Oscar made regular visits to Everett to see Marie and get to know her family. Their relationship flourished, and Oscar and Marie quickly began courting. Most of their time together was spent doing ministry work with Brother Jack.[117] In early 1924, Oscar proposed marriage, and Marie accepted. They set a wedding date for June 1924, but it was delayed when Marie's father, Jay, fell deathly ill, and Marie had to work to support the family. After Jay's recovery and subsequent return to work, Oscar and Marie set a new wedding date. They were married on September 17, 1924, in the basement of Marie's parent's home.[118] Rev. Idell H. Wood, the new pastor of the Pentecostal Mission in Everett, officiated the ceremony.[119]

Although Oscar Knutson and Jack Nelson occasionally worked together in later decades, 1924 marked the end of their regular ministry partnership. Both Knutson and Nelson got married in 1924, and they parted ways amicably, with their wives—their new ministry partners—at their sides.[120] Brother Jack and his wife Jessie remained in Seattle and contin-

---

Minister Dismissed," 13; *Daily Herald*, "Missions" (Dec. 3, 1921), 11; *Daily Herald*, "Missions: Consolidated Pentecostal Mission," 11; *Daily Herald*, "Church News" (Oct. 13, 1922), 13.

116. The consolidated Pentecostal Mission in Everett welcomed several evangelists in the early 1920s, not just Jack Nelson and his ministry associates, who visited on multiple occasions. In May 1922, the Pentecostal community in Everett welcomed Charles Simmonett, former Pentecostal pastor of Lethbridge, Canada, who assisted Rev. Joseph Lantz with planting the Pentecostal church in Great Falls, Montana. Then, in January 1923, Reverend Lantz himself visited Everett and held some evangelistic services at the Pentecostal Mission. *Daily Herald*, "Church News" (May 12, 1922), 13; *Daily Herald*, "Church News" (Jan. 23, 1923), 10.

117. Oscar and Marie Knutson, oral history interview with Wayne Warner, Sept. 5, 1983, audio recording, Flower Pentecostal Heritage Center.

118. Oscar and Marie Knutson, oral history interview with Wayne Warner, Sept. 5, 1983, audio recording, Flower Pentecostal Heritage Center; Knutson, *His Loving Care*, 29–30.

119. Index to Marriage Records, Snohomish County, Washington, Washington State Digital Archives; *Daily Herald*, "Pentecostal Mission" (July 5, 1924), 12; *Daily Herald*, "Pentecostal Mission" (Aug. 23, 1924), 12.

120. Handwritten reflections on Oscar Knutson's early ministry with Jack Nelson,

ued evangelistic work in the area.[121] Oscar and Marie also lived in Seattle, where Oscar worked as a carpenter and waited for the call of God into new ministry work.[122] As Oscar and Marie waited for the Lord's direction, they began their family with the birth of their daughter, Fern Marie Knutson, on February 22, 1926.[123]

Oscar M. Knutson archival collection, box 2, folders 14, 16.

121. R. L. Polk & Co., *Seattle City Directory, 1933*; *Tacoma Daily Ledger*, "Olaf Solberg," 12.

122. R. L. Polk & Co., *Seattle City Directory, 1925*.

123. Knutson, *His Loving Care*, 30; handwritten family history notes, Oscar M. Knutson archival collection, unprocessed box.

3

"I've Found the Way"

I've found the way, a wondrous way,
The way to life's eternal day;
A way that needs no sunlight ray,
The Lamb's the light, the Scriptures say.
—O. M. Knutson, "I've Found the Way"

THE CALL OF GOD for which Oscar and Marie Knutson had been waiting came in early 1927, when Oscar's older sister, Inga K. Johnson, contacted them with an urgent request to come to Great Falls, Montana, and assist her and her husband with rehabilitating a local Pentecostal rescue mission whose pastor had recently departed.[1] Inga, who had been living in Great Falls after her marriage in May 1920 to John A. Johnson, a railroad foreman with Norwegian heritage, was concerned about the rescue mission's ability to continue operating, as well as the Pentecostal witness in Great Falls.[2] Although Rev. Joseph Lantz's Pentecostal fellowship—renamed the City Gospel Mission in 1923—was continuing to minister in the Great Falls community, another Pentecostal preacher had started the rescue mission

---

1. Knutson, *His Loving Care*, 30–31.
2. *Great Falls Tribune*, "Johnson-Knudson," 9; *Great Falls Tribune*, "Marriage Licenses," 13; Knutson, *His Loving Care*, 31.

only to abandon it without paying any bills.³ It was a scandal, to be sure, and to make matters worse, it was not the only incident of its kind in Great Falls in the 1920s. Since Oscar Knutson had left for Seattle in fall 1922, the Pentecostal community in Great Falls had been wounded on multiple occasions by persons claiming spiritual authority to preach the gospel and represent Jesus but whose lives and actions were marked by dishonesty and immorality.⁴

Such problems were nothing new, of course. The early church was quite familiar with the presence of malicious individuals who corrupted the witness of the gospel because they tried to use the message of Jesus for personal gain, so much so that the New Testament writers actually assigned specific terminology—*false teachers, false apostles,* or *false prophets*—to describe such persons and warn faithful Christians against them. In his Sermon on the Mount, Jesus himself warned his followers to "beware of false prophets who come to you in sheep's clothing but inwardly are ravaging wolves."⁵ Jesus' words were later echoed by the apostles Peter, John, and Jude, and perhaps most notably by the apostle Paul, who warned of "false apostles, deceitful workers, disguising themselves as apostles of Christ."⁶ Relating such persons to Satan who "disguises himself as an angel of light," Paul wrote that false teachers "disguise themselves as servants of righteousness."⁷

Reflecting on Pentecostal hucksters and charlatans in Great Falls, Montana, in the 1920s, Oscar Knutson drew on the scriptural parlance of describing such persons as "wolves." Knutson noted that such persons were "a common problem in those days of the Pentecostal movement. Pentecostal people sometimes had difficulty recognizing the wolves when they came around. Often they had little contact with other Pentecostal churches except those nearby. This made it easier for the wolves to slip in and sometimes cause much trouble."⁸

---

3. *Great Falls Leader,* "City Gospel Mission," 6; Knutson, *His Loving Care,* 31.

4. Knutson, *His Loving Care,* 32; *Great Falls Tribune,* "Denounces Her 'Healer' Spouse as 'Bad Actor,'" 10; *Great Falls Tribune,* "Hold 'Healer' on Complaint in Check Chase," 6; *Great Falls Tribune,* "Evangelist to 'Purge Self of Sin' by Pleading Guilty," 5; *Independent-Record,* "'Evangelist' Held at Great Falls on Charge of Larceny," 12.

5. Matt 7:15, HCSB.

6. 2 Cor 11:13, HCSB.

7. 2 Cor 11:14–15, HCSB.

8. Knutson, *His Loving Care,* 32.

He Will Lead Me

Although mountain passes were still closed due to inclement winter conditions, Oscar and Marie Knutson, together with their one-year-old daughter, Fern, left Seattle for Great Falls. When they arrived, Oscar immediately took up pastoral leadership of the rescue mission, evaluated its financial situation, and established a plan for rehabilitation.[9] At the forefront of Knutson's plan was to recover and reestablish the integrity of the Pentecostal witness in Great Falls. To that end, Oscar agreed to serve as pastor of the rescue mission for two months, on the condition that he would not be paid for his pastoral work.[10] Instead, he would find another way to support himself and his family, which would allow the rescue mission to use all incoming funds for paying off outstanding bills and proceed with general operations for at least a few more months. In Knutson's mind, "This would prove that [the Pentecostal folk at the rescue mission] were honest even if the [former] preacher was not."[11]

According to Knutson's later reflections, his plan for the rescue mission was successful. Knutson got a job with a local building contractor for a few months while also holding church services and attending to general operations for the rescue mission, which was renamed the Interdenominational Gospel Station.[12] The bills were paid off quickly, and the integrity of the Pentecostal community was restored. "A black blot had been erased!" Knutson wrote.[13] Admittedly, despite this success, the rescue mission closed in the summer of 1927. In late May, Knutson had submitted a petition to the city council to permit Pentecostal street-meetings, but his request was formally denied.[14] It seems that this lack of support from the city led Oscar, his sister Inga, Reverend Lantz, and other local Pentecostal leaders to reflect on the needs of the Great Falls community at large and reorient their time and resources accordingly for the sake of the gospel.[15]

---

9. Knutson, *His Loving Care*, 30–31.
10. Knutson, *His Loving Care*, 32–33.
11. Knutson, *His Loving Care*, 32–33.
12. Knutson, *His Loving Care*, 33; *Great Falls Tribune*, "Interdenominational Gospel Station," 18.
13. Knutson, *His Loving Care*, 33.
14. *Great Falls Tribune*, "O. M. Knutson Requested," 3; *Great Falls Leader*, "Petition of O. M. Knutson," 3; *Great Falls Tribune*, "Request of O. M. Knutson," 3.
15. Knutson, *His Loving Care*, 33.

"I've Found the Way"

After the rescue mission closed, Oscar and Marie Knutson returned to Washington State, where they could be near their respective parents—Oscar's in Seattle, and Marie's in Everett—while still pursuing local ministry opportunities. In late February 1928, Marie's father, Jay Baldwin, died.[16] Shortly thereafter the Baldwin family moved back to Michigan, although Marie's mother, Cora May Baldwin, spent the next few years moving back and forth, alternating between being near family in Pontiac, Michigan, and having responsibility for the operations of some girls' homes in Seattle and Tacoma, Washington.[17] Similarly, over the next decade and a half, Oscar and Marie Knutson's ministry work took them back and forth between the Pacific Northwest and the Midwest as they sought to preach the gospel and establish and strengthen local Pentecostal fellowships along the way.

On October 8, 1929, Lloyd Oscar Knutson was born to Oscar and Marie Knutson in Seattle, Washington.[18] This joyful arrival of a second child came just weeks before their lives—and the lives of many around the world—took a radical turn. In late October 1929, the Great Depression hit. Held by historians to be the largest global economic crisis of the twentieth century, the impact of the Great Depression was felt deeply on the local level. Prices fell, production slowed, unemployment skyrocketed, and businesses floundered or folded. As the economy collapsed, people's spirits followed. It was a difficult time.[19]

Despite the chaos and change of the Great Depression, Oscar and Marie Knutson remained steadfast in their faith and entrusted themselves to God. They also "agreed that if we had any personal needs while in the service of the Lord, we would tell no one but the Lord. In that way we would know, when the answer came, that it was from the Lord and not from someone who might feel obligated to help us."[20] Although by no means critical of human sympathy or generosity, Oscar and Marie established this "policy"

---

16. *Daily Herald*, "Jay Neil Baldwin," 14.

17. Handwritten reflections on Baldwin family history, Oscar M. Knutson archival collection, unprocessed box; *Daily Herald*, "Postal Aid Sought in Locating Family," 8.

18. Knutson, *His Loving Care*, 30; *Daily Herald*, "Lloyd O. Knutson," 12.

19. Garraty, *Great Depression*, 9.

20. Knutson, *His Loving Care*, 6.

between the two of them because "we prefer to see the hand of the Lord in it because it shows that He is with us and careth for us."[21]

Although Oscar and Marie Knutson's decision to refrain from disclosing or discussing personal needs with anyone but the Lord was not necessarily representative of normative practice within the Pentecostal movement—nor of Christian tradition more broadly—it does reflect a uniquely Pentecostal concern about hearing from God directly. According to historian Grant Wacker, early Pentecostals desired "to be guided solely by God's Spirit in every aspect of their lives, however great or small."[22] Oscar and Marie Knutson were no different in this respect. This impulse was, after all, none other than one of the primary theological underpinnings of Pentecostalism, namely, "a yearning simply to know the divine mind and will as directly and purely as possible, without the distorting refractions of human volition, traditions, or speculations."[23]

In addition to the desire to hear from God directly and have assurance of his presence and activity in their lives, Oscar and Marie Knutson's decision to bring their needs to God alone was, especially during the Great Depression, an expression of deep faith and sincere confidence in the Lord. Moreover, it was steeped in scriptural exhortation. "Cast all your anxiety on [the Lord]," the apostle Peter wrote in his First Epistle, "because he cares for you."[24] Jesus framed the matter similarly in his Sermon on the Mount: "I tell you, do not worry about your life, what you will eat or drink; or about your body, what you will wear . . . . Look at the birds of the air; they do not sow or reap or store away in barns, and yet your heavenly Father feeds them. Are you not much more valuable than they? . . . Seek first his kingdom and his righteousness, and all these things will be given to you as well."[25] Jesus' words especially resonated with Oscar, who later reflected on God's provision for him and his family by referencing this very section of the Sermon on the Mount: "He who sees the sparrows surely watches over His own, and often He does things in a way that shows that He *is* watching."[26]

21. Knutson, *His Loving Care*, 35–36.
22. Wacker, *Heaven Below*, 12.
23. Wacker, *Heaven Below*, 11.
24. 1 Pet 5:7, NIV.
25. Matt 6:25–26, 33, NIV.
26. Knutson, *His Loving Care*, 46.

"I've Found the Way"

In 1930, Oscar and Marie were called to leave Seattle again and embark on new ministry work. Returning to Montana with two children under four years old, the Knutsons first held evangelistic meetings at the newly forming Pentecostal church in Livingston and then in the modest Pentecostal fellowship in Billings.[27] Then, in late June, after visiting Great Falls for a couple of days, they held two weeks of services in Augusta, which Oscar later described as "the moonshine town" and "very ungodly."[28] According to Oscar's reflections on their time in Augusta, "quite a number of folk came out to the services, but there was no real response to the Gospel. Not one was saved."[29] Consequently, the Knutson family did not spend much time in Augusta before moving on to other ministry opportunities. Even so, Oscar viewed the experience not as a failure, but rather through the lens of Jesus' parable of the sower. Although Oscar and Marie did not witness any conversions in Augusta, "many heard the Gospel. The seed was sown. We may not know till we get *home* what kind of soil the seed fell in."[30] These reflections indicate a two-fold theological understanding from this parable of Jesus, namely, the real, dynamic power of the word of God to transform lives as well as the importance of human responsibility to receive and obey the gospel.

After Augusta, the Knutsons proceeded to Fairfield, Montana, where they spent the next three months holding evangelistic services and investing in the local community to which Oscar had once belonged. While in Fairfield, Oscar, Marie, and the children stayed on the old homestead formerly owned by Oscar's parents, Andrew and Elvina Knutson. While also doing ministry work, Oscar took a temporary job with the US Reclamation Service, supervising a government irrigation project that would ensure that local farmers would have water for their crops in the spring.[31] The irrigation project concluded "before the frost," and the Knutson family returned to Great Falls for the winter.[32] As a result of their Pentecostal meetings in Fairfield, "at least two found the Lord," Oscar recalled.[33] Although the Knutsons did not plant a Pentecostal church in Fairfield, a local carpenter

---

27. Knutson, *His Loving Care*, 33; Roset et al., *Assemblies of God in Montana*, 51.
28. Knutson, *His Loving Care*, 33–34.
29. Knutson, *His Loving Care*, 34.
30. Knutson, *His Loving Care*, 34.
31. Knutson, *His Loving Care*, 36–37.
32. Knutson, *His Loving Care*, 37.
33. Knutson, *His Loving Care*, 37.

named Carl A. Beardsley continued their labors. Beardsley and his family began holding gospel meetings in their home in 1930, which led to the establishment of a humble Pentecostal fellowship in 1931.[34] In 1935, the church—which became known as the Fairfield Gospel Tabernacle—built its first formal building and, in 1941, gained membership in the Assemblies of God denomination.[35]

Upon returning to Great Falls, Montana, in late 1930, Oscar and Marie Knutson collaborated with Oscar's sister Inga Johnson to reopen the Pentecostal rescue mission which she and her husband restarted on a seasonal basis back in February 1929.[36] Known as the Glad Tidings Rescue Mission, its mission was to serve the substantial local population of men who needed food and shelter—"and, of course, the Gospel"—largely due to unemployment and other hardship.[37] Although poverty was not an uncommon reality—Jesus himself noted to his disciples in the first century that "the poor you will always have with you"[38]—the onset of the Great Depression had significantly increased the rate of poverty and, thus, the need for a rescue mission to be operating within the local community.

It was not just the local Pentecostal community in Great Falls that was attuned to the hardship of the Great Depression, however. Everyone was experiencing its effects, and city and county leaders sought to address these multifaceted challenges. Oscar Knutson noted in later reflections that "there was no welfare program at that time," and it was not uncommon for those in need to go "from house to house and store to store begging for food."[39] When the Pentecostal community in Great Falls approached the city leadership to seek guidance on reopening the rescue mission, they immediately found support from not just the city but county commissioners

---

34. Fairfield Heritage Committee, *Boots and Shovels*, 10, 124–25; Garrett, "History of the Montana District Council," 47.

35. Garrett, "History of the Montana District Council," 47; correspondence to Fairfield Gospel Tabernacle indicating affiliation with the Assemblies of God, Apr. 20, 1941, Flower Pentecostal Heritage Center.

36. *Great Falls Tribune*, "Glad Tidings Rescue Mission," 7; *Great Falls Leader*, "Glad Tidings Rescue Mission," 4.

37. *Great Falls Tribune*, "Glad Tidings Rescue Mission," 7; *Great Falls Leader*, "Glad Tidings Rescue Mission," 4; Knutson, *His Loving Care*, 39.

38. Matt 26:11, NIV.

39. Knutson, *His Loving Care*, 40.

as well. To assist the Glad Tidings Rescue Mission, Cascade County offered to pay for two storefront buildings—one for providing food and shelter for those in need and one for holding church services. Additionally, the county promised to "furnish heat and lights" and to provide "an old gas restaurant-type cook stove," along with some cots, tables, and other necessary equipment and supplies.[40] "We would only have to provide the food," Oscar remembered.[41] As it turned out, a local vegetable dealer gave the rescue mission lots of free potatoes and vegetables that were "not nice enough to put in stores, yet were not spoiled."[42] The rescue mission also acquired lots of day-old bread from local bakeries and plenty of soup bones and meat from various local butchers. Moreover, "hamburger was then selling retail for as little as three pounds for 25 cents," while "eggs were three dozen for 25 cents." The rescue mission was "never short of food," Oscar recalled.[43]

The Glad Tidings Rescue Mission reopened on November 1, 1930, with Oscar Knutson's sister Inga Johnson serving as pastor and Oscar himself serving as assistant pastor.[44] Both served in a volunteer capacity, as did other rescue mission workers, who assisted with day-to-day operations. The rescue mission operated until May 30, 1931, before closing for the season. During that period, "more than 10,000 meals were served by the mission," according to a local newspaper article.[45] Additionally, among other things, the mission was able to provide "fuel, rent payments, groceries, Christmas baskets and clothing" to those in need of them.[46] In addition to its "welfare" work, the Glad Tidings Rescue Mission held church services "practically every evening during the winter."[47] In total, the rescue mission's operating expenses for the season were a mere 475 dollars, which was supplied through charitable donations from various churches, clubs, businesses, organizations, and individuals within the Great Falls community.[48]

40. Knutson, *His Loving Care*, 40.
41. Knutson, *His Loving Care*, 40.
42. Knutson, *His Loving Care*, 41.
43. Knutson, *His Loving Care*, 41.
44. *Great Falls Tribune*, "Glad Tidings Rescue Home Opens Again," 10; *Great Falls Tribune*, "Rescue Mission," 24; *Great Falls Tribune*, "Glad Tidings Mission Will Resume Soon," 3.
45. *Great Falls Tribune*, "Glad Tidings Mission Will Resume Soon," 3.
46. *Great Falls Tribune*, "Glad Tidings Mission Will Resume Soon," 3.
47. *Great Falls Tribune*, "Glad Tidings Mission Will Resume Soon," 3.
48. *Great Falls Tribune*, "Glad Tidings Rescue Home Opens Again," 10; *Great Falls Tribune*, "Glad Tidings Mission Will Resume Soon," 3. Four hundred seventy-five dollars

The Glad Tidings Rescue Mission was significant as a local expression of the kind of tangible care for the vulnerable and needy expected of God's people throughout the holy Scriptures. The New Testament alone contains several rather sharp statements meant to call Christians to action in this regard. The apostle James went so far as to write that "pure and undefiled religion before our God and Father is this: to look after orphans and widows in their distress, and to keep oneself unstained by the world."[49] Similarly, the apostle John wrote that "if anyone has this world's goods and sees his brother in need, yet closes his eyes to his need, how can God's love reside in him?"[50] The early church took such words seriously and even became known for its organized efforts to help those whose lives were marked by poverty, sickness, violence, abandonment, and other hardship and suffering.[51] Church history is replete with examples of this kind of tangible care for those in need, and Pentecostalism shares in this robust heritage of Christian charity.

In addition to participating in the perennial Christian tradition of charity, the Glad Tidings Rescue Mission was historically significant because it featured a unique (and rather early) example of a woman serving as pastor, while a man served as her assistant pastor. The fact that Inga Johnson and Oscar Knutson were sister and brother perhaps made their ministerial relationship more intuitive and less surprising, but even so, to have a female pastor in Montana in the 1930s was nevertheless striking. Although women have served in a variety of important ministry capacities throughout church history, it has not been traditional Christian practice to ordain women to formal clerical roles. Female ordination became more prolific in the nineteenth and twentieth centuries among certain ecclesial bodies and denominational traditions—including, and especially, Pentecostalism—but broadly speaking, women pastors nonetheless remain a minority among clergy even in the present. This reality makes Inga Johnson's

---

in 1930 dollars is the equivalent of a little more than nine thousand dollars in 2024 dollars.

49. Jas 1:27, HCSB. Traditionally, the Epistle of James is held to have been written by James the "brother of the Lord," who was a pillar of leadership in the early church, came to be counted among the apostles, was made the first bishop of the church at Jerusalem, and presided at the Council of Jerusalem in AD 50, as recorded in Acts 15. This James is not to be confused with James the son of Zebedee or James the son of Alphaeus, who were two of Jesus' twelve apostles.

50. 1 John 3:17, HCSB.

51. Sittser, *Resilient Faith*, 146–50.

pastoral ministry, along with that of Oscar Knutson's other female ministry partners, significant.

In late spring 1931, the Knutson family returned to Seattle, Washington, to hold some church services with Brother Jack Nelson and to visit Oscar's parents. Then, in summer 1931, the Knutsons embarked for Custer, Montana, from which they had received a call to visit and hold Pentecostal meetings.[52] Along the way, the Knutsons stopped briefly in Butte, Montana, where they visited the Laughery family, whom Oscar had met while ministering with Brother Jack in Black Diamond, Washington, in 1923. The Laughery family had "surrendered to the Lord"—that is, converted to become Christians— in Black Diamond, and Mrs. C. B. Laughery, the matriarch of the family, was divinely healed of bone tuberculosis and abdominal cancer after being anointed by oil and prayed for by Nelson and Knutson.[53] In a short article published in *The Pentecostal Evangel* in 1928, Mrs. Laughery wrote of her experience in Black Diamond and noted that God had not only healed her body but also baptized her with the Holy Spirit:

> I am happy in the service of the King . . . I am altogether unworthy of God's goodness, but I write my testimony with the hope that it may help some other suffering one to prove Him as I have done— the Friend that never fails, always present to save and heal. I have been following Jesus nearly five years and the way grows sweeter as the days go by.[54]

Oscar was pleased to see Mrs. Laughery and her family in Butte and was delighted to find them "happily serving the Lord."[55]

After Butte, the Knutsons proceeded on with their journey and stopped briefly in Billings before finally arriving in Custer. In Custer, Oscar collaborated with retired blacksmith Peter Larson to hold evangelistic services in an old schoolhouse near the Larson family homestead.[56] According to Knutson's reflections, they held services in the schoolhouse for

---

52. Knutson, *His Loving Care*, 45.

53. Knutson, *His Loving Care*, 20–21; Laughery, "Healed of Cancer and Tuberculosis," 7.

54. Laughery, "Healed of Cancer and Tuberculosis," 7.

55. Knutson, *His Loving Care*, 47.

56. *Melstone Messenger*, "Peter Larson Retires," A1; Knutson, *His Loving Care*, 47–48.

two weeks in August 1931. Many people came, and "several were saved in the meetings."[57] In addition to several conversions, the Knutsons witnessed "some real rejo[i]cing in the little school house" due to the divine healing of a blind woman with severe arthritis. Oscar recalled that the woman's son had "asked us to pray for her arthritis because she was in intense pain, but the Lord not only healed her arthritis, he healed her eyes also!"[58]

Upon concluding two weeks of evangelistic meetings in Custer, the Knutson family returned to Billings, Montana, to hold services at the modest local Pentecostal mission pastored by Rev. Annie B. Applegate, an ordained female evangelist of the Assemblies of God denomination whom they had met previously.[59] Born Anna Belle Tong in Kansas in March 1872, Annie spent much of her early life in Missouri, where she married John Applegate in November 1887.[60] The Applegates had three children and lived in Kansas for several years before moving back to Missouri for a time.[61] Although much of Annie's biography is unclear, it is clear that she understood herself to have a "special calling" from the Lord to preach.[62] On July 19, 1905, Annie was ordained in the Gospel Church by Rev. D. R. Hays and began pursuing ministry.[63] Around 1915, she and her family moved to Billings, Montana.[64] On March 2, 1918, Applegate was re-ordained, and in 1922, her ordination was recognized by the Assemblies of God.[65] From 1922 to 1924, Applegate operated as a traveling Pentecostal evangelist and preached at various locations in Montana and Wyoming.[66] In 1925, she planted an

  57. Knutson, *His Loving Care*, 49.
  58. Knutson, *His Loving Care*, 49.
  59. Knutson, *His Loving Care*, 49.
  60. Annie B. Applegate, State of Montana Certificate of Death, 1935, Ancestry.com; Annie Tong and John Applegate, Marriage License, 1887, Ancestry.com; *Billings Gazette*, "Local Woman Dies of Heart Attack," 5.
  61. *Billings Gazette*, "Local Woman Dies of Heart Attack," 5.
  62. Ordination documents, in "Deceased Ministers—Applegate, Annie Belle," archival record file, Flower Pentecostal Heritage Center.
  63. Ordination documents, in "Deceased Ministers—Applegate, Annie Belle," archival record file, Flower Pentecostal Heritage Center.
  64. *Billings Gazette*, "Local Woman Dies of Heart Attack," 5.
  65. Ordination documents, in "Deceased Ministers—Applegate, Annie Belle," archival record file, Flower Pentecostal Heritage Center.
  66. *Hardin Tribune*, "Mrs. M. A. Bartells," A6; Applegate, "Reports from the Field:

"I've Found the Way"

Assembly of God mission in Billings and pastored it for the next decade while also continuing her evangelistic ministry.[67]

Women like Annie Applegate and Inga Johnson have always been important in church history. Although there are unfortunate exceptions, Christianity as a whole has historically affirmed the dignity of women in a way that is largely unparalleled by other religious and cultural settings. The biblical account of God's creation of the world establishes humanity as being comprised of both men and women, who are described as complementary equals, both made in the image of God.[68] Although the holy Scriptures are replete with examples of brokenness within male-female relationships due to the destructive presence of sin, the Scriptures also bear witness to the restoration of human relationships in Jesus, which includes the affirmation of female dignity in a highly patriarchal world. As the apostle Paul wrote to the first-century Galatian church: "There is no Jew or Greek, slave nor free, male or female; for you are all one in Christ Jesus."[69]

The apostle Paul's vision for the equality and complementarity of men and women in the church comes directly from Jesus himself, who was born of a woman, Mary.[70] The incarnation of Jesus is perhaps the greatest divine affirmation of womanhood, for in the womb of the Virgin Mary, the almighty, uncontainable, eternal God chose to dwell. Indeed, it was there in the womb of Mary that the physical body of Jesus was knit together. Jesus' divinity and humanity are equally imperative for his role as Savior of the world, and significantly, Jesus received his human nature from Mary, his mother.[71]

Jesus likewise affirmed the dignity of women during his earthly ministry. While other first-century Jewish rabbis only welcomed men as

---

Billings, Mon.," 14; Applegate, "Reports from the Field: Billings, Mont.," 12.

67. *Billings Gazette*, "Assembly of God" (May 17, 1925), 14; *Billings Gazette*, "Assembly of God" (Jan. 3, 1926), 14; *Billings Gazette*, "Pentecostal Assembly of God" (May 9, 1926), 16; *Billings Gazette*, "Assembly of God" (Aug. 21, 1927), 26; *Billings Gazette*, "Pentecostal Assembly of God" (Feb. 5, 1928), 18; *Billings Gazette*, "Assembly of God Mission" (Aug. 22, 1931), 4; *Billings Gazette*, "Assembly of God Mission" (Dec. 30, 1933), 5.

68. Gen 1:26–27, 2:20–24.

69. Gal 3:28, HCSB.

70. Luke 1:26–35, 2:1–7.

71. Church tradition is replete with further theological reflections on the relationship between Jesus and his mother, Mary. In addition to the biblical narrative, the Creed of the Council of Chalcedon (AD 451) and the Athanasian Creed (late fifth–early sixth century) clarify that Jesus received his human nature from Mary.

disciples, Jesus invited women to follow him and taught them just as he did his male disciples. Several women also served as benefactors for Jesus' earthly ministry.[72] At his crucifixion, when Jesus' male disciples had scattered and abandoned him, his female disciples were present at the foot of the cross.[73] These faithful women also visited Jesus' (empty) tomb, became the first witnesses of his resurrection, and were commissioned to preach this good news before any male disciples received the same charge.[74] This was an especially noteworthy action because in first-century Jerusalem, the testimony of women had no standing in legal proceedings. Jesus' commissioning of women to preach of his resurrection is significant because, contrary to the patriarchal culture of the day, it marks divine affirmation of women sharing in gospel ministry.

Women played a significant role throughout the New Testament, not just in the Gospels. Women were a significant constituency of those present for the great outpouring of the Holy Spirit at Pentecost, and served the early church in a variety of capacities.[75] Women were apostles, prophetesses, and deaconesses. Women also ran robust charity ministries and facilitated regular worship by turning their homes into meeting places for house churches.[76] It is noteworthy that several women are named throughout the epistles of the apostle Paul. Paul did much ministry work with women and counted their collaboration and labors in the gospel as equally valuable to his own.[77] Admittedly, there are a few passages in the New Testament—mostly from the writings of the apostle Paul, actually—that have raised significant discussion concerning women's place and ministry in the church.[78] Traditionally, these scriptural passages have been understood to clarify formal church offices and limit ordination to men, although by no means jettisoning the important lay ministry work done by both women and men. It is unfortunate and tragic that on many occasions, these passages have

---

72. Luke 8:2–3.
73. Matt 27:55–57; Mark 15:40–41; Luke 23:49.
74. Matt 28:1–10; Mark 16:1–7; Luke 24:1–11; John 20:1, 11–18.
75. Acts 1:14–15, 2:1–4.
76. Rom 16:1–15; Acts 9:36–42, 21:8–9; 1 Cor 11:1–5, 16:19; Phil 4:2–3; 2 Tim 4:19; Phlm 1:2. More extensive discussions on women in the New Testament and early church have been published elsewhere. For further consideration of this subject, see Gupta, *Tell Her Story*.
77. Phil 4:2–3.
78. 1 Cor 14:33–40; 1 Tim 2:11–12.

been, and are currently, also used to stifle and subordinate women and suppress their service to God.

Just as women were a significant constituency of the early church and served in a variety of ministry capacities, so too were women prolific within the context of nascent Pentecostalism, as well as earlier revivalist traditions. Women revivalists such as Phoebe Palmer and Maria Woodworth-Etter—the latter of whom published books that were personally impactful for Marie Knutson and her parents, Jay and Cora May Baldwin—were known for their fiery preaching and evangelism, which gave precedent for what became commonplace within the early Pentecostal movement.[79] Woodworth-Etter's ministry—which often drew crowds in the thousands—was especially significant, as it featured prolific charismatic experiences, ecstatic expressions, and healing miracles that became characteristic of the Pentecostal tradition.[80] Moreover, Woodworth-Etter, whose ministry began decades before the Azusa Street Revival in 1906, ultimately embraced Pentecostalism herself as it began to take shape in the early twentieth century.[81]

Early Pentecostalism tended to support women in ministry, in both lay and ordained capacities, but not because it sought to overturn or jettison holy Scripture, as opponents of the Pentecostal movement argued. Early Pentecostals were, after all, extremely focused on the Bible. They understood the Bible to be God's word written and thus authoritative and true.[82] Early Pentecostals were committed to following the Bible, but they often took a different interpretive tack on the issue of women's ordination than other more traditional ecclesial bodies. This interpretive difference was largely because Pentecostals were more focused on charismatic experiences and giftings than on traditional ecclesial forms and structures.[83] Besides, if the Holy Spirit moved in power and raised up a woman to be a pastor or minister, who could object? Who could deny the work of God?

---

79. Oscar and Marie Knutson, oral history interview with Wayne Warner, Sept. 5, 1983, audio recording, Flower Pentecostal Heritage Center.

80. Estrelda Alexander, "Women," in Stewart, *Handbook of Pentecostal Christianity*, 215; Jacobsen, *Thinking in the Spirit*, 16–17.

81. Anderson, *To the Ends of the Earth*, 94, 96–97.

82. Anderson, *To the Ends of the Earth*, 119–20, 122; Scott A. Ellington, "Scripture: Finding One's Place in God's Story," in Vondey, *Routledge Handbook of Pentecostal Theology*, 65.

83. Estrelda Alexander, "Women," in Stewart, *Handbook of Pentecostal Christianity*, 213.

The early Pentecostals saw themselves as continuing, or participating in, that great outpouring of the Holy Spirit at Pentecost, as recorded in the Acts of the Apostles. In Acts 2, the Holy Spirit fell upon all who were gathered in the upper room in Jerusalem—both men and women. Acts 2 was, after all, the realization of God's promise given through the prophet Joel: "After this I will pour out my Spirit on all humanity; then your sons and your daughters will prophesy . . . I will even pour out my Spirit on the male and female slaves in those days."[84] Since women were included in the great outpouring of the Holy Spirit at Pentecost, and since the New Testament bears witness to women in the early church speaking in tongues, prophesying, and exercising other charismatic gifts, early Pentecostals largely embraced women in a variety of ministry capacities.

Annie Applegate, Inga Johnson, and even Jack Nelson's ministry associate Mary Sanders were representative of the ubiquity of women in ministry within nascent Pentecostalism. Nevertheless, it should be noted that Pentecostals were not without reservations concerning women's ordination. There were still some difficult New Testament passages to navigate, which seemed to restrict women from having leadership in the church over men.[85] Furthermore, as Pentecostals began to embrace more denominational organization and structure, they often became less favorable toward women's ordination. In short, organization and structure often competed with charismatic experience and giftings. For example, the Assemblies of God, which recognized Annie Applegate's ordination as an evangelist in 1922, originally held several formal restrictions regarding female ordination. When the denomination was founded in 1914, women comprised one-third of its ministers and two-thirds of its missionaries.[86] However, the Assemblies of God did not originally ordain women as pastors or elders, which meant women were unable to hold voting privileges within the denomination's General Council. Women "ministers" in the Assemblies of God were, technically speaking, only evangelists and thus had limitations on their ministry work.[87]

---

84. Joel 2:28, 29, HCSB.

85. Particularly 1 Tim 2:12, in which the apostle Paul wrote: "I do not allow a woman to teach or to have authority over a man; instead, she is to be silent" (NIV).

86. Estrelda Alexander, "Women," in Stewart, *Handbook of Pentecostal Christianity*, 216–17; Anderson, *Introduction to Pentecostalism*, 274.

87. Wacker, *Heaven Below*, 166.

Annie Applegate's ordination papers reflect the early policy of the Assemblies of God to only ordain women as evangelists and missionaries. Even so, in her local context in Billings, Montana, she operated as both a pastor and evangelist. Like many other female ministers within the early Pentecostal movement, however, Applegate's pastoral ministry was not aimed at resisting restrictive policies of the denomination that held her ordination papers. Instead, it was aimed at doing the work to which the Lord had called her. Applegate's perspective is reflected in one of her "reports from the field" posted in *The Pentecostal Evangel* in May 1923:

> The Lord is still working, and the devil is stirred. There seem to be a few hungry hearts here and a few who are standing true, for which I praise the Lord. I have been out in other fields, and the Lord wonderfully blessed the work. I just returned from Powell, Wyoming, where I held a 3-weeks meeting. Three received the Baptism according to Acts 2:4, and more were at the altar seeking the ful[l]ness of God. To Him be all the glory. I will soon be out again for Him to other fields, as these northwestern states are such a hard, needy field. I covet the prayers of the saints that I may have strength and means to press the battle on for the Lord, and that many souls may get saved and filled with the Spirit.[88]

While female ordination has been, and continues to be, a topic of significant conversation and debate among Christians, Oscar Knutson was evidently unconcerned about the matter. His theological writings do not reflect any engagement with it, and available biographical information indicates that he collaborated in ministry with many people, including multiple women, over the course of his life. Knutson's primary female ministry associates were his sister Inga Johnson and Annie Applegate of Billings, but of course, Oscar's lifelong ministry companion was none other than his beloved wife, Marie.

---

88. Applegate, "Reports from the Field: Billings, Mon.," 14.

4

"He Will Lead Me"

He will lead me thro' the waters,
He will lead me by the hand,
He will still the rolling billows;
Lead me safe to glory's strand.

—O. M. Knutson, "He Will Lead Me"

After two weeks of evangelistic services in Billings, Montana, with Rev. Annie Applegate in August 1931, the Knutson family returned briefly to Custer, Montana, for a "water baptismal service" and then began driving east for Pontiac, Michigan, intending to visit Marie's mother and siblings.[1] The trip to Michigan took longer than expected and revealed the very present and bitter reality of the Great Depression, as well as the abiding goodness and grace of God. Despite the hard times, Oscar's reflections consistently speak of God's providence regarding finances, not to mention other needs. For Oscar and his family, the difficult conditions of the Great Depression made room for significant scriptural reflection, as well as sincere faith and trust in the Lord, which only led to deeper lifelong confidence in him.

Throughout the Great Depression, God took care of the Knutson family on several occasions, providing them with just what they needed and

1. Knutson, *His Loving Care*, 49.

right when they needed it. The Lord stretched their finances—often just a few dollars—to meet their immediate physical needs so that they never went hungry. God also provided jobs for Oscar to support his family, especially when they would not be able to be supported through their ministry work. In addition to many stories of financial provision, Oscar recorded several anecdotes of God providing for him and his family in other ways. "True, there were some hardships to endure," Knutson recalled later, "but it brought such great blessings to see the hand of the Lord work things out in supernatural ways."[2]

Back in early 1930, while doing ministry in Augusta, Montana, Oscar wore out his only suit of clothes and did not have money to purchase a new one. He was also unable to obtain press-on patches from the local store and, at the recommendation of the storekeeper, tried to make do with some patching cement, to no avail.[3] The next morning, however, Knutson visited the local post office and found that a suit of clothes had arrived in the mail for him from a friend and ministry partner in Seattle, "a colored preacher"—probably Rev. Lee Henson—who, Oscar noted, "did not know that I needed a suit just then."[4] According to Oscar's reflections, the preacher friend had been gifted the suit, and "the Lord had laid it on his heart to send it to me."[5]

In July 1930, while driving eastward over the Bitterroot Mountains on their way to Custer, Montana, the Knutsons ran out of food, but at lunchtime just happened to find "a fresh loaf of bread, still sealed in wax paper" on the side of the road.[6] "Who dropped that loaf of bread up in the mountains in a place where we could find it at just exactly noon?" Oscar considered.[7] "We are sure we know, the One who watches over His own."[8] Shortly after this experience, while still on their way to Custer, the Lord miraculously kept the Knutsons' 1926 Ford Model T automobile running miles beyond its gas tank capacity when there was no opportunity to get fuel while driving through middle-of-nowhere prairie in Montana.[9]

2. Knutson, *His Loving Care*, 101.
3. Knutson, *His Loving Care*, 34–35.
4. Knutson, *His Loving Care*, 35.
5. Knutson, *His Loving Care*, 35.
6. Knutson, *His Loving Care*, 46.
7. Knutson, *His Loving Care*, 46.
8. Knutson, *His Loving Care*, 46.
9. Knutson, *His Loving Care*, 47.

In addition to finances, clothing, food, and fuel, God provided rest to the Knutson family. Oscar recalled that while they were on their way to Michigan in fall 1931, he, Marie, and their children had to spend the night just off the road, somewhere near Rapid City, South Dakota.[10] It was midnight, and there was no formal place to stay, so Oscar gathered "dead grass that had been burned by the severe drought" and used it to make beds for his family.[11] Apparently, he and his family rested well that night but discovered in the morning that over half of the "grass" was not prairie grass after all, but rather long, pointy, cactus needles.[12] "We slept all night on it without getting stuck once!" Knutson noted.[13] "It made me think of when they pressed a crown of thorns onto the head of our Lord and Saviour. His head was pierced by the thorns. Here we had slept on long thorns, and somehow the Lord must have protected us. He suffered, we rested."[14]

Although perhaps not as life changing as miracles of radical divine healing, small yet timely miracles like these of bread, clothing, transportation, and rest strengthen faith. Like God providing manna in the wilderness for his people, these comparatively modest miracles of providing bread and clothes speak to Jesus' own words from the Sermon on the Mount, that his followers must simply seek first God's kingdom and his righteousness, and God would take care of their daily necessities—food, clothing, shelter, and the like.[15] In a book of life reflections published in 1979 or 1980, Oscar described this as God's "loving care," that is, the Lord's daily provision and affection for those who trust in him.[16]

The Knutson family passed through Mitchell, South Dakota, on their way to Michigan in fall 1931. In Mitchell, "we broke our last $5.00 bill, filled our gas tank, and then went to a grocery store to get some bread," Oscar wrote.[17] As they started driving again, however, it seemed as though God was directing them to further ministry work along the way. Oscar "felt strongly"

---

10. Knutson, *His Loving Care*, 49.
11. Knutson, *His Loving Care*, 49.
12. Knutson, *His Loving Care*, 49–50.
13. Knutson, *His Loving Care*, 50.
14. Knutson, *His Loving Care*, 50.
15. Matt 6:31–33.
16. Knutson, *His Loving Care*.
17. Knutson, *His Loving Care*, 50.

that they ought to pause their trip eastward to Michigan and instead drive north to Huron, South Dakota.[18] "Even though we knew nothing about Huron, I just could not get it off my mind," Oscar remembered.[19] "However, I said nothing to Marie about it and just started driving east. But after driving a mile or two Marie said, 'I think we are going in the wrong direction. I feel like we should go north to Huron.'"[20] Oscar "took this as a verification of our leading," and promptly changed course for Huron.[21]

The Knutson family arrived in Huron, South Dakota, in early September 1931. There, they discovered that the local Assembly of God church had been "broken up" for several months and was desperately in need of healing.[22] Founded as the Full Gospel Assembly in fall 1927, the church had originally flourished under the pastoral leadership of Rev. William E. Menzies.[23] In mid 1928, however, Reverend Menzies resigned, perhaps to pursue other ministry opportunities.[24] By January 1929, Rev. G. H. Rake was installed as pastor, and within months the name of the church was changed to Huron Gospel Tabernacle.[25] A charismatic leader who wanted to "stir up the whole town," Rake launched a large revivalist campaign of special services, radio programs, and visiting evangelists.[26] "His campaign fell flat," however, and Rake attributed its failure to sin within his own congregation.[27] While Rake advertised Huron Gospel Tabernacle as "the church that makes you feel welcome," he began causing divisions within his own fellowship while seeking to root out "Mr. Sin."[28] In late April 1931,

18. Knutson, *His Loving Care*, 50.
19. Knutson, *His Loving Care*, 50.
20. Knutson, *His Loving Care*, 50.
21. Knutson, *His Loving Care*, 50.
22. Oscar and Marie Knutson, oral history interview with Wayne Warner, Sept. 5, 1983, audio recording, Flower Pentecostal Heritage Center.
23. *Daily Plainsman*, "Full Gospel Assembly" (Oct. 14, 1927), 14.
24. *Daily Plainsman*, "Full Gospel Assembly" (June 1, 1928), 5; Knutson, *His Loving Care*, 53–54.
25. *Daily Plainsman*, "Full Gospel Tabernacle" (Jan. 18, 1929), 6; *Daily Plainsman*, "Huron Gospel Tabernacle" (May 31, 1929), 7.
26. Knutson, *His Loving Care*, 53–54; *Daily Plainsman*, "Full Gospel Tabernacle" (Feb. 8, 1929), 12; *Daily Plainsman*, "Tomorrow on Your Radio . . . 9:00—Gospel Tabernacle," 4; *Daily Plainsman*, "Revival Service Continues Here," 12.
27. Knutson, *His Loving Care*, 54.
28. *Daily Plainsman*, "Huron Gospel Tabernacle" (Dec. 27, 1929), 6; *Daily Plainsman*, "Huron Gospel Tabernacle" (Jan. 10, 1930), 5; *Daily Plainsman*, "Huron Gospel Tabernacle" (May 1, 1930), 3; Knutson, *His Loving Care*, 54.

Rake resigned to become the pastor of another Assemblies of God church in Milford, Nebraska, and left the Huron congregation in shambles.[29]

With the support and assistance of local lay leaders, Oscar and Marie Knutson began holding evangelistic services five evenings a week at Daum's Hall, the building in which the church had been meeting since its founding in 1927.[30] Attendance was low at first, but slowly grew. Oscar noted that as attendance increased, seating within the sanctuary space reflected previous church divisions. One group of former church members sat up front, while another group sat at the back. Knutson continued holding services, pastorally seeking to facilitate reconciliation.[31] Concerning this experience, he reflected:

> The conditions there looked almost hopeless, but nothing is impossible for the Lord. God's love, so wonderfully manifested in Jesus our precious Lord and Saviour, is the only power that can melt the stony hearts. Never the hammer. There could never be real fellowship among those people until their hearts were first melted before the Lord, and until they would seek the Lord in true repentance. Bitterness had to be cleansed from their hearts, and be replaced by the Love of Christ before *Eph 4:3, 13*, could operate fully in their hearts. Our first aim was to treat all alike. Manifest true Christian love for all alike. Then preach the Word in love.[32]

Oscar Knutson witnessed the beginning of reconciliation about a month after arriving in Huron. Spiritual healing and church growth followed. Before long, a significant constituency of non-English-speaking newcomers joined the church, previously hailing from a Mennonite community north of Huron which "spoke German with some Russian mixed in."[33] Knutson soon recognized the need for a new pastor who could speak both English and "the German-Russian language," and the Lord evidently provided an answer when a letter arrived from Rev. H. G. Schmid, a German-speaking pastor with an extensive ministry background, inquiring about the church in Huron.[34] Knutson invited Reverend Schmid and his

---

29. *Milford Review*, "Rev. G. H. Rake New Pastor Here," 1; *Daily Plainsman*, "Huron Gospel Tabernacle" (May 1, 1931), 12; Knutson, *His Loving Care*, 54.
30. *Daily Plainsman*, "Evangelists to Hold Meetings Next Week," 3.
31. Knutson, *His Loving Care*, 54–55, 57.
32. Knutson, *His Loving Care*, 57–58.
33. Knutson, *His Loving Care*, 58–59.
34. Knutson, *His Loving Care*, 59.

wife to visit and hold evangelistic services and found them to be a good fit for the congregation.³⁵

Born in Germany in May 1869, Henry G. Schmid immigrated to the United States in 1887.³⁶ Schmid settled in the Midwest, where he attended college in 1900 and afterward became a pastor and served various German-speaking congregations.³⁷ In 1906, Schmid married Maria Martha Schmidt in Stockton, California, and they subsequently moved to Minnesota, where they started their family and continued doing ministry in German-speaking Methodist Episcopal congregations. Around 1912, the Schmid family moved to the Pacific Northwest, and for the next few years, Reverend Schmid pastored German Methodist Episcopal congregations in Richfield, Seattle, and Tacoma, Washington. In November 1916, Reverend Schmid became the pastor of the German Methodist Episcopal Church in Rathdrum, Idaho, and remained there until late July 1918, when he departed after objecting to a city-wide patriotic celebration of news of German defeats at the Second Battle of the Marne in war-torn Europe.³⁸

Reverend Schmid's reservations about American patriotism during World War I seem to have sparked his subsequent ecclesial transition. Between 1925 and 1929, Reverend Schmid served as pastor of the German Baptist Church in Startup, Washington.³⁹ After living briefly in Alameda, California, and Monroe, Washington, respectively, Reverend Schmid moved to Stanwood, Washington.⁴⁰ It was there in 1931 that, according to Oscar Knutson, Reverend Schmid was pastoring a Pentecostal church and received news of the German-Russian speaking congregation in Huron, South Dakota.⁴¹ After coming to Huron and holding church services, the congregation "literally fell in love with the Schmid[s]," Oscar wrote.⁴²

---

35. Knutson, *His Loving Care*, 59–60.

36. Henry G. Schmid, "Twelfth Census of the United States, Schedule No. 1—Population," 1900, Ancestry.com; Henry G. Schmid, "Thirteenth Census of the United States, 1910—Population," Ancestry.com.

37. "Twelfth Census of the United States, Schedule No. 1—Population," 1900, Ancestry.com; "Thirteenth Census of the United States, 1910—Population," Ancestry.com.

38. *Silver Blade*, "German Divine Quits," 1.

39. *Daily Herald*, "Ministers Elect Officers at First Meeting," 4; *Daily Herald*, "Startup" (July 19, 1929), 9; *Daily Herald*, "Startup" (Aug. 19, 1929), 8.

40. *Daily Herald*, "Startup" (Mar. 12, 1930), 4; *Daily Herald*, "Startup" (May 2, 1930), 10; *Daily Herald*, "Startup" (Nov. 9, 1930), 10.

41. *Daily Herald*, "Stanwood," 11; Knutson, *His Loving Care*, 59.

42. Knutson, *His Loving Care*, 59–60.

Knutson turned over spiritual leadership of the church to Reverend Schmid in December 1931, and the congregation "unanimously accepted Brother Schmi[d] as their new pastor."[43]

As the Knutson family prepared to leave Huron, South Dakota, they received a letter requesting that they hold evangelistic meetings in Belknap, Illinois. Although they still intended to celebrate Christmas with Marie's family in Pontiac, Michigan, they answered the call.[44] Along the way, the Knutsons stopped briefly in Mitchell, South Dakota, to visit with fellow Pentecostal traveling evangelist Rev. A. D. Guth, who had also recently visited them in Huron.[45] Reverend Guth, whom Oscar had met in Great Falls, Montana, in 1921, had become a dear friend of Oscar and his family, as well as something of a spiritual mentor and regular ministry associate.

Born in Tazewell County, Illinois, in September 1881, Aaron D. Guth was the youngest of twelve children born to German immigrants Peter and Fannie Guth (née Birkey).[46] In 1891, the Guth family moved to Reno County, Kansas, where they joined the local Mennonite farming community in the town of Enterprise.[47] Around 1906, Aaron Guth moved to Los Angeles, California, with his older brother Noah and there became involved in the Pentecostal movement after visiting the Azusa Street Mission and receiving the baptism of the Holy Spirit.[48] In 1915, Aaron left California and became a Pentecostal evangelist after attending a ministry convention in Chicago.[49] Over the next several years, Guth held Pentecostal revival

43. Knutson, *His Loving Care*, 60.

44. Knutson, *His Loving Care*, 60, 62.

45. Knutson, *His Loving Care*, 59–61.

46. Aaron D. Guth, Indiana State Board of Health, Certificate of Death, 1948, Ancestry.com; Aaron Guth, "Twelfth Census of the United States, Schedule No. 1—Population," 1900, Ancestry.com; Find a Grave, "Rev Aaron D. Guth," obituary.

47. *Sterling Kansas Bulletin*, "Obituary of Peter Guth," 4; *Hutchinson News*, "Peter Guth," 12; "Twelfth Census of the United States, Schedule No. 1—Population," 1900, Ancestry.com; *Sterling Kansas Bulletin*, "Enterprise," 4.

48. *Los Angeles Times*, untitled article indicating transfer of property to A. D. Guth, 80; *Los Angeles Times*, "Real Estate Record," 27; handwritten and typewritten reflections on Oscar Knutson's early life, Oscar M. Knutson archival collection, box 2, folder 14.

49. *Great Bend Tribune*, "Local Happenings," 8. It is significant to note that this newspaper clipping indicates that A. D. Guth was a friend of Harry Van Loon, who was connected to both William Howard Durham and Frank J. Ewart, two major figures within early Pentecostalism. Van Loon was known as Durham's "right hand man" and worked

meetings in multiple states, including Nebraska, Missouri, and Montana.[50] Between 1917 and 1918, Guth moved to Sterling, Kansas, but continued his ministry work.[51] Around the same time, Guth compiled and published a Pentecostal songbook called *Selected Gospel Songs*, which he used during his revival services.[52] In March 1920, Guth held evangelistic services at Rev. Joseph Lantz's Pentecostal mission in Great Falls, Montana, and returned to

---

closely with Ewart while Durham was alive, as well as after Durham's death in 1912. Andrew K. Gabriel, "William Howard Durham," in Stewart, *Handbook of Pentecostal Christianity*, 65; Frodsham, "Wonderful Life Ended," 2. William Howard Durham, originally a Baptist pastor in Chicago, visited Los Angeles in 1907 and received the baptism of the Holy Spirit at the Azusa Street Mission. He returned to Chicago and subsequently turned his Baptist church into a major hub of the early Pentecostal movement. Richard M. Riss, "Durham, William H.," in Burgess and van der Maas, *New International Dictionary*, 594. In 1911, Durham left Chicago and planted his own Pentecostal mission in Los Angeles that rivaled the Azusa Street Mission. Gabriel, "William Howard Durham," in Stewart, *Handbook of Pentecostal Christianity*, 68. Durham was theologically different than many other early Pentecostals, however, because he did not hold to the radical Holiness doctrine of sanctification which taught that people were made holy—that is, cleansed from sin and their propensity to it—in one immediate, instantaneous act of God in their lives, subsequent to their conversion experience (which was its own great work of God). Instead, Durham proposed an alternative understanding of sanctification, in which people are progressively made more holy by ongoing participation in what he described as the "Finished Work of Calvary." Durham's Finished Work theology was so controversial that it became the source of one of the early schisms within the early Pentecostal movement. David A. Reed, "Finished Work Controversy," in Stewart, *Handbook of Pentecostal Christianity*, 84–87. When Durham died in 1912, pastoral leadership of his Los Angeles mission fell to Frank J. Ewart and Harry Van Loon. Ewart and Van Loon, "Special Notice," 16. Ewart, like Durham, became another major figure within the early Pentecostal movement. Just two years after Durham's death, Ewart became a staunch supporter of the "Jesus Only" movement, which denied the traditional trinitarian formula for water baptism, arguing instead that water baptism should be done only "in the Name of Jesus." Anderson, *Introduction to Pentecostalism*, 46–48. Based on a misunderstanding of the descriptions of water baptism in the Acts of the Apostles, the Jesus Only doctrine—originally known as "the New Issue"—also caused schism among early Pentecostals. The Assemblies of God denomination was formed with an explicitly trinitarian statement of faith, while other groups propagated the non-trinitarian position that has become known presently as Oneness Pentecostalism. Admittedly, while A. D. Guth did not become a major Pentecostal leader on the level of Durham or Ewart, his indirect connection to them via Van Loon is indeed intriguing.

50. *Twice-A-Week Times*, "Pentecostal Revival . . . ," 6; *Milford Review*, "Pentecostal Assembly," 1; *Twice-A-Week Times*, "Pentecost Church . . . [sic]," 2; *Twice-A-Week Times*, "Revival Meeting," 3; *Louisiana Press-Journal*, "Special Meetings," 1; *Daily Inter Lake*, "Pentecostal Mission," 2.

51. Aaron D. Guth, World War I Draft Registration Card, 1918, Ancestry.com.

52. Guth, *Selected Gospel Songs*.

hold additional meetings in June 1921.[53] During this latter visit, Guth met Oscar Knutson and gave fifty copies of his songbook to help the Pentecostal church in Great Falls.[54]

Rev. A. D. Guth, who was a single man his whole life, continued his traveling evangelism throughout the 1920s, holding Pentecostal tent meetings and revival services at local churches in multiple states, particularly Oregon and Montana, but even so far as Ontario, Canada.[55] Significantly, in March 1926, Guth held services at Rev. Annie Applegate's Pentecostal mission in Billings, Montana.[56] Newspaper clippings throughout the 1920s describe Guth as "a man of wide experience and a forceful speaker" who preached "the old time religion"—salvation, Holy Spirit baptism, divine healing, and the Second Coming of Christ.[57] While not affiliated with any one formal Pentecostal denomination, Guth evidently held to trinitarian theology and baptismal formula.[58] From 1924 to 1930, in addition to his work as a traveling evangelist, Guth edited and wrote articles for a publication called *The Full Gospel Testimony*.[59] In the 1930s, Guth continued his

---

53. *Great Falls Tribune*, "South Side Sunday School Chapel," 29; *Great Falls Tribune*, "Pentecostal Mission Holds Its Services," 9.

54. Handwritten and typewritten reflections on Oscar Knutson's early life, Oscar M. Knutson archival collection, box 2, folder 14.

55. *Daily Inter Lake*, "Pentecostal Mission," 2; *Great Falls Leader*, "South Side S. S. Chapel," 13; *Great Falls Tribune*, "Pentecostal Mission Holds Its Services," 9; *Montana Record-Herald*, "Pentecostal Tent Meetings," 9; *Waterloo Region Record*, "Faith Mission," 3; *Butte Miner*, "Evangelistic," 11; *Capital Journal*, "Hear Evangelist," 5.

56. *Billings Gazette*, "Assembly of God" (Mar. 21, 1926), 16.

57. *Statesman Journal*, "Glad Tidings Mission," 6; *Louisiana-Press Journal*, "Special Meetings," 1; *Capital Journal*, "Glad Tidings Mission," 6.

58. *Capital Journal*, "Glad Tidings Mission," 6. This is significant, as a major schism occurred within early Pentecostalism over the doctrine of the Trinity, and even today, many people who identify themselves as Pentecostals do not hold to traditional trinitarian doctrine. The phenomenon is presently known as Oneness Pentecostalism. For some historical context, see chapter 4, n49. Rev. A. D. Guth's personal commitment is additionally indicated in the periodical *The Full Gospel Testimony*, of which he was the editor for several years. Each issue of the periodical begins with a list of theological affirmations, one of which is: "Water baptism administered in the name of the Father, and of the Son, and of the Holy Ghost. Mat. 28:19."

59. *Full Gospel Testimony* 1.8 (Aug. 1924); *Full Gospel Testimony* 2.1 (Jan. 1925); *Full Gospel Testimony* 2.2 (Mar. 1925); *Full Gospel Testimony* 2.3 (July 1925); *Full Gospel Testimony* 2.4 (Oct. 1925); *Full Gospel Testimony* 2.5 (Dec. 1925); *Full Gospel Testimony* 2.6 (Mar. 1926); *Full Gospel Testimony* 2.7 (June 1926); *Full Gospel Testimony* 3.1 (Jan. 1927); *Full Gospel Testimony* 3.6 (Feb. 1930); *Full Gospel Testimony* 3.7 (July 1930).

evangelistic ministry.[60] In late 1931, Guth visited the Knutson family in Huron, South Dakota, and, as a fluent German speaker himself, affirmed the Pentecostal testimonies of the German-speaking congregants who could not share testimonies in English.[61] After visiting Huron, Guth left to hold evangelistic services in Mitchell, South Dakota. Guth was still in Mitchell when the Knutsons left Huron, and they visited him briefly before proceeding to other ministry work.[62]

While several figures impacted and influenced Oscar Knutson's life and ministry, Rev. A. D. Guth was certainly one of the most significant. Guth and Knutson met in 1921, a very formative time in Knutson's life, and Knutson's ministry seems to have been largely informed by Guth's example. Although he maintained connection to his family in Kansas, Guth devoted his life to traveling evangelism. Guth generally did not stay in one place to do ministry for an extended period of time. Evidently, he preferred to keep moving, although he regularly revisited faith communities to check on their spiritual well-being, likely inspired by the missionary journeys of the apostle Paul. Knutson, likewise, maintained familial connections in the Pacific Northwest and the Midwest, while devoting much of his life—as well as that of his wife and children—to traveling evangelism. Even when pastoring or planting churches, Knutson generally did not spend a lot of time in each place. His longest pastorate in one location was six years, although he too revisited faith communities often to check in with them and see how they were doing.

In addition to much traveling, Guth focused on ministering to smaller communities, in contrast to those constituencies of the Pentecostal movement who, rightly or wrongly, focused on urban centers, seeking to draw larger crowds. Higher attendance at church services and revival meetings could, admittedly, draw a greater volume of people to the Lord in one event. However, from a more critical standpoint, higher attendance was also a more reliable way for preachers or evangelists to get more money and gain

---

60. *Sault Star*, "Penticostal Tabernacle [sic]," 9; *Butte Gazette*, "Revival Meetings," 5; *Daily Plainsman*, "Pentescotal Mission [sic]," 3; *Hutchinson News*, "Full Gospel Mission (Pentecostal)," 7; *Frontier and Holt County Independent*, "Revival Meetings," 1; *Wells Mirror*, "Wells Gospel Tabernacle" (Mar. 21, 1935), 6.

61. Knutson, *His Loving Care*, 59. Admittedly, while Oscar Knutson did not expressly name Rev. A. D. Guth as the German-speaking evangelist that visited them in Huron, South Dakota, the details offered, together with other biographical information known about Guth, indicate that he was this visitor.

62. Knutson, *His Loving Care*, 60–61.

He Will Lead Me

a measure of fame. Guth's goal was not to make money nor to make a name for himself. Largely interested in rural communities and in on-the-ground, local ministry, Guth's mission was to see souls saved. Every soul mattered, including—and maybe even particularly—those forgotten or on the margins, and those whom others deemed apparently unimportant. In the Acts of the Apostles, Jesus empowered his disciples with the Holy Spirit to be his witnesses in Jerusalem, in Judea and Samaria, and "to the ends of the earth."[63] For Guth and Knutson, this commission of Jesus resonated to the tune of many local communities in various nooks and crannies of Washington, Oregon, Montana, Michigan, South Dakota, Minnesota, Iowa, Nebraska, and so on. Knutson, like Guth, was interested in doing the Lord's work—nothing more, nothing less. He was not interested in amassing fame or fortune but was instead focused on an incarnated vision of ministry on the local level and living a life in full service to Christ.

Driven by Jesus' own mission "to seek and save the lost," this shared vision of on-the-ground, local-level ministry was accomplished by Guth and Knutson in similar ways.[64] In addition to regular traveling evangelism and preaching and pastoring among smaller, often rural, communities, Guth and Knutson shared an interest in doing ministry through music and through writing, printing, and publishing. Early in his ministry career, Guth compiled a gospel songbook to aid him in his ministry work. Knutson, who was introduced to both Guth and his songbook in 1921, began formal ministry with Brother Jack Nelson in 1922 by leading music at their various evangelistic meetings. Music played a big role throughout Knutson's evangelistic and pastoral ministry, to the point that he eventually inherited Guth's songbook, revised it, and, with his own printing press, published the new edition of the songbook along with other similar songbooks for decades. Furthermore, as Knutson's family grew, they became more and more involved in music ministry together, singing and playing a wide variety of instruments during church services—guitar, accordion, banjo, and a rather eclectic stringed instrument known as an octofone, described in a 1930 newspaper clipping as a "Haw[ai]ian guitar."[65]

Guth's printing ministry, particularly his writing and editing of various theological articles, likewise provided Knutson a pattern to follow. In the latter half of his life, Knutson wrote and published various gospel tracts and

---

63. Acts 1:8, NIV.
64. See Luke 19:10, NIV.
65. *Augusta News*, "Church News," 8.

short but pithy theological pamphlets and books, in addition to songbooks and other ministry-related materials, all with his own printing press. As with preaching and pastoral ministry, Guth's and Knutson's respective music ministries, and their writing, printing, and publishing ministries, were all done for the sake of the gospel—for the express purpose of saving souls, equipping the faithful, and building up the local church.

After their brief visit with Reverend Guth in Mitchell, South Dakota, the Knutsons proceeded to Sioux City, Iowa, where they visited a Pentecostal mission that Reverend Guth had helped plant several years prior. Reverend Guth had heard that one of the pastors of the mission was "getting involved in some off doctrines" and requested that Oscar visit the mission and investigate the reports.[66] Knutson did so and sent a message to Guth confirming the reports. The Knutson family then proceeded to Ferguson, Iowa, and held evangelistic services for a week at the town's modest local Pentecostal mission. "Only a very few came to the services, but the Lord blessed," Oscar wrote.[67]

The Knutson family arrived in Belknap, Illinois, in late October or early November 1931. In freezing weather, and with a mere twenty-five cents left, they nevertheless trusted the Lord's provision and began holding evangelistic services. "There were some at Belknap who had been seeking the Baptism of the Holy Spirit for many years but yet had not received," Oscar recalled.[68] However, "soon after the special meetings started, the Lord began to bless. Some received their baptism at the alt[a]r, others received it sitting in their seats during the meeting. I never have seen another meeting like those at Belknap," Knutson reflected.[69]

The Knutsons spent three weeks holding revival meetings in Belknap, Illinois. As they were concluding these services, Rev. A. D. Guth contacted them by letter and requested that they join him in establishing a church among the budding local Pentecostal community in Estherville, Iowa.[70] The Knutsons, who were already committed to spending the holi-

---

66. Knutson, *His Loving Care*, 61.
67. Knutson, *His Loving Care*, 61.
68. Knutson, *His Loving Care*, 62–63.
69. Knutson, *His Loving Care*, 63.
70. Knutson, *His Loving Care*, 63; *Calvary Gospel Assembly*, 7.

days with Marie's family in Pontiac, Michigan, agreed to come after the start of the new year.[71]

After a restful holiday visit with the Baldwin family, the Knutsons left for Estherville, Iowa, picking up Rev. A. D. Guth in Dearborn, Michigan, along the way.[72] It had been arranged that they would arrive in Estherville to hold the community's first formal church service on January 2, 1932, but inclement weather conditions—namely, a serious Iowa blizzard—kept them from arriving until January 7.[73] In Estherville, the Knutsons found a reserved but winsome community of Pentecostal Christians which had been forming among a handful of local farming families for the last few years, mostly led by former Lutheran layman William Guge, a member of the prominent Guge clan.[74] Since early 1930, Guge had been facilitating regular Pentecostal prayer gatherings in homes, due to interest in the Estherville community based on the testimony of his sister-in-law Effie Guge of Marshalltown, Iowa, who in December 1928 received divine healing for a severe incurable illness, as well as a radical "born again" experience and the baptism of the Holy Spirit.[75] Effie Guge, the wife of William Guge's younger brother John, traveled to Estherville to share her experiences with the rest of the Guge family and other members of the Estherville community. "Sister Guge just could not keep all this to herself. She had to tell others!" Oscar wrote in later reflections.[76] Although family and friends in Estherville who heard Effie's testimony belonged to churches of other denominations—Lutheran, Methodist, and Presbyterian—conversations about these Pentecostal experiences propagated, and interest grew.[77]

Soon, other members of the Estherville community began having their own "born again" experiences, and some even received the baptism of the Holy Spirit.[78] They testified to these experiences among their respective fellowships and then began meeting regularly in homes for prayer.[79]

71. Knutson, *His Loving Care*, 63.
72. Knutson, *His Loving Care*, 64–65.
73. *Calvary Gospel Assembly*, 7; Knutson, *His Loving Care*, 65.
74. *Calvary Gospel Assembly*, 6; Knutson, *His Loving Care*, 67.
75. *Calvary Gospel Assembly*, 6, 8; Knutson, *His Loving Care*, 67.
76. Knutson, *His Loving Care*, 67.
77. Knutson, *His Loving Care*, 67; *Calvary Gospel Assembly*, 6.
78. *Calvary Gospel Assembly*, 6.
79. *Calvary Gospel Assembly*, 6.

While William Guge was the primary figure leading these prayer gatherings, various Pentecostal ministers—Rev. A. D. Guth, in particular—visited with some regularity and held evening services in people's homes.[80] The Pentecostal community continued to grow, and in 1931, it became clear that a more formal gathering space was necessary, along with more formal pastoral leadership.[81] A building was purchased in early December 1931, and preparations were made for a church to be established.[82]

When Reverend Guth and the Knutsons arrived, they assisted with making the church building ready for worship and then began holding services.[83] The name "Full Gospel Mission" was selected for the new fellowship, and Oscar Knutson was installed as its first formal pastor.[84] Reverend Guth, beloved by the Estherville community, assisted with services for two weeks and during that time also wrote out a statement of faith for the church:

> The [Full Gospel] Mission has no creed other than the New Testament, the faith is therefore based directly on the teachings of Christ and the apostles: namely, *Repentance* and *Faith* toward *God*: *Regeneration* or the *New Birth*: *Baptism* of the *Holy Ghost*: *Water Baptism By Immersion*; *Divine Healing*; the *Literal Return of the Lord*; *Special Observance of the Sermon on the Mount*[,] love and peace toward all mankind; love your enemies; bless them that curse you; do good to them that hate you; and pray for them that despitefully use, et cetera . . . . The work has never been incorporated. The unity is maintained by observing the Scriptures directly rather than through organization.[85]

The statement of faith of the Estherville Full Gospel Mission may be a bit non-traditional in terms of Christian ecclesiology—rejecting historic creeds, formal ecclesial organization, and the like—but it was largely representative of many independent Pentecostal churches of its time. It also raises some interesting points for reflection concerning the theology of the church, particularly from a Pentecostal standpoint.

First, the statement of faith expresses devout loyalty to the holy Scriptures, especially to the New Testament, which contains and bears witness

---

80. *Calvary Gospel Assembly*, 6.
81. *Calvary Gospel Assembly*, 6.
82. *Calvary Gospel Assembly*, 6–7.
83. Knutson, *His Loving Care*, 66.
84. *Calvary Gospel Assembly*, 6–7; Knutson, *His Loving Care*, 63, 66.
85. *Calvary Gospel Assembly*, 7–8.

to the teaching of Jesus and his apostles.[86] This reflects a particular understanding of Scripture, which holds a unique place of authority in the church, and for the church—a place that may not be claimed by anything else. In this way, the Pentecostal understanding of the relationship between Scripture and the church is clarified. Scripture does not submit to the church. The church submits to Scripture.

Second, the statement of faith is deeply christocentric, that is to say, it affirms that Jesus—and faith and obedience to him—is central to ecclesial identity. The Full Gospel articulation offers a uniquely Pentecostal flavor to this christological ecclesiology. The church is only the church insofar as it *is* the body of Jesus, the One who is Savior, Sanctifier, Baptizer with the Holy Spirit, Healer, and Soon-Coming King. Furthermore, as a local expression of the one body of Christ, the statement of faith understands that the local church—in this case, the Estherville Full Gospel Mission—must manifest its identity as Jesus' body *through* its faith and obedience to him. Emphasis is thus placed on the seminal teaching of Jesus, the Sermon on the Mount, which must be embodied. The Sermon on the Mount is, however, more than just obedience to Christ's commands. It is a way of life—*the* way of life. It is also key to the designation of the fellowship as a "mission," because as a Full Gospel fellowship, it holds an eschatologically driven missiological focus and purpose. As a local expression of Jesus' body, the local church must be a faithful representation of Jesus. In doing so, it shares in his mission to bring redemption to the whole world.

Third, the statement of faith appeals to the apostolicity of the Full Gospel theological formula, which essentially connects its uniquely Pentecostal identity to Pentecost itself, that great outpouring of the Holy Spirit upon the apostles in the upper room in Jerusalem. In this way, Pentecostal ecclesiology finds connection to the New Testament church. Jesus' apostles are those that Jesus himself empowered with the Holy Spirit and commissioned to be his witnesses. From a Pentecostal standpoint, then, the church's identity is apostolic. The church is not simply the body of Christ; it is also the temple of the Holy Spirit. It is the community of those who have been anointed with the Holy Spirit and commissioned by Christ to be his witnesses. The church is thus expected to manifest the power, presence, gifts,

---

86. Although the Estherville Full Gospel Mission's statement of faith only expressly mentions fidelity to the New Testament and says nothing of the Old Testament, it is highly unlikely that the community rejected the Old Testament. Jettisoning the Old Testament in some kind of Marcionite fashion would be significantly uncharacteristic of early Pentecostals.

and fruit of the Holy Spirit, whom the Lord has poured out upon all flesh and sent forth to renew the face of the earth.

Finally, the statement of faith discloses a resistance to formal ecclesial organization and structure. The ecclesiological reflection is that the church does not belong to man; it belongs to God. Reservations concerning formal order reflect an impulse to protect the church from becoming a mere human entity. The Estherville Full Gospel Mission was, in this way, especially representative of a common theme among the early Pentecostal movement—the belief that organization and structure were largely inimical to the movement of the Holy Spirit. Institutionalism hampered revival.[87] Even so, the statement of faith reflects confidence in unity with the greater body of Christ, as a physical assembly committed to the same mission of the gospel and empowered with the same Holy Spirit to accomplish it.

Oscar Knutson continued pastoring the Full Gospel Mission in Estherville, Iowa, after Reverend Guth departed for other ministry work. The church flourished under Knutson's pastoral leadership and grew significantly.[88] While pastoring in Estherville, Knutson also held street meetings in various nearby towns, especially Superior, Iowa, and Windom, Minnesota.[89] Knutson's evangelism in Windom was particularly significant, as he was

---

87. As a matter of historical reality, practical necessities eventually forced the issue. Pentecostal denominations formed, albeit with a diversity of organizational forms. Some denominations, like the Church of God in Christ, embraced a hierarchical ecclesial structure. Others, like the Assemblies of God, attempted to blend a kind of presbyterian polity on the denominational level with that of a quasi-congregational polity on the local level. Still other Pentecostal fellowships, however, remained independent and unincorporated, believing this to make for a purer form of worship in which they could hear from God directly, uninhibited by man-made organizations, rules, and traditions. This independent model, which largely affirmed an egalitarian, congregational form of polity, was especially common among Scandinavian free Pentecostal fellowships, which tended to resist the more authoritarian models of their state church counterparts in Europe. Dwight J. Wilson, "Ecclesiastical Polity," in Burgess and van der Maas, *New International Dictionary*, 596–97. As a Pentecostal fellowship composed of people of mostly German and Norwegian heritage, the Full Gospel Mission in Estherville, Iowa, was, not surprisingly, free church congregational in its orientation. Knutson, *His Loving Care*, 65–66.

88. *Calvary Gospel Assembly*, 9; Knutson, *His Loving Care*, 68, 72–73.

89. *Calvary Gospel Assembly*, 7.

joined by Rev. Clarence W. Hart, whom he had originally met while doing ministry with Brother Jack Nelson in Black Diamond, Washington.[90]

Born in New York in February 1894, Clarence Hart moved to Canada in 1911 and married Scottish immigrant Annie Qua around 1914.[91] Their daughter Phyllis was born in Lethbridge, Alberta, Canada, in 1915.[92] According to a 1916 Canadian census record, the Harts were affiliated with the Presbyterian church.[93] In 1921, Clarence's religious affiliation was with the Methodist church, while Annie and Phyllis remained Presbyterian.[94] In 1922, the Harts moved to the United States and settled in Black Diamond, Washington.[95] There, Clarence apparently discontinued the family's religious activities and participation.[96] When Jack Nelson and Oscar Knutson came to Black Diamond, however, Phyllis was at their first service.[97] "Mama would [also] like to go to church," she explained to them, "but Daddy won't let her."[98] Despite Clarence's disapproval, Annie Hart was present with her daughter Phyllis at the next service.[99] Eventually, Clarence, who did not get home from work until eight o'clock each night, threatened to beat Annie for attending the Pentecostal services.[100] Recognizing the severity of the situation, the Pentecostal community in Black Diamond prayed over it fervently.[101] When Annie returned home from the service the same night, she found that Clarence had repented of being an abusive husband and

---

90. Knutson, *His Loving Care*, 71.

91. Clarence W. Hart, Washington State Department of Health, Certificate of Death, 1947, Ancestry.com; 1916 Canada Census of Manitoba, Saskatchewan, and Alberta, Ancestry.com; Annie Hart, Missouri Division of Health, Certificate of Death, 1964, Ancestry.com.

92. 1916 Canada Census of Manitoba, Saskatchewan, and Alberta, Ancestry.com.

93. 1916 Canada Census of Manitoba, Saskatchewan, and Alberta, Ancestry.com.

94. Clarence Hart, "Population," 1921 Census of Canada, Ancestry.com.

95. Phyllis Ann Hart, border crossings from Canada to US, June 1922, Eastport, Idaho, Ancestry.com.

96. Knutson, *His Loving Care*, 20.

97. Knutson, *His Loving Care*, 20.

98. Knutson, *His Loving Care*, 20.

99. Knutson, *His Loving Care*, 21.

100. Knutson, *His Loving Care*, 24.

101. Knutson, *His Loving Care*, 25.

"surrendered and gave his heart to the Lord."[102] Clarence reconciled with Annie and Phyllis, and the family "rejoiced in the Lord, together."[103]

Sometime after Clarence Hart's repentance and conversion experience in Black Diamond, he went into ministry and became a Pentecostal pastor.[104] According to Oscar Knutson, Reverend Hart's first pastorate was in Bridgeport, Washington, where he pastored for about five years.[105] In December 1931, while still pastoring in Bridgeport, Reverend Hart also held evangelistic services in nearby Coulee City, Washington.[106] "A true Holy Spirit revival stirred the community," which sparked the beginning of what became a thriving Assembly of God church in Coulee City.[107] In 1932, Reverend Hart and his family left the Pacific Northwest, visited the Knutsons in the Midwest, joined Oscar in holding street meetings in Windom, Minnesota, and subsequently took charge of the Pentecostal ministry activities in the town.[108]

While Rev. Clarence Hart continued ministering in Windom, Oscar Knutson continued pastoring the Full Gospel Mission in Estherville. The congregation in Estherville continued to grow and flourish, but in late 1931, Oscar resigned due to poor health.[109] Although Knutson and his family had grown to love the people of Estherville—"I do not know anyplace with finer people to pastor than at Estherville," he later wrote—it gave them an opportunity to return to the Pacific Northwest, spend the holidays with Oscar's parents, and even hold services in the Seattle vicinity.[110]

On their way back to Seattle, the Knutsons stopped for a few days in Huron, South Dakota. They also held two weeks of Pentecostal meetings in Sioux City, Iowa, and in Naper, Nebraska, respectively.[111] While the Knutsons held services at Naper Pentecostal Church, its pastor, Rev. Linus Heidt, visited Estherville and held two weeks of services.[112] In February 1933,

---

102. Knutson, *His Loving Care*, 25.
103. Knutson, *His Loving Care*, 25.
104. Knutson, *His Loving Care*, 25.
105. Knutson, *His Loving Care*, 25.
106. *Spokesman-Review*, "Revival Meetings Opened," 8.
107. Tannenberg, *Let Light Shine Out*, 66–67.
108. Knutson, *His Loving Care*, 71–72.
109. *Calvary Gospel Assembly*, 9.
110. Knutson, *His Loving Care*, 72–73.
111. Knutson, *His Loving Care*, 73.
112. *Calvary Gospel Assembly*, 9.

Reverend Heidt answered a call to become the pastor of the congregation in Estherville and served well in that capacity for about five years before proceeding on to other ministry work.[113] The same month that Reverend Heidt accepted the pastorate of the Full Gospel Mission, the Estherville community celebrated the wedding of Oscar Knutson's younger sister Harda to Martin Guge, the younger brother of William Guge.[114] Over the next several years, while pursuing other ministry work, Oscar Knutson and his family returned to visit Estherville on multiple occasions, both to hold services and to visit with friends and family.[115]

---

113. *Calvary Gospel Assembly*, 9–11; Knutson, *His Loving Care*, 73.

114. *Estherville Daily News*, untitled article noting the wedding of Martin Guge and Harda Knutson, 2; handwritten family history notes, Oscar M. Knutson archival collection, unprocessed box.

115. Knutson, *His Loving Care*, 73.

5

"Thou Art My All"

Thou art my friend, my close companion ever.
Earth's path diverge as comrades onward vend.
Friends may depart but Thou wilt leave me never.
I trust in Thee, Thou art my all in all.

Thou art my all,
Thou wilt forsake me never.
Thou art my all, fulfilling all my need.
There is no power on earth that can us sever:
I'll follow Thee wherever Thou doth lead.
—O. M. Knutson, "Thou Art My All"

EARLY 1933 FOUND THE Knutson family in the Pacific Northwest. That spring, Oscar Knutson held revival meetings at a newly planted Pentecostal fellowship in Davenport, Washington, while Marie and the children remained in Seattle for school.[1] On his way back to Seattle after concluding services in Davenport, Oscar stopped in Bridgeport, Washington, to visit

---

1. Knutson, *His Loving Care*, 74.

the church that Rev. Clarence W. Hart had formerly pastored for several years. In Bridgeport, Knutson discovered that the Pentecostal church in town had recently lost its pastor—presumably, Reverend Hart's successor—and like the church in Huron back in 1931, it was seriously wounded by division and congregational strife.[2] At the request of local lay leadership, Knutson agreed to move to Bridgeport temporarily, serve as pastor, and attempt to facilitate reconciliation among the congregation. As in Huron, Knutson noted in his reflections that reconciliation was a tough job, as "no one can be won by using a hammer! It must be done with love."[3] Even so, Knutson pastored in Bridgeport over the summer and left after harvest concluded in the fall. During that time, "the Lord began to work," and Knutson's labors bore good fruit.[4] The congregation was reconciled, and a new pastor, Rev. Frank Edgemon, was installed.[5]

Born in Rosalia, Washington, in May 1892, Franklin Ross Edgemon was the son of wheat farmer Samuel S. Edgemon and his wife Sarah (née Durham).[6] Raised in a rural agricultural context, Frank Edgemon took up wheat farming as his own occupation and for many years lived in the town of Mold, just north of Coulee City, Washington, where his family had moved around 1903.[7] In 1915, Frank married Mildred E. Allen of Amber, Washington, and the couple had two children.[8] Around 1930, the Edgemon family started becoming involved in the local Pentecostal community in Bridgeport, Washington. Although he still maintained the family farm in Mold, Frank began to feel a call to ministry.[9] In summer 1931, Edgemon led a water baptismal service for Coulee City's forming Pentecostal fellowship, at which forty-five people were baptized. Then, on December 31, 1931, he

2. Knutson, *His Loving Care*, 74–75.
3. Knutson, *His Loving Care*, 75.
4. Knutson, *His Loving Care*, 75–76.
5. Knutson, *His Loving Care*, 76–77.
6. Frank R. Edgemon, Certificate of Death, 1954, Washington State Digital Archives.
7. Tannenberg, *Let Light Shine Out*, 68; Franklin Edgemon, "Twelfth Census of the United States, "Schedule No. 1—Population," 1900, Ancestry.com; Frank Edgemon, "Thirteenth Census of the United States, 1910—Population," Ancestry.com; Frank Edgemon, "Fourteenth Census of the United States, 1920—Population," Ancestry.com; *Spokesman-Review*, "Coulee City," 6.
8. Frank Edgemon and Mildred Allen, Certificate of Marriage, 1915, Washington State Digital Archives.
9. Frank R. Edgemon, "Fifteenth Census of the United States, 1930—Population Schedule," Ancestry.com; Tannenberg, *Let Light Shine Out*, 68.

agreed to serve as the church's pastor.¹⁰ As Edgemon began pursuing ministry, he and his wife felt as though it was time to give up farming and focus exclusively on pastoring. While in Bridgeport in 1933, Edgemon shared as much with Oscar Knutson. In conversation together, Knutson noted that Edgemon was "a sensible man, nearing forty," who was already known and liked among the Pentecostal community in Bridgeport.¹¹ Edgemon also seemed to be "sound in doctrine," and he was a good preacher.¹² The Bridgeport Pentecostal community soon called Edgemon to be their pastor, and he accepted the call. After harvest in 1933, Edgemon retired the farm and was installed as pastor in Bridgeport. According to Knutson, Edgemon "pastored the church for many years, and d[id] well."¹³

Having spent most of 1933 in the Pacific Northwest, the Knutson family returned to the Midwest in the fall to hold revival services in various locations. After spending Christmas with the Baldwins in Pontiac, Michigan, the Knutsons continued their evangelistic ministry.¹⁴ In early 1934, they held a few weeks of Pentecostal meetings in Ohio, Illinois, and Iowa, respectively, before proceeding on to South Dakota, and then North Dakota.¹⁵ In the spring of 1934, the Knutsons spent a week holding meetings in the town of Bowman, North Dakota, having "received a very hearty welcome" from Pentecostal farmer Alfred Moor and his family.¹⁶ In later reflections, Oscar noted the faith and joy of the Pentecostal community in Bowman, which he found remarkable given the brutal economic conditions of the Great Depression on the local agricultural community. Discouraged by the North Dakotan Dust Bowl, many farmers had declined to plant crops that spring, believing that "it was useless to sow seed in the dust."¹⁷ The Moor family, however, along with some other Pentecostal farming families, decided to plant anyhow, as an act of faith. "It is my part to sow the seed," Alfred Moor

---

10. Tannenberg, *Let Light Shine Out*, 68.
11. Knutson, *His Loving Care*, 76.
12. Knutson, *His Loving Care*, 76.
13. Knutson, *His Loving Care*, 76–77.
14. Knutson, *His Loving Care*, 77.
15. Knutson, *His Loving Care*, 77–78.
16. Knutson, *His Loving Care*, 80–81; Rodgers, *Northern Harvest*, 107n191.
17. Knutson, *His Loving Care*, 80–81.

told Oscar. "It's the Lord's part to make them grow."[18] According to Oscar's later reflections:

> That evening, not long after we arrived, the clouds began to roll in, and they had a good soaking rain. All the farmers rushed to prepare their ground and sow their seed. But by the time they had plowed and worked their ground and got their seed in, much of the moisture was gone. However, Bro[ther] Moor and most of the Pentecostal folk who had sown early got a fairly good crop, whereas the others got very little.[19]

In summer 1934, the Knutson family returned to the Pacific Northwest, and while Marie and the children remained in Everett, Washington, Oscar continued pursuing evangelistic ministry. After briefly holding revival services in Pendleton, Oregon, Oscar traveled to Ellensburg, Washington, where he visited Tom Overland, "an old friend" from the Seattle area.[20] Born in Norway in April 1898, Thomas Thor Overland immigrated to the United States in 1912.[21] Overland settled in Seattle, and in November 1920, he married Tressie G. Brown.[22] Tom and Tressie Overland had four children and remained in Seattle for several years before moving to Ellensburg in the early 1930s.[23] Tom was a baker by trade, but in 1934 he felt "burdened" to plant a Pentecostal church in nearby Kittitas, Washington.[24] Knowing that Oscar

---

18. Knutson, *His Loving Care*, 81.

19. Knutson, *His Loving Care*, 81.

20. Knutson, *His Loving Care*, 81.

21. Thomas Overland, "Declaration of Intention," US naturalization paperwork, 1929, Ancestry.com; Thomas Overland, "Fifteenth Census of the United States, 1930, Population Schedule," Ancestry.com.

22. Thomas Thor Overland, World War I Registration Card, 1918, Ancestry.com; Marriage Certificate for Thomas Overland and Tressie G. Brown, 1920, Washington State Digital Archives.

23. Thomas Overland, "Fifteenth Census of the United States, 1930, Population Schedule," Ancestry.com; "Sixteenth Census of the United States, 1940," Ancestry.com; Knutson, *His Loving Care*, 81.

24. Knutson, *His Loving Care*, 81; Thomas Thor Overland, World War I Registration Card, 1918, Ancestry.com; "Fifteenth Census of the United States, 1930, Population Schedule," Ancestry.com; "Sixteenth Census of the United States, 1940," Ancestry.com; *Kittitas Assembly of God Church History: 50th Anniversary, 1937–1987*, by Church History Committee and Pastor Gary R. Fountain, in "*Churches*—General II" archival file, Ellensburg Public Library.

Knutson had significant ministry experience, he discussed the matter with him. Oscar was already committed to return to Everett and spend time with Marie and the children, but afterward, he agreed to come back and assist Overland's efforts in Kittitas.[25]

Oscar Knutson returned to Kittitas in late 1934, and for about three weeks assisted Tom Overland and his family with revival meetings in Kittitas, held in a former meat market building that they had rented and renovated together. It was a successful endeavor and marked the beginning of what became a thriving Assembly of God church in Kittitas.[26] Although planted during the Great Depression, "the people shared food, time and what money they had," according to a fifty-year church anniversary publication.[27] "The church grew, because God was with them to move and to bless."[28]

In the spring of 1935, the Knutson family traveled back to the Midwest to pursue further evangelistic ministry and for the next few months held revival services in several states.[29] That summer, while passing through Michigan on the way to Wisconsin, the Knutsons stopped to visit an old family friend of Marie's from White Bluffs, Washington, who insisted that they go to Muskegon Heights, Michigan, and try to help the local Pentecostal church, which was "in very bad shape."[30] According to Oscar's recounting

25. Knutson, *His Loving Care*, 82.

26. Knutson, *His Loving Care*, 82; *Kittitas Assembly of God Church History: 50th Anniversary, 1937–1987*, by Church History Committee and Pastor Gary R. Fountain, in "*Churches—General II*" archival file, Ellensburg Public Library.

27. *Kittitas Assembly of God Church History: 50th Anniversary, 1937–1987*, by Church History Committee and Pastor Gary R. Fountain, in "*Churches—General II*" archival file, Ellensburg Public Library.

28. *Kittitas Assembly of God Church History: 50th Anniversary, 1937–1987*, by Church History Committee and Pastor Gary R. Fountain, in "*Churches—General II*" archival file, Ellensburg Public Library.

29. Knutson, *His Loving Care*, 82–83.

30. Oscar and Marie Knutson, oral history interview with Wayne Warner, Sept. 5, 1983, audio recording, Flower Pentecostal Heritage Center. Muskegon Heights, Michigan, should not be confused or conflated with Muskegon, Michigan. The latter is located about a mile and half north of the former. Muskegon had a Pentecostal church called the Full Gospel Assembly of God, which was set in order by the Assemblies of God denomination in early May 1923. It flourished for over seventy-five years, especially under the pastoral leadership of its founding pastor, Rev. Marcus Horness, who pastored the church from May 1923 until his retirement in December 1947. *Central Assembly of God, 1923–1998*, 9–13. A letter from May 1923, written by William Lambert Brant,

in a 1983 oral history interview, the church in Muskegon Heights had "just got done kicking their pastor out, because he was caught in open sin."[31] The church was "desperate" to find a new pastor but had not found success.[32] The Knutsons agreed to go, and after becoming acquainted with the church and the financial mess caused by its former pastor, Oscar agreed to take up the pastorate and try to facilitate recovery.[33]

Although economic conditions were difficult, the Lord provided a way for the Pentecostal church in Muskegon Heights. As a first order of business, Oscar Knutson saw to it that as money came in, outstanding bills were paid off.[34] Knutson also ensured that new and ongoing operating expenses were fully covered.[35] Financial recovery began to materialize between August and September 1935, and by January 1936 the church even had surplus funds in its treasury.[36]

Although Oscar Knutson did not directly discuss his time in Muskegon Heights, Michigan, in *His Loving Care*, his book of reflections on his life and ministry, this experience was significant to his spiritual biography for multiple reasons. First, along with previous experiences in Great Falls, Montana; Huron, South Dakota; Bridgeport, Washington; and Estherville, Iowa, it was another instance of concrete pastoral ministry, not just traveling evangelism. Second, similar to previous pastorates, Knutson's ministry

---

the associate district chairman of the Central District of the Assemblies of God, indicates that while the Pentecostal church in Muskegon had just affiliated with the General Council of the Assemblies of God, the smaller, nearby city of Muskegon Heights also had a Pentecostal church that was "considering the matter of Council fellowship also and a good spirit of cooperation between the two churches prevails." William Lambert Brant to J. W. Welch, May 5, 1923, courtesy of Glenn Gohr, reference archivist, Flower Pentecostal Heritage Center. Although further historical records concerning the Muskegon Heights church have apparently not survived, the church evidently operated until its pastoral embezzlement scandal in the mid 1930s.

31. Oscar and Marie Knutson, oral history interview with Wayne Warner, Sept. 5, 1983, audio recording, Flower Pentecostal Heritage Center.

32. Oscar and Marie Knutson, oral history interview with Wayne Warner, Sept. 5, 1983, audio recording, Flower Pentecostal Heritage Center.

33. Oscar and Marie Knutson, oral history interview with Wayne Warner, Sept. 5, 1983, audio recording, Flower Pentecostal Heritage Center.

34. Oscar and Marie Knutson, oral history interview with Wayne Warner, Sept. 5, 1983, audio recording, Flower Pentecostal Heritage Center.

35. Oscar and Marie Knutson, oral history interview with Wayne Warner, Sept. 5, 1983, audio recording, Flower Pentecostal Heritage Center.

36. Oscar and Marie Knutson, oral history interview with Wayne Warner, Sept. 5, 1983, audio recording, Flower Pentecostal Heritage Center.

in Muskegon Heights was largely a healing ministry for the local church. Oscar's charge was to pastor a wounded congregation that needed repair as a community. Oscar confronted that brokenness directly and labored faithfully for restoration.

Perhaps the most personally significant part of Oscar Knutson's time in Muskegon Heights, however, was that it was the beginning of a ministry shift for him, which came to fruition a decade and a half later. While pastoring in Muskegon Heights in 1935, Knutson acquired his first printing press and began dabbling in printing ministry.[37] Operating out of the basement of the Muskegon Heights church building with a small hand-power press purchased for thirty-five dollars, Knutson began publishing gospel tracts, as well as a Pentecostal paper featuring testimonies and short essays that functioned as printed sermons, which he titled *The Good News*.[38] Knutson distributed these print materials free of charge, as they assisted with local ministry work.[39] Although printing was a fairly new endeavor for Knutson, it was not entirely unfamiliar. Back in Augusta, Montana, in 1930, Knutson had gained some previous printing experience assisting the local newspaper publisher with proofreading and setting type.[40] Having this experience made for a smoother learning process, as Knutson did some preliminary printing of his own in Muskegon Heights and pondered what it could look like to pursue gospel work through printing and publishing.

Due to an apparent scarcity of available historical evidence, the rest of the story of the Pentecostal church in Muskegon Heights, Michigan, is unclear. However, Oscar Knutson published his third issue of *The Good News* from Muskegon Heights in March 1936, which speaks to the timeline at least in part. In spring 1936, the Knutson family left Muskegon Heights and returned to Seattle, where Oscar continued his printing ministry. In June 1936, Oscar published the fourth issue of *The Good News* from his parent's address at 8017 Second Avenue NE, Seattle. He published the fifth issue from the same address in November 1936.[41] Oscar also continued

37. Oscar and Marie Knutson, oral history interview with Wayne Warner, Sept. 5, 1983, audio recording, Flower Pentecostal Heritage Center; Knutson, *His Loving Care*, 95; *Ken Rock Herald*, "Published 20,000 Books!," 1.

38. Scrapbook featuring items printed by Oscar Knutson, courtesy of Phillip W. Knutson; Oscar and Marie Knutson, oral history interview with Wayne Warner, Sept. 5, 1983, audio recording, Flower Pentecostal Heritage Center.

39. Knutson, *His Loving Care*, 95.

40. Knutson, *His Loving Care*, 95.

41. Scrapbook featuring items printed by Oscar Knutson, courtesy of Phillip W.

his evangelistic ministry and in August 1936 visited and held services at the Full Gospel Tabernacle in Cut Bank, Montana, an Assemblies of God church that Oscar's sister Rev. Inga Johnson planted in spring 1935.[42]

For most of their traveling evangelism in the 1920s and 1930s, the Pentecostal revival services held by Oscar Knutson and his family took place in local churches, in available buildings or storefronts, or on the street.[43] In 1937, however, the Knutsons purchased a tent for "Gospel meetings."[44] As they were living in Seattle, with Oscar working as a carpenter, the Knutsons held initial tent meetings on the West Coast.[45] Then, in 1938, they headed eastward, stopping first in Kettle Falls, Washington, "a strongly Catholic town," according to Oscar's reflections.[46] "As soon as we pitched the tent, some Catholic young men threatened that they would run us out of town in three days," Oscar wrote.[47] In addition to disruptions by some antagonistic "young fellows," the Knutsons experienced some intimidation in Kettle Falls, including a close call from some would-be arsonists.[48] In his reflections, Oscar only connected this resistance to religious animosity, but it is possible that such strong objections may also have been racially motivated. After all, it was more than just Oscar and his family who were present to hold Pentecostal tent meetings in Kettle Falls. Rev. Lee Henson, an African American preacher friend from Seattle, had accompanied the Knutsons to Kettle Falls to assist with services.[49]

Born in Bennswill, South Carolina, in July 1880, Lee Elliott Henson married Ellen Jefferson of Norwoodville, Iowa, in February 1905. In the 1910s, the Hensons moved to Seattle, where Lee—a former coal

---

Knutson.

42. *Cut Bank Pioneer Press*, "At the Churches," 1; Garrett, "History of the Montana District Council," 46; Roset et al., *Assemblies of God in Montana*, 32.

43. Oscar and Marie Knutson, oral history interview with Wayne Warner, Sept. 5, 1983, audio recording, Flower Pentecostal Heritage Center.

44. Knutson, *His Loving Care*, 83.

45. R. L. Polk & Co., *Seattle City Directory, 1937*; Knutson, *His Loving Care*, 83.

46. Knutson, *His Loving Care*, 83.

47. Knutson, *His Loving Care*, 83.

48. Knutson, *His Loving Care*, 83.

49. "Food Shower—Kettle Falls, Wn.," photograph of Knutson family and Rev. Lee Henson in Kettle Falls, Washington, ca. 1938–39, courtesy of Bernice M. Fergus.

miner—worked as a laborer. Sometime between 1918 and 1920, the couple seems to have separated. Lee appears to have remained in Seattle, working as a mechanic. Henson got involved with the local Pentecostal community in Seattle and eventually met Oscar Knutson, who became a close friend and partner in ministry. Henson may have been among the Pentecostal people of color from Seattle who visited Knutson and Brother Jack Nelson in Black Diamond, Washington, who narrowly escaped a racist lynch mob. Henson, also a friend of Oscar's parents, was almost certainly the "colored preacher" who sent Oscar the new suit of clothes while he was ministering in Augusta, Montana, in 1930.

Oscar Knutson and Lee Henson worked together and supported one another on several occasions. One anecdote in particular stands out. In summer 1934, while Knutson was away from his family holding revival meetings in Silverton, Oregon, Henson served as a significant support to Marie during a medical emergency that occurred with the Knutson's four-year-old son, Lloyd. According to Oscar's retelling, Lloyd had fallen out of a tree while playing and broke his arm at the elbow. It was a severe injury, however, as the elbow was "turned half ways around" and prevented blood circulation to his arm.[50] "Lloyd was rushed to the hospital," but the next morning, medical professionals informed Marie—who was unable to remain at the hospital with Lloyd—that they would have to amputate Lloyd's arm.[51] Marie appealed, and the procedure was delayed until one o'clock that afternoon.[52] While Oscar "rac[ed] for home as fast as I could," Reverend Henson and some other local "saints" gathered at Oscar's parents' house and prayed fervently for hours that God would intervene.[53] At noon, Reverend Henson asked Marie to call the hospital and inquire about Lloyd, but the medical staff still reported no blood circulation. According to Oscar, "Marie continue[d] to call every few minutes. Then, five minutes to one o'clock Bro[ther] Henson said, 'Marie, call again.' She did, and the doctor said, 'The blood has just begun to circulate. We will not have to amputate.'"[54] It was a miracle to be sure, and while God received all the praise and thanksgiving, Reverend Henson's ardent prayers, robust faith,

50. Knutson, *His Loving Care*, 100.
51. Knutson, *His Loving Care*, 100.
52. Knutson, *His Loving Care*, 100.
53. Knutson, *His Loving Care*, 100.
54. Knutson, *His Loving Care*, 100.

and steady presence conveyed a deep care for the Knutson family that was never forgotten.

Sometime in the early 1930s, Lee Henson became the pastor of the Full Gospel Mission on Ballard Avenue in Seattle. Given his pastoral responsibilities, it is unclear as to how long he assisted the Knutsons in Kettle Falls before he returned home. Regardless, in fall 1938, the Knutsons paused their tent meetings in Kettle Falls due to weather constraints and resumed in spring 1939.[55] Despite the early resistance to their tent meetings in Kettle Falls, the labors of the Knutson family and Rev. Lee Henson were fruitful. "We had good results," Oscar wrote.[56] The young men who had initially sought to shut down the meetings eventually ceased their disruptions and even attended some services themselves. Additionally, the Pentecostal community in Kettle Falls—originally just composed of Marie's eldest sister, Vera May Blair (née Baldwin), and her family—grew and became established as a formal church community.[57] Considering their work in Kettle Falls complete, the Knutson family continued their evangelistic ministry eastward, holding tent meetings as far as South Dakota and Iowa.[58]

World War II broke out in September 1939, and as the nations of the world rushed to respond, the Knutson family remained diligent and steadfast in their ministry work. With the chaos of conflict raging on such a large scale, people needed the gospel more than ever. The Knutsons continued holding tent meetings into the early 1940s, although they kept permanent residence in Seattle, where Oscar worked as a carpenter and building contractor.[59] In 1940, the Knutsons lived at 4226 Linden Avenue, and in 1941, they moved to 8717 Dayton Avenue, where they remained for the next couple of years.[60]

---

55. Knutson, *His Loving Care*, 84.

56. Knutson, *His Loving Care*, 84.

57. Knutson, *His Loving Care*, 84; handwritten family history notes, Oscar M. Knutson archival collection, unprocessed box.

58. Knutson, *His Loving Care*, 84.

59. R. L. Polk & Co., *Seattle City Directory, 1940*; "Sixteenth Census of the United States, 1940," Ancestry.com; R. L. Polk & Co., *Seattle City Directory, 1941*; R. L. Polk & Co., *Seattle City Directory, 1942*.

60. R. L. Polk & Co., *Seattle City Directory, 1940*; "Sixteenth Census of the United States, 1940," Ancestry.com; R. L. Polk & Co., *Seattle City Directory, 1941*; R. L. Polk & Co., *Seattle City Directory, 1942*.

Oscar Knutson continued his publishing ministry from the Dayton Avenue address, printing a variety of gospel tracts and other like materials under the name "The Full Gospel Press."[61] The print materials reflect Knutson's evangelistic theological convictions, with gospel tract titles such as "Redeemed Through the Blood," "The Door Is Open," "A Free Gift to You," "Jesus Is Coming Soon," and "Have You Been Endued with Power?"[62] More than just exhortations for individuals to repent and turn to Jesus, however, these tracts reflect a more corporate vision for spiritual renewal and revival. In one such tract, Oscar wrote: "*Surely* it is the desire of every one that we should have the blessing of God upon this land of ours; but knowing that there is always a condition with every promise in God's Holy Word, let us see what it is, and then meet it."[63] Knutson subsequently outlined the scriptural witness concerning who and how God blesses, concluding with a call to national repentance: "*America!* Repent, awake to righteous, and God will surely deliver us."[64] Published in the middle of World War II, a time in which patriotic fervor ran high, Knutson did not simply assume divine favor upon the United States. Instead, he kept himself scripturally grounded and worked to point others, not to confidence in their nation, but to faith in Jesus Christ, in whom true salvation is found.

The United States formally entered World War II in December 1941, which forced Oscar Knutson to consider war, and the possibility of military service, from a Christian standpoint. Sometime after the United States joined the conflict, Knutson wrote and published a twenty-three-page pamphlet entitled *The Christian and War*, in which he articulated what he believed wholeheartedly to be God's viewpoint on the matter. Written exclusively for "those who are the Blood bought Saints of God who love the Lord with all their heart, and who desire to go through with God regardless of the cost," the pamphlet argued that true Christians have no business participating in war, or in anything that leads to the death of others.[65] Instead, true Christians should be only concerned about life in Christ,

---

61. Gospel Tracts, "Full Gospel Press," Oscar M. Knutson archival collection, box 2, folder 4.

62. Gospel Tracts, "Full Gospel Press," Oscar M. Knutson archival collection, box 2, folder 4.

63. Gospel Tracts, "Full Gospel Press," Oscar M. Knutson archival collection, box 2, folder 4.

64. Gospel Tracts, "Full Gospel Press," Oscar M. Knutson archival collection, box 2, folder 4.

65. Knutson, *Christian and War*, 1.

meaning they must be entirely committed to serving Jesus and willing to suffer for the sake of the gospel. More than just an apology for Christian pacificism, *The Christian and War* offered a robust expression of Knutson's theology of suffering and discipleship and a call for Christians to become more deeply rooted in God. In the foreword, Knutson expressed his hope that the pamphlet would "make God's Word on the war question clear," as well as edify faithful Christians and lead to repentance those who had, in Knutson's view, capitulated to a sinful, worldly perspective.[66]

Filled with scriptural references and reflections, *The Christian and War* was brief yet thorough. For Oscar Knutson, war was nothing more than a "horrible pit" and a "maelstrom of death and horror" caused by lust and other worldly affections.[67] By contrast, true Christians are regenerate people, born of God. True Christians are not of this world and have "put away" lust and other sinful affections. Moreover, true Christians are filled with the fruit of the Holy Spirit and have a "sheep nature."[68] How could one "of a meek, lowly and contrite heart" participate in bloodshed and violence?[69] As for those who might defend military service as a necessary means toward establishing "permanent peace" in the world, Knutson affirmed that Jesus alone will bring the peace for which the whole created order longs.[70] Nations of the world do not need to do Jesus' job for him, nor should they try.

But what about obedience to the government? Does not God establish all governing authorities? Engaging with these questions, Oscar Knutson explored Israel's rejection of God's rule and her subsequent idolatry with Baal and other deities.[71] Knutson also noted the governments that executed innocent Christians in the New Testament period and in the early history of the church, not to mention the Roman government, which executed Jesus himself. Were these governments divine? How about twentieth-century Germany, Italy, or Japan?[72] And what about the United States going to war with the former? Would that not carry "house divided" ramifications? If governments are not all divinely established, then who is to say which ones

---

66. Knutson, *Christian and War*, 1.
67. Knutson, *Christian and War*, 3, 5.
68. Knutson, *Christian and War*, 3–4.
69. Knutson, *Christian and War*, 3–5.
70. Knutson, *Christian and War*, 3.
71. Knutson, *Christian and War*, 6.
72. Knutson, *Christian and War*, 6.

are and which ones are not?[73] With rhetorical boldness, Knutson wrote: "All unregenerated, or unsaved people[,] are of their father[,] the devil.... Can a government of unregenerated men, ruling over mostly unregenerated people, be divine? If they are, then their father the devil must be divine also."[74] Far from suggesting that God has nothing to do with government, however, Knutson argued that government is vital to human existence on earth.[75] After all, the "intended purpose" of government, "when rightly administered, is to do good, and not to do harm."[76] Obedience to government must be qualified, though. Like Jesus' apostles, Christians must obey "the laws of the land in all things pertaining to the natural man," but must refrain from doing so when such behavior would require them to "compromise on the Word of God."[77]

What about war itself, though? Does God sanction it? Not in the New Testament, Oscar Knutson argued. Instead of "an eye for an eye," Jesus charged his followers: "If they smite you on one cheek then turn the other."[78] Moreover, Jesus commanded his disciples to "love your enemies, bless them that curse you, [and] do good to them that hate you."[79] According to Knutson, if a Christian went out to war and "c[a]me face to face with a man from the enemy forces ... he would love his soul, (not his sins) and would do all in his power to win that soul for God ... he could not kill him and send his never dying soul to hell."[80] In this way, true Christians would follow after Jesus, whose example was never violence, Knutson argued. Even in the Garden of Gethsemane, Jesus rebuked his disciple Peter for taking a sword and cutting off the ear of a man who had come to arrest him. Knutson went so far as to suggest that Jesus "made sure that one of his disciples had a sword so he could set an example before us."[81] As Jesus himself said, "all they that live by the sword shall perish by the sword."[82]

---

73. Knutson, *Christian and War*, 6.
74. Knutson, *Christian and War*, 8.
75. Knutson, *Christian and War*, 8.
76. Knutson, *Christian and War*, 8, 9.
77. Knutson, *Christian and War*, 8, 9.
78. Knutson, *Christian and War*, 9; see Matt 5:38, 39, KJV.
79. Knutson, *Christian and War*, 9–10; see Matt 5:44, KJV.
80. Knutson, *Christian and War*, 10.
81. Knutson, *Christian and War*, 10.
82. Knutson, *Christian and War*, 10–11; see Matt 26:52, KJV.

But, one might argue, how about self-defense? "What a foolish question for one who professes to be a [C]hristian to ask," Oscar Knutson wrote.[83] Such a question, he asserted, reflects a profound lack of faith. "Where is their God? Has he gone on a journey, or is he asleep? Is he sick abed so that he cannot help them?"[84] Knutson's words rang sharp, yet utterly confident, as he proceeded to quote the Scriptures: "The God I serve is a living God ... [He is my] Refuge and Strength, a very present help in trouble.... The Lord is my Rock and my Fortress, and my Deliverer; my God, my Strength, in whom I will trust: my buckler, and the horn of my salvation, and my high tower."[85] From Knutson's perspective, those concerned about self-defense were simply "shallow [C]hristians," and did not "live close enough to God to be under his sheltering and protecting arm."[86] True Christians would not entertain such fears. Rather, their confidence in God is such that they would entrust themselves to him, uncompromising, even unto death.

The self-defense question, for Oscar Knutson, seemed to reveal a deeper theological issue—the meaning of Christian discipleship and the reality of suffering in the Christian life. As one who had witnessed and experienced great hardship in his own life, Knutson understood that faith in Jesus would not prevent people from experiencing suffering.[87] Instead, there is a "cost" to discipleship, to use the parlance of German theologian Dietrich Bonhoeffer, who wrote about such matters in 1937, just a few years prior to Knutson's publication of *The Christian and War*. Since Jesus' life was marked by suffering, true Christians could expect the same. In the context of World War II, American Christians could expect to suffer in some capacity for choosing to be conscientious objectors, and such hardship should not be feared or avoided.[88] All too often, though, it had been feared and avoided by professing Christians. "O you jellyfish backboned [C]hristians, how do you ever expect to make the pearly gates of Heaven?" Knutson wrote.[89] "You have been receiving the blessings of God and you

83. Knutson, *Christian and War*, 11.
84. Knutson, *Christian and War*, 11.
85. Knutson, *Christian and War*, 11; see Pss 46:1; 18:2.
86. Knutson, *Christian and War*, 12.
87. At risk of making an overly anachronistic comparison, the theological content of *The Christian and War* suggests that if Knutson had been familiar with the teachings known presently as the "health and wealth" gospel, the Word of Faith movement, or the Prosperity Gospel, he would have opposed them vehemently.
88. Knutson, *Christian and War*, 12.
89. Knutson, *Christian and War*, 13.

continually ask for more, but yet refuse to carry the cross, and walk up Golgotha's hill with your Lord and Saviour."[90]

For Oscar Knutson, the answer was faith in Jesus and obedience to the holy Scriptures. "The question of whether you will be persecuted or not is a question you should not consider at all if you feel in your own heart that you desire to obey the Word of God," Knutson argued.[91] "You should rather ask God to give you grace and strength for every trial and test you may be called upon to bear."[92] Knutson went so far as to suggest that "[a] true [C]hristian is the greatest asset of defense any nation can possess, whether they realize it or not."[93] Concretely speaking, Knutson suggested that Christians who were drafted should work at non-military labor without pay or go into non-combatant service and provide medical assistance to the wounded.[94] For regular civilians, Knutson recommended supporting the Red Cross or other relief work financially, while refraining from buying war bonds that would be "receive[d] back with interest later."[95] Additionally, Knutson asserted that under no circumstances could a true Christian contribute financially to, or participate in the manufacture of, firearms, bombs, planes, or other military implements that would be used to kill. "Before God it is equally as bad to make the weapons as it is to use them . . . . The blood will be on your skirts regardless of which way you get it there."[96]

Oscar Knutson's final word in *The Christian and War* was a call to prayer, repentance, and sincere faith and obedience to God, given through a typified Abraham and Lot from the thirteenth chapter of the book of Genesis. When the two kinsmen parted ways, "Lot chose the best [portion of land] from the natural view point, but it took him toward Sodom."[97] By comparison, "Abraham took what was left, but it brought him a wonderful promise, and an inheritance . . . . To this day Abraham stands as a monument of faith and obedience."[98] True Christians must be like Abraham, not

90. Knutson, *Christian and War*, 13.
91. Knutson, *Christian and War*, 18.
92. Knutson, *Christian and War*, 18.
93. Knutson, *Christian and War*, 16.
94. Knutson, *Christian and War*, 17, 19.
95. Knutson, *Christian and War*, 19.
96. Knutson, *Christian and War*, 15.
97. Knutson, *Christian and War*, 23.
98. Knutson, *Christian and War*, 23.

like Lot, Knutson asserted. "If you are willing to dull your conscience a little, and interpret the Word of God to suit your need, so that you can reap in all the comforts and riches of this world, even though you may have to taint yourselves a little to do so; you are a Lot type [C]hristian. Remember your end," Knutson warned.[99] Instead, true Christians should "wish to go all the way with your God, and wish only to do according to his precious Word."[100] Furthermore, Knutson exhorted the faithful, "do not let yourselves be misled by the compromising leaders of the professing church, or by anyone else. Take your stand on God's Holy Word, and then stand there, and God will see you through[. You will] more than conque[r] in Christ Jesus."[101]

---

99. Knutson, *Christian and War*, 23.
100. Knutson, *Christian and War*, 23.
101. Knutson, *Christian and War*, 23.

6

"Praise the Lord"

Praise the Lord, praise the Lord, praise the Lord,
For His Mercy endureth forever;
Praise the Lord, praise the Lord, praise the Lord,
For His Mercy endureth forever.

Sing of His wonderful love to me,
Jesus who died upon Calv'ry's tree,
Risen, He liveth, my King to be,
Praise the Lord, praise the Lord, praise the Lord.
—O. M. Knutson, "Praise the Lord"

In early November 1941, just a month prior to the United States' entrance into World War II, Oscar Knutson attended the West Coast Convention of the Independent Assemblies of God, an unincorporated fellowship of (mostly Scandinavian) Pentecostal churches and ministers who shared a preference for local church autonomy and voluntary collaboration over formal denominational affiliation.[1] Formed in St. Paul, Minnesota, in 1922,

1. Gross, "Marvelous Revival," 19–20; Mead and Hill, *Handbook of Denominations*,

the Independent Assemblies of God had merged with a similar body, the Scandinavian Assemblies of God in the United States, Canada, and Foreign Lands, in 1935.[2] Knutson may have been involved with the Independent Assemblies of God as early as the 1920s, and certainly by the 1930s and 1940s.[3] Admittedly, the exact nature of Knutson's affiliation with the Independent Assemblies of God is unclear, but it was evidently a useful ministry connection for him. Throughout his life, Knutson never committed himself to any one Pentecostal denomination, preferring instead to work with anyone who was "sound in doctrine" and committed to the same Pentecostal ministry vision.[4] In this way, Knutson's connection to the Independent Assemblies of God makes sense, although the same also could be said of his connection to the Assemblies of God, with which he collaborated on several occasions even though he was not a formal Assemblies of God minister.

Hosted by the Rev. John W. Moseid's Bethel Assembly in Tacoma, Washington, the West Coast Convention of the Independent Assemblies of God ran for five days and included a meaningful array of teaching, preaching, Bible study, fellowship, worship, and prayer.[5] Notably, Brother Jack Nelson attended the convention, along with many other Pentecostal ministers and missionaries.[6] According to some reflections published in the official periodical of the Independent Assemblies of God, *Herald of Faith*, the convention was "a glorious time of feasting and fellowship in the Holy Ghost," in which several attendees "accepted Christ as their personal Saviour, one received the Baptism of the Holy Ghost, and many were refilled with the Holy Ghost."[7] Admittedly, Oscar Knutson did not personally write

---

277–78; Jones, *Guide to the Study of the Pentecostal Movement*, 570.

2. Mead and Hill, *Handbook of Denominations*, 277–78; Jones, *Guide to the Study of the Pentecostal Movement*, 570, 627.

3. Rodgers, *Northern Harvest*, 107n191; Gross, "Marvelous Revival," 20.

4. Oscar and Marie Knutson, oral history interview with Wayne Warner, Sept. 5, 1983, audio recording, Flower Pentecostal Heritage Center.

5. Gross, "Marvelous Revival," 19.

6. Gross, "Marvelous Revival," 20.

7. Gross, "Marvelous Revival," 19–20. The language of being "refilled" with the Holy Spirit was common within the Pentecostal theological context and referred to a renewal or refreshment of the Spirit of God within a person who had previously received the baptism of the Holy Spirit. This "refilling" was, generally, to equip a person for further ministry work. Although this experience happened in the context of private prayer, it normatively occurred during public worship services. Those describing said worship services would typically state that the Holy Spirit was present, as evidenced by the number of (a) conversion experiences, (b) instances of divine healing, (c) persons "reclaimed,"

about his experiences at this convention, but his collaboration in ministry with some of the attendees over the next few years—including the convention's host pastor and acting chairman, Rev. John W. Moseid, along with his younger brother, Rev. C. Albert Moseid—indicate that it was a meaningful and productive experience for him.

Although Oscar Knutson opposed war from a biblical and theological standpoint, the United States' entrance into World War II meant that he still had to be registered for potential military service.[8] Participating in the third round of draft registration in February 1942, Knutson's registration card describes him as a forty-one-year-old self-employed builder and minister with brown hair, blue eyes, and light complexion, about 5' 10," and approximately 145 pounds. At the time of registration, Knutson was still living at 8717 Dayton Avenue in Seattle, and he listed his father, Andrew Knutson, as the person who would always know his address.[9] Admittedly, Oscar Knutson was never drafted for military service, but his draft registration

---

that is, rededicated to serving Christ, presumably after a period in which they had not been serving him faithfully, (d) Holy Spirit baptisms, and (e) persons "refilled" with the Holy Spirit. In 1980, Frances P. Hoy, an Assemblies of God minister residing in Costa Mesa, California, wrote an article about the significance of being refilled with the Holy Spirit. "The Scripture teaches that an effective witness for the gospel must be frequently refreshed by refillings of the Spirit," she wrote. "In Acts 2:4 we read that the early disciples were filled with the Spirit, but in Acts 4:31 they were refilled. Peter was filled with the Spirit on the Day of Pentecost (Acts 2:4), but as he stood before the Sanhedrin he was refilled (Acts 4:8). Paul was filled with the Spirit in Damascus (Acts 9:17), but he was refilled at Paphos (Acts 13:9)." Hoy, "Renewal of the Spirit," 28. J. Roswell Flower, who became one of the "founding fathers" of the Assemblies of God, published part of his own testimony in 1910, which included the following experience: "While asking the blessing at the supper-table, the power of God fell on me and I was compelled to go off alone with God where He dealt with me in a very precious way for some hours. Then the following week He filled me and refilled me and laid me under His mighty power half a dozen times." Flower, "God Honors Faith," 1. While the early Pentecostal movement held that speaking in tongues was the initial evidence of the baptism of the Holy Spirit, it is unclear whether speaking in tongues always accompanied the experience of being refilled with the Holy Spirit. Hoy's description, along with the scriptural references provided, do not clarify this point. If anything, they suggest that being refilled with the Holy Spirit was not necessarily another "tongues" experience, but rather a kind of personal spiritual revival—a movement of the Holy Spirit within a person to embolden them to preach the gospel in a powerful and effective manner.

8. Fold3 Military Records, "US, WWII Draft Registration Cards, 1940."
9. Oscar Marius Knutson, World War II Registration Card, 1942, Ancestry.com.

card is historically significant for providing personally descriptive details that would not be available otherwise.

Oscar Knutson and his family continued their evangelistic ministry in 1942, although they kept their permanent residence in Seattle. In spring 1942, the Knutsons visited the Full Gospel Mission in Estherville, Iowa, where they held several weeks of revival meetings with Rev. Lawrence F. Guge, who had been ordained and installed as pastor in late 1938, some months after Rev. Linus Heidt resigned.[10] In June and July 1942, the Knutsons also visited Reverend Heidt, who was then pastoring the Independent Pentecostal church in Sioux Falls, South Dakota, and conducted "'old time' gospel services" in their "Big Brown tent," according to local newspaper clippings.[11]

Oscar Knutson's ministry work shifted from tent meetings to pastoral ministry in Okanogan, Washington, in 1943. On Tuesday, August 17, 1943, Knutson and his family set up their evangelistic tent on a local skating rink lot just one block west of the county courthouse in Okanogan and began holding "old fashioned gospel meetings."[12] Although initial attendance was modest, turnout increased.[13] Meetings occurred every Tuesday through Friday at eight p.m., and Sundays at three p.m.[14] Oscar led most of the meetings, although a handful of ministry colleagues visited and assisted with services on occasion.[15] By the time the weather became too cold for tent meetings, regular attendance had grown to seventeen people, with children in the majority.[16] Oscar found that the local Townsend Hall at 305 Tyee Street was available three Sundays per month and rented it for services.

---

10. *Estherville Daily News*, "Rev. O. M. Knutson," 1; *Calvary Gospel Assembly*, 11.

11. *Argus-Leader*, "Independant Pentecostal [sic]," 4; *Argus-Leader*, "Evangelist O. M. Knutson," 4; *Argus-Leader*, "Independent Pentecostal," 5.

12. *Okanogan Independent*, "Old Fashioned Gospel Meetings at the Big Brown Tent"; "Town of Okanogan" page from 1959 Metsker map of Okanogan County, Okanogan County Historical Society; *Okanogan Independent*, "Outdoor Skating Rink Is Recreation Center"; *Okanogan Independent*, "Work Goes Ahead on Skating Rink." Credit is due to Barry I. George, volunteer at the Okanogan County Historical Society, for identifying the skating rink location of Oscar Knutson's initial tent meetings in Okanogan.

13. Knutson, *His Loving Care*, 86.

14. *Okanogan Independent*, "Old Fashioned Gospel Meetings at the Big Brown Tent."

15. *Okanogan Independent*, "Robert G. Smyth."

16. Knutson, *His Loving Care*, 86.

However, because the rental agreement still left the growing Pentecostal community without a formal gathering space one Sunday per month, they began praying for God to make a more reliable meeting location available.[17]

In December 1943, Oscar Knutson noticed that the building at 521 Second Avenue South in Okanogan was being vacated and put up for sale.[18] Built in September 1940, the building was a former bowling alley that had closed down, likely due to economic difficulties associated with World War II.[19] As recently as September 1943, the former bowling alley had also been used to board seasonal fruit laborers.[20] Upon inquiry, Knutson negotiated the terms of sale down to a total price of forty-two hundred dollars, with a down payment of one thousand dollars and monthly mortgage payment of thirty-five dollars.[21] Admittedly, Knutson only had a little over fifty dollars in cash—not nearly enough to cover the down payment. As an act of faith, however, Knutson put down the cash he had as earnest money and secured the sale of the building with the understanding that the down payment money would have to be paid within the next two days.[22]

A few minutes after leaving the real estate broker's office, Knutson had a chance meeting with Harry Rasmussen, a local Okanogan man who had attended some of the Pentecostal meetings.[23] Rasmussen inquired if Knutson had heard about the former bowling alley and if he had considered purchasing it for the forming Pentecostal community in Okanogan. Knutson disclosed details concerning the purchase offer, the terms, and the earnest money, to which Rasmussen then asked about the down payment. After Knutson told Rasmussen that he did not know where the money was

---

17. Knutson, *His Loving Care*, 86; *Okanogan Independent*, "Congregation Buys Second Ave. Building," 1.

18. Knutson, "Okanogan, Wash.," 27–28; Knutson, *His Loving Care*, 86–87.

19. "NAPA Building," *Okanogan Business Directory*, 56, courtesy of Barry I. George of the Okanogan County Historical Society.

20. "NAPA Building," *Okanogan Business Directory*, 56, courtesy of Barry I. George of the Okanogan County Historical Society; *Okanogan Independent*, "Congregation Buys Second Ave. Building," 1.

21. Knutson, *His Loving Care*, 86.

22. Knutson, *His Loving Care*, 87.

23. Knutson, *His Loving Care*, 87; warranty deed, vol. 112, pp. 397–400, Feb. 12, 1944, indicating purchase and transfer of property from W. F. Schmidt to trustees of the Full Gospel Christian Assembly, Okanogan County Auditor's Office, courtesy of Barry I. George of the Okanogan County Historical Society. According to deed paperwork, Harry Rasmussen had become one of the trustees of the Full Gospel Christian Assembly of Okanogan.

going to come from, Rasmussen promptly told Knutson that he would supply it. "Thus, by the grace of God, we got the building," Knutson rejoiced.[24]

Although formal deed paperwork was not signed until February 12, 1944, the Okanogan Pentecostal community—which had become organized as the "Full Gospel Christian Assembly" under the pastoral leadership of Oscar Knutson—was able to begin using the former bowling alley for regular church services in January 1944.[25] Additionally, in early to mid January, Rev. C. Albert Moseid of Seattle, a ministry colleague of Oscar's who was affiliated with the Independent Assemblies of God, visited and held special services for the Okanogan congregation.

The son of Norwegian immigrant Knut J. Moseid and his wife, Maria Aase (née Severtson), Charles Albert Moseid was born in November 1892 in Marshall County, Minnesota.[26] Moseid, who often went by his middle name, Albert, became involved in the Pentecostal movement in the early decades of his life. From 1917 to 1922, he was listed in the minister's directory of the Assemblies of God, although on his World War I draft registration card, Moseid identified himself as a traveling evangelist affiliated with the Pentecostal Assemblies of the World—a striking paradox, given the discrepancy on trinitarian theology between the two denominations.[27] In 1918, Albert married Ella Mathilda Brun of Dunn County, Wisconsin.[28] With permanent residence in Colfax, Wisconsin, the couple had two

---

24. Knutson, *His Loving Care*, 87.

25. Warranty deed, vol. 112, p. 397, Feb. 12, 1944; *Okanogan Independent*, "Full Gospel Christian Assembly" (Jan. 6, 1944).

26. Charles Albert Moseid, World War II Draft Registration Card, 1942, Ancestry.com; John W. Moseid, Washington State Department of Health, Certificate of Death, 1965, Ancestry.com.

27. Assemblies of God General Council Ministers Directories, 1917–22, Consortium of Pentecostal Archives. Admittedly, Albert Moseid is not in the 1918 Assemblies of God Minsters Directory, but there is an "Alfred Moseid." It seems likely this was an error and that "Alfred Moseid" is actually Albert Moseid; Charles Albert Moseid, World War I Draft Registration Card, 1918, Ancestry.com; David A. Reed, "Pentecostal Assemblies of the World," in Burgess and van der Maas, *New International Dictionary*, 965.

28. *Dunn County News*, "Applications for marriage licenses," 5. Interestingly, Ella M. Brun was the sister of Elma O. Brun, who married fellow Pentecostal evangelist Rev. Elmer C. Erickson, the primary founder of the Independent Assemblies of God, decades-long pastor of the Duluth Gospel Tabernacle in Duluth, Minnesota, and the original editor of *The Full Gospel Testimony*, the publication which Rev. A. D. Guth edited for several years. *Dunn County News*, "Mrs. E. C. Erickson," 14; Joseph Colletti, "Erickson, Elmer C.," in Burgess and van der Maas, *New International Dictionary*, 600. In several primary sources, Ella's last name has been anglicized as "Brown."

children together, Eunice and Alberta, and they also pursed Pentecostal evangelistic ministry together.[29] Notably, from 1918 to 1922, Ella was herself listed in the Assemblies of God minister's directory as an ordained evangelist in good standing.[30]

Tragically, Ella M. Moseid died of illness in March 1923, leaving Albert Moseid as a single parent of both a toddler and an infant.[31] In the wake of Ella's untimely death, Albert lived with his in-laws in Cumberland, Wisconsin, but nevertheless continued his Pentecostal ministry work.[32] By 1935, Albert had become the pastor of the Superior Gospel Tabernacle in Superior, Wisconsin.[33] He also appears to have remarried in the late 1930s, and over the next decade had two more children—Calvin and Chester—with his new wife, Ella Louise (née Larsen).[34] Although Albert Moseid did not continue his formal affiliation with the Assemblies of God, he helped found the Independent Assemblies of God in 1922, alongside his brother, Rev. John W. Moseid; his brother-in-law, Rev. Elmer C. Erickson; and a fellow Pentecostal ministry colleague, Rev. A. C. Valdez. In addition to the Independent Assemblies of God, Rev. Albert Moseid's appearances in the Pentecostal periodical *Sanningens Vittne* indicate that he worked with the Scandinavian Assemblies of God, which later merged with the Independent Assemblies of God in 1935.[35] By 1940, Albert Moseid and his family moved to Seattle, Washington, where Albert served as pastor of the Ballard

29. Albert Moseid, "Fourteenth Census of the United States, 1920—Population," Ancestry.com; *Dunn County News*, "Mr. and Mrs. Albert Moseid" (Apr. 21, 1921), 11; *Dunn County News*, "Mr. and Mrs. Albert Moseid" (Dec. 22, 1921), 9.

30. Assemblies of God General Council Ministers Directories, 1919–22, Consortium of Pentecostal Archives.

31. *Dunn County News*, "Colfax," 11; "Fifteenth Census of the United States, 1930—Population Schedule," Ancestry.com.

32. Charles A. Moseid, "Fifteenth Census of the United States, 1930—Population Schedule," Ancestry.com; *Dunn County News*, "Albert Moseid" (Apr. 19, 1923), 13; *Dunn County News*, "Albert Moseid" (Aug. 2, 1923), 10; *Dunn County News*, "Pentecostal meetings," 10; *Star Tribune*, "Full Gospel Mission, Pentecostal," 10.

33. R. L. Polk & Co., *Superior (Douglas County, Wisconsin) City Directory, 1935*.

34. Charles Moseid, "Sixteenth Census of the United States, 1940," Ancestry.com; Charles A. Moseid, "1950 Census of Population and Housing," Ancestry.com; Calvin Sanford Moseid, Certificate of Marriage, 1971, Washington State Digital Archives; Chester Albert Moseid, Certificate of Marriage, 1975, Washington State Digital Archives.

35. Boze, "Denominational Organization," 6; Nilson, "Utländska Missionen," 6; Berglund, "Resebrev," 6; Hedeen, "Tacoma, Washington," 5. *Sanningens Vittne*, which means "Witness to the Truth," was a Swedish-language paper and the official periodical of the Scandinavian Assemblies of God.

Pentecostal Tabernacle on Jones Avenue and collaborated in ministry work with his older brother, Rev. John W. Moseid, in nearby Tacoma, Washington.[36] Albert Moseid was still pastor of this Seattle congregation in early 1944 when he visited and held special services at Oscar Knutson's Full Gospel Christian Assembly in Okanogan, Washington.

On Monday, January 17, 1944, the Full Gospel Christian Assembly held "a big fellowship meeting and dedication service" to dedicate the former bowling alley "to the service of the Lord."[37] Rev. C. Albert Moseid preached the dedication message, and several friends and ministry associates from Omak, Washington—particularly, Rev. Andrew S. Teuber—attended the ceremony. Over the next few years, the former bowling alley building proved to be a tremendous blessing to the Full Gospel Christian Assembly in Okanogan. According to Oscar Knutson's later reflections: "People began to come in greater numbers. Some were getting saved and bapti[z]ed in the Holy Spirit. The Lord blessed, and there was victory in the camp. And before we had been there a year, we had the largest attendance of any church in town."[38] In addition to holding regular church services in what became the main assembly hall, Knutson held regular Sunday school and Bible study sessions in the facility and even set up his print shop at the rear of the building, maintaining the name "The Full Gospel Press." As a local newspaper clipping put it, "Mr. Knutson not only preaches but also publishes the Gospel."[39]

The Full Gospel Christian Assembly continued to flourish under Oscar Knutson's pastoral leadership over the next few years. In addition to regular church services, Sunday school sessions, Bible studies, and prayer meetings, the Okanogan congregation had special visits by multiple Pentecostal pastors and missionaries. In late February 1944, just after the church formally purchased the former bowling alley, it welcomed "consecrated missionary" Erma Roth to visit and speak about her ministry work in Venezuela,

---

36. Charles Moseid, "Fifteenth Census of the United States, 1940," Ancestry.com; Charles Albert Moseid, World War II Draft Registration Card, 1942, Ancestry.com; R. L. Polk & Co., *Seattle City Directory*, 1943.

37. *Okanogan Independent*, "Full Gospel Christian Assembly" (Jan. 13, 1944), 5.

38. Knutson, *His Loving Care*, 87–88.

39. *Okanogan Independent*, "Congregation Buys Second Ave. Building," 1.

South America.[40] Furthermore, in January 1945, Pentecostal evangelist Karl Kristensen and his wife visited the Full Gospel Christian Assembly and held special services for a couple of weeks. Originally from Sweden, the Kristensens had served as missionaries to the Belgian Congo in Africa for the past twenty years and had settled in the United States after wartime conditions in Europe prevented them from returning home.[41]

In early April 1945, the Full Gospel Christian Assembly hosted "[a] big three day fellowship and Bible conference meeting."[42] Open to both laypersons and ordained ministers, the conference primarily featured large-group discussion and Bible study. Perhaps most notable were several discussions that welcomed all present to participate in considering matters such as the distinction between "personal calling" and "leading by God," the difference between "a real Biblical revival" and "a substitute," the meaning of hope in Christ, the meaning of sanctification, and whether "our security in God [is] conditional or unconditional."[43] In writing about the event, Oscar Knutson noted that "these subjects were discussed in a wonderful spirit of fellowship and harmony."[44] While the conference had many noteworthy attendees, Rev. John W. Moseid and Rev. C. Albert Moseid were present as featured preachers, indicating Knutson's ongoing collaboration with them.[45]

The older brother of Albert Moseid, John William Moseid was born in Marshall County, Minnesota, in October 1890.[46] Like Albert, John seems to have become involved in the Pentecostal movement in the early decades of his life. In 1915, John married Mabel Anderson of Berlin, Minnesota, and a year later, their son Phillip was born. Together, the Moseid family pursued Pentecostal ministry work.[47] On his World War I Draft Registration Card, dated June 1917, John described himself as a "minister of the gospel," employed by "The Lord."[48] In January 1922, John helped found

---

40. *Okanogan Independent*, "Full Gospel Christian Assembly" (Feb. 24, 1944), 6.
41. *Okanogan Independent*, "Missionaries to Hold Meetings."
42. Knutson, "3-Day Fellowship Bible Conference," 12.
43. Knutson, "3-Day Fellowship Bible Conference," 12.
44. Knutson, "3-Day Fellowship Bible Conference," 12.
45. Knutson, "3-Day Fellowship Bible Conference," 12.
46. John W. Moseid, Washington State Department of Health, Certificate of Death, 1965, Ancestry.com.
47. *People's Press*, untitled article noting the wedding of John W. Moseid and Mabel J. Anderson, 12.
48. John W. Moseid, World War I Draft Registration Card, 1917, Ancestry.com.

the Independent Assemblies of God, together with his brother, Rev. Albert Moseid, and their friends and ministry associates Rev. E. C. Erickson and Rev. A. C. Valdez. Like Albert, John Moseid also worked with the Scandinavian Assemblies of God in the 1920s and 1930s.[49]

Tragically, Mabel Moseid died of illness in August 1925, leaving John a single parent of their nine-year-old son.[50] Despite this loss, John Moseid continued his Pentecostal ministry work in Minnesota, becoming assistant pastor of the Full Gospel Pentecostal Assembly in Minneapolis, together with Rev. John Feuk.[51] In March 1928, John Moseid remarried. As in his previous marriage, Moseid's new wife, Mabel Florence Peterson, was a strong support in ministry.[52] Rev. John Moseid continued pastoring alongside Rev. John Feuk until 1936, when Reverend Feuk resigned from their church—renamed the Full Gospel Temple in the early 1930s—to embark on other ministry work.[53] With Reverend Feuk's departure, Reverend Moseid took up full pastoral leadership of the church, which was subsequently renamed Bloomington Temple. Over the next few years, Rev. John Moseid pastored Bloomington Temple while also traveling to pursue evangelistic work.[54] In 1938, he accepted the pastorate of Salem Full Gospel Church in Brooklyn, New York, while the church's pastor, Rev. A. W. Rasmussen, made a year-long trip to Europe.[55] After Reverend Rasmussen's return in fall 1939, Reverend Moseid left Brooklyn and pursued traveling evangelism for a few months before accepting a call to pastor the Bethel Pentecostal Assembly in Tacoma, Washington, in 1940.[56] Reverend Moseid, whose second wife Mabel died in 1945, pastored in Tacoma until 1951 and collaborated with Oscar Knutson on multiple occasions throughout the 1940s.[57]

49. Boze, "Denominational Organization," 6.
50. *Ellendale Eagle*, "Mrs. John Moseid," 1.
51. *Minneapolis Journal*, "Full Gospel Assembly Pentecostal," 5.
52. *Minneapolis Star*, "Marriage Licenses," 19; *News Tribune*, "Mrs. John W. Moseid," 12.
53. *Minneapolis Star*, "Pastor of Gospel Church Resigns," 5.
54. *Star Tribune*, "Evangelist Services," 14; *Minneapolis Star*, "Smith Brothers Revival Meetings," 8; *Friend Tribune*, "Rev. John Moseid," 1.
55. *Minneapolis Star*, "Bloomington Gets Pastor," 7; *Tacoma Times*, "Rev. J. W. Moseid Will Preach Here," 19; Moseid, "Greeting from Pastor John Moseid," 10.
56. Moseid, "Greeting from Pastor John Moseid," 10; Hedeen, "Tacoma, Washington," 5.
57. *News Tribune*, "Mrs. John W. Moseid," 12; R. L. Polk & Co., *Tacoma City Directory, 1951*; *News Tribune*, "Rev. John W. Moseid," 37.

"Praise the Lord"

Sadly, Oscar Knutson's regular rhythms in Okanogan were interrupted by the death of his eldest sister, Inga Kristine Johnson, on June 30, 1945.[58] Inga, a mere forty-six years old, succumbed to ovarian cancer in Seattle, where she had been visiting her parents since May 1945.[59] Inga's death was undoubtedly a significant blow to the whole Knutson family, not to mention her own husband and children. Even so, she left behind a tremendous legacy. A remarkable woman of God, Inga had done ministry among several church communities in Montana for many years, mostly Assemblies of God churches. Furthermore, both of her sons, John A. Johnson Jr. and Everett A. Johnson, were themselves Assemblies of God ministers in Fort Benton, Montana.[60] If Oscar wrote down any reflections concerning Inga's death, they do not seem to have survived. However, in a scrapbook album, Oscar did preserve a handwritten letter of condolences from a local Okanogan family, the Shepards, which in relation to Inga acknowledges the reality of death and grief but also points to the hope of resurrection:

> Dear friends, [w]e have heard of your bereavement, and our sympathy goes out to you and yours. But we know your sorrow is not as the sorrow of one that has lost a dear one that had no hope beyond the grave. Your loss is her gain. So we'll say, "Oh death, where is thy sting[?] Oh grave where is thy victory[?]"[61]

In early January 1947, just after celebrating the holidays, the Knutson family left Okanogan to take a trip "in the interest of the Independent Full Gospel Assemblies, and Gospel Publication work."[62] Over the next few months, the Knutsons traveled by car through Oregon, California, Arizona, New Mexico, Texas, Oklahoma, Kansas, Indiana, and Kentucky, among other states, before returning to Okanogan. Along the way, they made stops for

---

58. Inga Kristine Johnson, Certificate of Death, 1945, Washington State Digital Archives.

59. *Great Falls Tribune*, "Mrs. Inga Johnson Dies in Seattle," 9.

60. *Great Falls Tribune*, "Mrs. Inga Johnson Dies in Seattle," 9.

61. The Shepards to the Knutsons, July 2, 1945, Oscar M. Knutson archival collection, unprocessed box.

62. *Okanogan Independent*, "Local Pastor and Family to Take Trip," 8; *Okanogan Independent*, "Local Pastor and Family Home from Trip South," 3.

evangelistic meetings, sometimes for as much as three weeks at a time. During their absence, local layman Arthur Buckingham preached and conducted services for the Full Gospel Christian Assembly back in Okanogan. It was "a fine trip," according to a local newspaper clipping published upon their return.[63] The Knutsons reported mostly rainy weather, "even in dry Arizona."[64] Although evidently just a report of literal experiences, it might as well have been intended as something of a Pentecostal metaphor. After all, the early Pentecostal movement often spoke of the Holy Spirit coming down from heaven like rain, drawing on the words of the Old Testament prophet Joel: "Be glad, O sons of Zion, and rejoice in the Lord, your God; for he has given the early rain for your vindication, he has poured down for you abundant rain, the early and the latter rain, as before."[65] According to Pentecostal scholar Peter Althouse:

> Early Pentecostals articulated a theology of the latter rain, which validated their charismatic experiences of the Spirit's outpouring. Based in the agricultural climate of the Near East, an early rain falls for the planting of crops, and a latter rain falls to mature the crops preceding harvest. Based on this metaphor, early Pentecostals believed that the outpouring of the Holy Spirit and subsequent charismatic activity in the early church was the early rain, and the outpouring of the Spirit and restoration of charismatic activity at the dawn of the twentieth century was the latter rain, preparing the world for a great harvest of souls immediately preceding the return of Christ in glory to establish his kingdom reign.[66]

Oscar Knutson evidently shared this "latter rain" parlance and perspective, as did various ministry partners. In some typed notes for an unfinished project from the late 1980s or early 1990s entitled "Pentecost—Yesterday and Today," Knutson wrote: "Often the Azusa Street Mission is referred to as the high point of the Pentecostal Movement."[67] Significantly, next to this sentence, Knutson penciled the words, "lat[t]er day," likely intending to add

---

63. *Okanogan Independent*, "Local Pastor and Family to Take Trip," 8; *Okanogan Independent*, "Local Pastor and Family Home from Trip South," 3.

64. *Okanogan Independent*, "Local Pastor and Family Home from Trip South," 3.

65. Joel 2:23, RSV.

66. Peter Althouse, "Eschatology," in Stewart, *Handbook of Pentecostal Christianity*, 73–74.

67. Typed notes (with handwritten annotations), "Pentecost—Yesterday and Today," Oscar M. Knutson archival collection, box 2, folder 37.

"Praise the Lord"

this detail to a subsequent draft.[68] In some handwritten notes for the same project, Knutson wrote of "the lat[t]er day outpouring of the baptism of the Holy Spirit."[69] Rev. Andrew Teuber, a personal friend of Knutson and an important ministry coworker during Knutson's pastorate in Okanogan, also found the "latter rain" theological framework helpful. In the 1960s, he published a book entitled *Tongues of Fire*, in which he alluded to the Pentecostal experience of the baptism of the Holy Spirit as the "latter rain" and connected it to an exhortation from the Epistle of James in the New Testament: "Be patient, therefore, brethren, until the coming of the Lord. Behold, the farmer waits for the precious fruit of the earth, being patient over it, until it receives the early and the late rain. You also be patient. Establish your hearts, for the coming of the Lord is at hand."[70] According to Reverend Teuber: "G[od] is pouring out His Spirit upon believers in a greater measure than at any time since the days of the Apostles . . . . These are the days of the 'latter rain' which were prophesied to be before the coming of Christ."[71]

Oscar Knutson and his family returned to Okanogan in June 1947, getting back from their trip not a moment too soon. Around the same time that they returned, Okanogan County leadership contacted the Full Gospel Christian Assembly and requested to purchase the former bowling alley,

---

68. Typed notes (with handwritten annotations), "Pentecost—Yesterday and Today," Oscar M. Knutson archival collection, box 2, folder 37.

69. Handwritten notes on "Pentecost: Yesterday and Today, 1901–1990," Oscar M. Knutson archival collection, box 2, folder 36.

70. Teuber, *Tongues of Fire*, 7; Jas 5:7–8, RSV.

71. Teuber, *Tongues of Fire*, 7. The early Pentecostals embraced this "latter rain" theological framework quite ubiquitously, but interestingly, some articulated it differently than others. For example, Rev. Joseph Lantz of Great Falls, Montana, whose ministry was deeply formative for Oscar Knutson's early years in the Pentecostal movement, took a different interpretive tack. In a pamphlet entitled *Is the Baptism with the Holy Spirit Scriptural?* Lantz specifically quoted Joel 2:23 and wrote of Palestinian weather patterns and agricultural ramifications. However, drawing on the relationship between Passover and Pentecost in the context of Jewish ritual life, Lantz wrote that "the former rain is a figure of receiving Christ in salvation. The latter rain is a figure of receiving the outpouring of the gift of the Holy Spirit." Lantz, *Is the Baptism of the Holy Spirit Scriptural?*, 3, 8–10. Whereas most early Pentecostals interpreted Joel 2:23 as a prophetic word being fulfilled in their own day, and in its connection to the great outpouring of the Holy Spirit at Pentecost as recorded in Acts 2, Reverend Lantz utilized the same passage with more of a typological hermeneutic.

intending to turn the space into a welfare office.⁷² Offering more than twice what the church had paid for the building back in February 1944, the county also offered to furnish money and resources for the Okanogan congregation to build their own church building.⁷³ Although the offer meant giving up their beloved bowling alley building and going without a formal worship space for a time, it was also an opportunity full of potential and possibility. Moreover, acceptance of the offer would be an act of good faith with Okanogan County. "This sounded good to the church," Knutson wrote. "So we sold."⁷⁴ Trustees of the Full Gospel Christian Assembly—L. B. Allard, Harry Rasmussen, and Alexander Pfitzer—formally signed deed paperwork on July 21, 1947, transferring ownership of the former bowling alley to Okanogan County. In return, the county paid ninety-five hundred dollars, and although not documented in the deed paperwork, Knutson noted that the county also provided "all the sand and gravel we would need for concrete" for the upcoming building project.⁷⁵

In early July 1947, with the sale of the former bowling alley in process, the Full Gospel Christian Assembly began drafting plans for the construction of their new church building as well as looking for available property on which to build it.⁷⁶ At first, the congregation considered building on the corner of Fourth Avenue and Conconully Street but experienced significant resistance from local property owners with property adjacent to the lot. On July 21, the same day church trustees signed deed paperwork with the county, there was a two-and-a-half-hour public hearing concerning the proposal that drew a "record crowd"—so many attendees that the hearing had to be moved from the city hall to the county courthouse.⁷⁷ Ultimately, the proposal was declined, and the church proposed another location, three available lots at the corner of Fourth and Tyee Street. Another public

---

72. Knutson, *His Loving Care*, 89; *Okanogan Independent*, "Heavy Building Program Seen."

73. Knutson, *His Loving Care*, 89.

74. Knutson, *His Loving Care*, 89.

75. Warranty deed, vol. 112, pp. 399–400, July 21, 1947, indicating purchase and transfer of property from the trustees of the Full Gospel Christian Assembly to Okanogan County, Okanogan County Auditor's Office, courtesy of Barry I. George of the Okanogan County Historical Society; warranty deed, vol. 112, pp. 397–400, Feb. 12, 1944, indicating purchase and transfer of property from W. F. Schmidt to trustees of the Full Gospel Christian Assembly; Knutson, *His Loving Care*, 89.

76. *Okanogan Independent*, "Heavy Building Program Seen."

77. *Okanogan Independent*, "Public Hearing on Proposed Church."

hearing was held on August 6, this time with no objections expressed.[78] The Okanogan city council approved the proposal, the church was deeded the property on August 14, and the building project started shortly thereafter, with Oscar Knutson supervising the work.[79] Although the Okanogan congregation hoped to complete enough of the building project to hold services in the new structure by October 1947, construction seems to have taken a few months longer than expected.[80] Marginal notes in a Bible owned by Knutson indicate that the first church meeting in the (unfinished) new building was held on November 5, 1947.[81] The primary scriptural text for the occasion was from the book of the prophet Ezra:

> And when the builders laid the foundation of the temple of the LORD, they set the priests in their apparel with trumpets, and the Levites the sons of Asaph with cymbals, to praise the LORD, after the ordinance of David king of Israel. And they sang together by course in praising and giving thanks unto the LORD; because he is good, for his mercy endureth for ever toward Israel. And all the people shouted a great shout, when they praised the LORD, because the foundation of the house of the LORD had been laid.[82]

Death in the family again interrupted Oscar Knutson's regular rhythms in Okanogan, this time with the death of his father, Andrew O. Knutson, on December 8, 1947.[83] Seventy-five years old, Andrew Knutson had worked as a carpenter in Seattle for most of the last two and a half decades and along with his wife, Elvina, remained active in local Pentecostal circles since the early 1920s.[84] Although Oscar did not reflect extensively on

---

78. *Okanogan Independent*, "Church Application Gets Another Hearing"; *Okanogan Independent*, "Gospel Assembly to Build at 4th-Tyee."

79. Warranty deed, vol. 114, p. 203, Aug. 14, 1947, indicating purchase and transfer of property from Charles C. and Evalyn Rumbolz to the trustees of the Full Gospel Christian Assembly, Okanogan County Auditor's Office, courtesy of Barry I. George of the Okanogan County Historical Society; *Okanogan Independent*, "$14,000 Church Building Begun."

80. *Okanogan Independent*, "$14,000 Church Building Begun."

81. In the local newspaper, the weekly advertisement noting church services for the Full Gospel Christian Assembly indicates that in mid December, the Okanogan congregation was utilizing the basement of the new church building for services. *Okanogan Independent*, "Full Gospel Christian Assembly" (Dec. 18, 1947).

82. Ezra 3:10–11, KJV. Scriptural text directly taken from Bible owned by Oscar Knutson. Courtesy of Bernice M. Fergus.

83. Andrew O. Knutson, Certificate of Death, 1947, Washington State Digital Archives.

84. Oscar and Marie Knutson, oral history interview with Wayne Warner, Sept. 5,

his father's death in writing—in later reflections, he only briefly mentioned visiting Seattle for his father's funeral—he was obviously inspired by his father's experiences and relationship with the Lord.[85] While publishing gospel tracts in Seattle in the early 1940s, Oscar published a story from his father's life which he found to be a particularly significant testimony "that God ever watches over His own."[86] The same story was later added as the last anecdote of *His Loving Care*, Oscar's book of reflections on life and ministry.[87]

Titled "How God Used a Crow" in both the gospel tract and *His Loving Care*, the story takes place around 1900, when Oscar's father was the captain of a fishing boat on the North Sea.[88] One night, while the fishing boat was anchored far from shore and Andrew Knutson and his crew slept, a storm was brewing. Before it hit, however, Andrew awoke to a cacophony of incessant cawing and rapping at his window—a crow. "Now a crow is a land bird and has never been known to ever go as far out to sea as at this time," Oscar narrated.[89] Nevertheless, the crow was there and "perched itself on the window sill and began to fl[a]p its wings and make all the noise he know how to make."[90] Andrew's attempts to shoo the bird away failed, and as he left his cabin to go around to the other side of the window, he saw the storm approaching in the distance. Knowing the storm could be a fatal event, Andrew woke his crew and they swiftly sailed back to harbor, safe and sound.[91] While stubbornly persistent in awakening Andrew from his slumber, the crow flew away peacefully as soon as Andrew roused the crew and began sailing back to harbor. It was a miracle, according to Oscar. God had sent the crow to save his father. "He who could send a raven to feed Elijah, could also send a crow out to sea, and give him a courage that he does not naturally possess," Oscar wrote.[92]

1983, audio recording, Flower Pentecostal Heritage Center.

85. Knutson, *His Loving Care*, 91.

86. Gospel Tracts, "Full Gospel Press," Oscar M. Knutson archival collection, box 2, folder 4.

87. Knutson, *His Loving Care*, 103–5.

88. Knutson, *His Loving Care*, 103–4.

89. Knutson, *His Loving Care*, 104.

90. Knutson, *His Loving Care*, 104.

91. Knutson, *His Loving Care*, 104.

92. Knutson, *His Loving Care*, 104–5.

Construction continued on the Full Gospel Christian Assembly's new church building, and in early March 1948, the congregation was able to begin meeting for services on the main floor. Just a few months later, the building was complete. On Monday, July 19, 1948, nearly a year after the building project began, the Full Gospel Christian Assembly held a special dedication service for its new church building.[93] It was a joyous occasion. In addition to local attendees, Oscar Knutson invited many out of town guests, including Rev. Lee Henson, the Knutson's African American preacher friend from Seattle; the Moseid brothers, of Tacoma and Seattle, respectively; and Rev. Andrew S. Teuber of Wenatchee, Washington, a long-time friend and ministry colleague of Oscar's, along with his father, Rev. A. C. Teuber, and brother-in-law, Rev. Harold Hansen, both of Omak, Washington.[94] Marie Knutson's mother, Cora May Baldwin, also attended the dedication service. Perhaps most notably, according to a local newspaper article, Marie "served dinner and breakfast to all the out of town guests, who spent the night in Okanogan."[95]

In the final months of establishing the new church building on Fourth Avenue and Tyee Street in Okanogan, Oscar Knutson also began assisting Rev. Andrew S. Teuber's Assembly of God church in Wenatchee with its own church construction project. Initially, Knutson just offered advice on the plans for the new Wenatchee church building, but he eventually agreed to supervise construction itself.[96] The morning after the Okanogan congregation's dedication service of their new church building, Knutson left for Wenatchee to begin the new construction job.[97] It was a big commitment, admittedly, as Wenatchee was about ninety miles south of Okanogan. For the next few months, Knutson had to "leave home early every Monday morning," drive to Wenatchee and spend the week supervising the building project, then return home on Saturday to prepare for church services in Okanogan on Sunday.[98] Although it was a big commitment, Reverend Teuber was an old friend.[99] Furthermore, Knutson was always seeking to do the Lord's work, wherever he would call him.

93. *Okanogan Independent*, "Dedicate New Gospel Edifice, Monday, July 19," 1.
94. *Okanogan Independent*, "Full Gospel Christian Assembly Church Dedication," 14.
95. *Okanogan Independent*, "Full Gospel Christian Assembly Church Dedication," 14.
96. Knutson, *His Loving Care*, 90.
97. *Okanogan Independent*, "Full Gospel Christian Assembly Church Dedication," 14.
98. Knutson, *His Loving Care*, 90.
99. Knutson, *His Loving Care*, 90.

He Will Lead Me

Born in Tacoma, Washington, in July 1911, Andrew Simon Teuber was the youngest son of German immigrant and Congregational minister Rev. Adolph C. Teuber and his wife, Annie Irene (née Muhm).[100] Andrew's mother had received the baptism of the Holy Spirit in 1906, and his father had received the baptism of the Holy Spirit in 1907.[101] Undoubtedly, the Teubers met and befriended the Knutsons through mutual participation in local Pentecostal circles. Andrew Teuber lived with his parents in Tacoma until 1932, when he left to pursue ministry work. In December 1932, Teuber planted the Full Gospel Church in Cashmere, Washington, and began serving as its pastor.[102] In January 1934, he married Freda Schulz of Sacramento, California, and together they had three children.[103] Andrew Teuber received formal ordination by the Assemblies of God in June 1935.[104] The same year, he became the pastor of the Assembly of God church in Omak, Washington, a pastorate which he held for nearly a decade.[105] Although committed to the Omak congregation, Reverend Teuber held Pentecostal meetings in nearby towns, and in 1936 planted an Assembly of God church in Tonasket, Washington.[106] When Oscar Knutson was on his way to hold tent meetings in Okanogan in 1943, he first visited Reverend Teuber, who encouraged him to go to Okanogan.[107] Knutson continued collaboration with Reverend Teuber after planting the Full Gospel Christian Assembly in Okanogan. In early 1945, Reverend Teuber resigned his pastorate in Omak and accepted a call to pastor the Wenatchee Assembly of God church.[108]

---

100. Andrew Simon Teuber, World War II Draft Registration Card, 1940, Ancestry.com; Teuber, *Tongues of Fire*, 33, 35.

101. Teuber, *Tongues of Fire*, 33, 35.

102. "Ice and Snow No Barrier," 12.

103. Andrew Teuber and Freda Schulz, State of Washington, Certificate of Marriage, 1934, Ancestry.com; Andrew Teuber, "Fifteenth Census of the United States, 1940," Ancestry.com.

104. Andrew S. Teuber, ordination application, in "Deceased Ministers—Teuber, Andrew S.," archival record file, Flower Pentecostal Heritage Center; Assemblies of God General Council Ministers Directory, 1935, Consortium of Pentecostal Archives.

105. Andrew S. Teuber, ordination application, in "Deceased Ministers—Teuber, Andrew S.," archival record file, Flower Pentecostal Heritage Center; Assemblies of God General Council Ministers Directory, 1935, Consortium of Pentecostal Archives; Tannenberg, *Let Light Shine Out*, 107; *Omak Chronicle*, "Large Attendance at Full Gospel Daily Bible School"; Knutson, "3-Day Fellowship Bible Conference," 12.

106. Tannenberg, *Let Light Shine Out*, 96.

107. Knutson, *His Loving Care*, 85.

108. Knutson, *His Loving Care*, 89–90; Gerla, "To Omak Wash.," 28. Rev. R. J. Gerla

"Praise the Lord"

Although supervising work on the Wenatchee church building made for a rather busy season for him, Oscar Knutson had good support. Rev. Harold Hansen of Omak—Rev. Andrew Teuber's brother-in-law—was particularly helpful, as he agreed to lead services in Okanogan on weekdays so that Knutson did not have to drive back and forth between Okanogan and Wenatchee during the week.[109] A fellow Norwegian who immigrated to the United States and became a lifelong Pentecostal minister, Harold Emil Hansen was born in December 1881 in Tønsberg, Norway. Hansen's family immigrated to America in 1883 and settled in Alameda County, California.[110] As a young man, Harold became a machinist and eventually moved to Honolulu, Hawaii, where he married Margaret Singe Tollefsen in early December 1906.[111] The couple soon became involved in the Pentecostal movement, and in 1912, Harold was superintendent of the Apostolic Faith Rescue Mission in Honolulu, although still working as a machinist.[112] In 1914, Harold and Margaret were ordained as missionaries of the Assemblies of God and in September went overseas to do missionary work in China and Japan.[113] Primarily based in Beijing, China—then known as Peking, China—the Hansens oversaw and ran the Assemblies of God missionary headquarters in the city for multiple years.[114] In April 1918, Mar-

---

succeeded Rev. Andrew Teuber as pastor of the Omak church, receiving pastoral leadership in February 1945. Significantly, at the Wenatchee Assembly of God Church, Reverend Teuber succeeded Rev. Reuben J. Carlson, son of Rev. Carl G. Carlson. Rev. Reuben Carlson left Wenatchee to pastor in Spokane. In 1953, he became the assistant district superintendent for the Northwest District of the Assemblies of God. In 1958, he became district superintendent and served in this capacity until 1971, after which he returned to pastor again in Wenatchee. Tannenberg, *Let Light Shine Out*, 182–85; Knutson, *His Loving Care*, 16.

109. Knutson, *His Loving Care*, 90.

110. "Twelfth Census of the United States, Schedule No. 1—Population," 1900, Ancestry.com. Admittedly, this census record says "Harl" or perhaps "Carl," rather than "Harold," but all of the other details—family members, birth date, immigration date, etc.—point to this being Harold Hansen.

111. Harold E. Hansen, "Thirteenth Census of the United States, 1910—Population," Ancestry.com; Harold Emil Hansen and Margaret Signe Tollefsen, Certificate of Marriage, 1906, Honolulu, Oahu, Ancestry.com.

112. R. L. Polk & Co., *Honolulu City Directory, 1912*.

113. Harold E. Hansen, ordination record card, in "Deceased Ministers—Hansen, H. E. (Harold E.)," archival record file, Flower Pentecostal Heritage Center; Hansen, "Peking, North China," 12, 16.

114. "Sister Florence Bush," 3.

garet returned the United States due to ill health, and Harold joined her in February 1919.[115]

Harold and Margaret Hansen returned to China in 1920 to continue their missionary work. About a year later though, on Easter Sunday in 1921, Margaret succumbed to illness.[116] After her death, Harold Hansen continued his Pentecostal missionary work in Beijing, and in June 1922, he married Letta Teuber, a fellow Assemblies of God missionary to China.[117] Born in Hebron, North Dakota, in April 1898, Letta was the older sister of Andrew Teuber.[118] As an ordained missionary of the Assemblies of God, Letta accompanied Harold and Margaret Hansen when they returned to China in March 1920 and took charge of regular Sunday school meetings in Beijing.[119] After their marriage in mid 1922, Letta and Harold continued their missionary work in China for the next few decades, and together they adopted a Chinese girl and had four biological children.[120]

In the 1930s, as war brewed between China and Japan, the United States ambassador called for Americans to leave China and offered opportunity for evacuation.[121] Believing that God had called them to China, however, the Hansens remained in Beijing through the Second Sino-Japanese War and into World War II. In 1941, the Hansens were taken as prisoners of war by Japanese forces, although they were permitted to continue doing ministry within Beijing city limits.[122] Eighteen months later, however, in 1942, all prisoners of war—including the Hansen family—were placed in a Japanese internment camp. It was not until October 1943 that a prisoner

---

115. Hansen, "Returning to Rest," 3.

116. Harold E. Hansen, US Passport Application, 1920, Ancestry.com; "Missionary Gleanings," 12; "Testing Days," 16; Margaret Signe Hansen, Report of Death of an American Citizen, American Consular Service, 1921, Ancestry.com.

117. Hansen, "Work in Peking, China," 3.

118. Letta T. Hansen, Certificate of Death, 1965, Washington State Digital Archives; Letta Teuber, "Fourteenth Census of the United States, 1920—Population," Ancestry.com.

119. "Missionary Gleanings," 12; Hansen, "Bro. and Sister Hansen Arrive in Peking, North China," 13.

120. Gladys Pearson, "China Revisited," *Pentecostal Evangel* (Mar. 21, 1982), in Wilson, *Early Pentecostal and Assemblies of God Missionaries*, n.p.

121. Gladys Pearson, "China Revisited," *Pentecostal Evangel* (Mar. 21, 1982), in Wilson, *Early Pentecostal and Assemblies of God Missionaries*, n.p.

122. Gladys Pearson, "China Revisited," *Pentecostal Evangel* (Mar. 21, 1982), in Wilson, *Early Pentecostal and Assemblies of God Missionaries*, n.p.

of war exchange permitted the Hansens to return to America.[123] Settling in Omak, Washington, where Letta's brother Andrew was pastoring, the Hansens remained in Okanogan County for the duration of the 1940s. As retired missionaries, they assisted with various local ministry needs, including covering for Oscar Knutson in Okanogan in 1948 while he was supervising the church building project in Wenatchee.[124]

The Wenatchee church building project concluded in late fall 1948, which permitted Oscar Knutson to again focus primarily on ministry in Okanogan. More than just regular preaching or publishing, however, doctrinal controversy within the broader Pentecostal world forced Knutson to consider carefully some rather fundamental theological issues—mostly pertaining to ecclesiology—and navigate it with his local congregation accordingly. In early 1948, the spiritual and theological movement that became known as the "New Order of the Latter Rain" was born in Saskatchewan, Canada, and sent shock waves through post-World War II North American Pentecostalism and beyond.[125] Described by the movement's leaders not as a mere spiritual renewal but as a reestablishment of the church itself, the movement drew on the "latter rain" parlance of the prophet Joel and sought to reawaken people from the perceived stupor of a dry and institutionalized Pentecostalism. Calling all (Pentecostal) Christians to abandon their denominational affiliations and ecclesial organizations, the Latter Rain Movement understood itself to be the spiritual fulfillment of the third great Israelite feast—the Feast of Tabernacles—seeing Passover fulfilled in Jesus' Passion and Pentecost fulfilled in the great outpouring of the Holy Spirit as described in Acts 2.[126] In addition to its provocative ecclesiological claims and Scripture hermeneutics, the Latter Rain Movement caused controversy due to its emphasis on the presence and authority of modern-day apostles and prophets, who allegedly had the power to bestow the Holy Spirit at

---

123. Gladys Pearson, "China Revisited," *Pentecostal Evangel* (Mar. 21, 1982), in Wilson, *Early Pentecostal and Assemblies of God Missionaries*, n.p.

124. Harold E. Hansen, World War II Draft Registration Card, 1942/1944, Ancestry.com; 1950 US Federal Census, Ancestry.com; Knutson, *His Loving Care*, 90.

125. Richard M. Riss, "Latter Rain Movement," in Burgess and van der Maas, *New International Dictionary*, 830.

126. Richard M. Riss, "Latter Rain Movement," in Burgess and van der Maas, *New International Dictionary*, 831; McClymond, "Latter Rain," in Wilkinson, *Brill's Encyclopedia of Global Pentecostalism*, 380.

will—even on those who had already experienced the baptism of the Holy Spirit—simply by laying their hands on people.[127]

By fall 1948, news of the Latter Rain Movement had reached far beyond Canada and raised serious questions pertaining to ecclesiology, authority, and the nature of revelation and religious experience, among other issues.[128] In response to the Latter Rain Movement, Oscar Knutson started a special Bible study with his Okanogan congregation to ensure that his flock was grounded in the holy Scriptures and resistant to doctrinal falsehood.[129] When asked about it in a 1983 oral history interview, Knutson stated confidently that when the Latter Rain Movement made its way to Washington State, it infiltrated some other churches—particularly in Seattle—but not his Okanogan congregation. "They never got into our church," Knutson asserted.[130]

In addition to facilitating a special Bible study with his Okanogan congregation, Oscar Knutson appears to have responded to the Latter Rain Movement's ecclesiological claims with a theological pamphlet entitled *The Glorious Church*. Nearly fifty pages, the pamphlet outlined Knutson's understanding of the nature and mission of the church, membership and leadership in the church, and related theological matters. Similar to his previous publication, *The Christian and War*, Knutson's *The Glorious Church* was concise yet thorough. It was also steeped in scriptural references and reflections, while located within a definitively Pentecostal theological framework.

Oscar Knutson opened his ecclesiological reflections in *The Glorious Church* with the assertion that "the aim and purpose of our Lord Jesus Christ is to present to himself a glorious church."[131] Referencing the apostle Paul's Epistle to the Ephesians, Knutson wrote that the whole purpose of Jesus' incarnation, death, and resurrection was, and is, to purchase and redeem for himself a people, the church.[132] Not simply individualistic in fo-

---

127. Michael McClymond, "Latter Rain," in Wilkinson, *Brill's Encyclopedia of Global Pentecostalism*, 380–81.

128. Martin W. Mittelstadt, "Latter Rain Movement," in Stewart, *Handbook of Pentecostal Christianity*, 138.

129. Oscar and Marie Knutson, oral history interview with Wayne Warner, Sept. 5, 1983, audio recording, Flower Pentecostal Heritage Center.

130. Oscar and Marie Knutson, oral history interview with Wayne Warner, Sept. 5, 1983, audio recording, Flower Pentecostal Heritage Center.

131. Knutson, *Glorious Church*, 3.

132. See Eph 5:27.

cus, Jesus' redemptive mission was, and is, corporate in nature. Admittedly, Knutson noted, "there are many man made churches, but there is only one Church, the Blood bought Church of the first born, written in Heaven."[133] From Knutson's perspective, ecclesial organizations, denominational structures, and theological movements—including the Latter Rain Movement, and even Pentecostalism more broadly—did not themselves constitute the church. Rather, the true church was composed of "God's Blood bought people regardless of what denomination, group, or fellowship . . . they belong to, or if they belong to none."[134]

Oscar Knutson's perspective that members of the church may be found in a variety of Christian denominations or ecclesial organizations— or even in none!—raises some important questions about church membership. What is the church? And how does one become a member of it? The apostle Paul wrote that the church is the "body" of Jesus and taught that "we were all baptized by one Spirit into one body."[135] Traditionally, this verse has been understood to refer to water baptism and thus sees water baptism as marking sacramental entrance into the church. From a radical Pentecostal perspective, this verse has been understood to refer to the baptism of the Holy Spirit, thus implying that only those who have received the baptism of the Holy Spirit are true members of the church.[136] Acknowledging both interpretations, Knutson took a different approach, holding that the baptism which Paul was referring to was none other than Jesus' "death on Calvary."[137] Referring to his crucifixion, Jesus told his disciples in the Gospel According to Luke: "I have a baptism to be baptized with."[138] Connecting this statement with the apostle Paul's teaching on baptism in his Epistle to the Romans, Knutson wrote that Christians are people who have been united to the body of Christ by virtue of their faith in Jesus, and specifically his atonement.[139]

Oscar Knutson's emphasis on the atonement—that is, the reconciliation of the whole created order to God, obtained and effected by the blood of Jesus, the death of Jesus, the cross, Calvary, etc.—also provided

---

133. Knutson, *Glorious Church*, 3.
134. Knutson, *Glorious Church*, 4.
135. 1 Cor 12:13, HCSB.
136. Knutson, *Glorious Church*, 16.
137. Knutson, *Glorious Church*, 16.
138. Luke 12:50, HCSB.
139. See Rom 6:3–11.

theological grounding for Knutson's convictions concerning the unity of the church, which in turn, was connected to his own trinitarian theology. For Knutson, the unity of the church was none other than a participation in the unity found in the relationship between the Father and the Son.[140] In the garden of Gethsemane, just before his betrayal, suffering, and death, Jesus himself prayed that his people—the church—would be one as he and the Father were one. According to Knutson, Jesus then purchased that unity through his atoning work on the cross.[141] Since Jesus purchased the church's unity, unity was not (and is not) based upon human efforts or organizing activities. Instead, the unity of the church was, and is, an objective reality that has been secured in Christ but must be apprehended through faith and obedience to him.[142] Once a person had surrendered their will to Jesus, Knutson held that he or she would receive the Holy Spirit. The Holy Spirit would then mystically unite the new person of faith to the body of Jesus and facilitate their participation in the fellowship between the Father and the Son, together with others who had likewise committed themselves to Christ.[143]

Oscar Knutson's understanding of the unity of the church as sharing in the fellowship of the Holy Trinity had ramifications for his convictions regarding the existence of various denominations, fellowships, and ecclesial organizations. If the church was constituted exclusively by fellowship with the triune God, then it was in its essence a divine organism, not a human organization.[144] Human organizations then, including various denominations or theological movements, could not themselves claim exclusive status as the true church.[145] According to Knutson, the true church was, and is, constituted by fellowship with the Father, the Son, and the Holy Spirit, not the strivings or efforts of finite and sinful humans. "We concede that any church which has not received, or which is not guided by the Holy Spirit must . . . have some form, or organization, as a substitute for the true guide that the Lord promised. I much prefer the genuine to any substitute man can invent."[146]

---

140. Knutson, *Glorious Church*, 6–7.
141. Knutson, *Glorious Church*, 8.
142. Knutson, *Glorious Church*, 8.
143. Knutson, *Glorious Church*, 21.
144. Knutson, *Glorious Church*, 8–9, 16.
145. Knutson, *Glorious Church*, 8–9, 16.
146. Knutson, *Glorious Church*, 22.

From Oscar Knutson's perspective, the disunity and differences among various ecclesial organizations and fellowships reflected merely human, and even sinful, origins.[147] After all, humans can be confused and divided, but not God. "The Holy Spirit teaches us the truth of God," Knutson wrote.[148] "He does not teach one doctrine to one denomination, and a different doctrine to another. He has only one doctrine to teach, and that is the doctrine of God, and it is always the same no matter to whom it is taught."[149] So what of visible divisions among Christians? Knutson's words were sharp but clear:

> When our doctrines differ it is a sure sign that someone is out of line with the Holy Spirit. We must then have been taught by something else, and not by the Spirit. The truth is that so many follow their own natural and carnal wisdom, and try to interpret the Word of God by their natural wisdom, and the result is confusion.[150]

Although critical of ecclesial organizations and denominational structures, Oscar Knutson acknowledged that the church had to take physical, visible form in some capacity. How else could the church share the gospel and witness to the world? Rather than emphasizing organizational strategies and structures, however, Knutson asserted that the church needs to keep her focus on God, trust him to do the things that are only his to do, and know her own role in relation to God and his redemptive mission. For example, regarding church membership, Knutson wrote that it is not the church's job to keep a list of names of people who belong to Christ, but God's. After all, "the Lord knoweth them that are His," and their names "are written in Heaven."[151] Noting that in the Acts of the Apostles, "the Lord added to the Church daily those who were being saved," Knutson argued that church membership was exclusively God's responsibility.[152] "There are many duties that are assigned to us; things that the Lord has told us plainly that we should do," Knutson acknowledged.[153] "But here[,] He does not say that we should do the adding: we make too many mistakes. Let us mind our

---

147. Knutson, *Glorious Church*, 24.
148. Knutson, *Glorious Church*, 24.
149. Knutson, *Glorious Church*, 24.
150. Knutson, *Glorious Church*, 24–25.
151. Knutson, *Glorious Church*, 20; see 2 Tim 2:19; Heb 12:23.
152. Knutson, *Glorious Church*, 21; see Acts 2:47.
153. Knutson, *Glorious Church*, 21.

own business, and do that which has been committed to us to do, and let the Lord do His. Surely He will not neglect His part, and no mistakes will be made."[154]

The subject of church government composed a significant portion of *The Glorious Church*. Such was an important issue, both because of the controversial claims of the Latter Rain Movement, but also because of the diversity of perspectives within the broader Pentecostal world. Some Pentecostal denominations, for example, were hierarchical in their ecclesiastical polity. Others were presbyterian in polity. Still others were congregational, and others were a mixture of multiple polities.[155] As far as Oscar Knutson was concerned, chief governance of the church rested with the triune God.[156] Scripturally however, for the health and mission of the church, the Lord established certain offices in the church and called and equipped certain people to fill those offices.[157] For Knutson, the important takeaway here was that such leaders were not elected and appointed by (finite and sinful) humans.[158] Instead, they derived their authority from God and executed their office faithfully. Titles, Knutson also noted, are often unimportant and unhelpful.[159] Faithfully fulfilling the office entrusted by God is what really mattered.

In his discussion of church offices, Oscar Knutson reflected on apostles, prophets, teachers, and elders.[160] Although he affirmed that Jesus' twelve apostles had a unique role that God had not given to anyone after them, Knutson nevertheless held that "if the Church was in Scriptural order we would have apostles today also."[161] Various ecclesial organizations recognized this too, Knutson observed.[162] How else would one make sense of the prevalence of bishops, overseers, or superintendents among various denominations? Unlike those who had been elected to their office by people, however, Knutson wrote that a true apostle was one "sent forth by the

---

154. Knutson, *Glorious Church*, 21.

155. Dwight J. Wilson, "Ecclesiastical Polity," in Burgess and van der Maas, *New International Dictionary*, 596.

156. Knutson, *Glorious Church*, 29.

157. Knutson, *Glorious Church*, 30.

158. Knutson, *Glorious Church*, 32.

159. Knutson, *Glorious Church*, 34.

160. See 1 Cor 12:28 and Eph 4:11, 12.

161. Knutson, *Glorious Church*, 31.

162. Knutson, *Glorious Church*, 31, 32.

Lord."[163] An apostle was "God's messenger to the Church" and the church's highest human authority.[164]

For Knutson, the office of prophet followed that of apostle. "The prophet is simply the mouthpiece of the Lord to the Church," Knutson wrote.[165] The prophet "has insight into spiritual things and speaks them forth to others."[166] Knutson acknowledged that in some cases, so-called prophets and prophecies could be a bit "fanatic."[167] However, "it takes God, and God alone, to produce the prophet," and "if it is of God it will be well balanced."[168] Although he held this prophetic office in high regard, Knutson noted that it was rare to find a true prophet of God.[169]

If prophets were rare, then teachers, which Oscar Knutson divided into three categories—evangelists, pastors, and teachers—were the most prevalent office in the church, if only because, in Knutson's estimation, it was so easy to become a teacher in the church without a genuine call from God.[170] Admittedly, Knutson did not reflect extensively on the office of teacher, but observed that in terms of ministry, it was highly contextual. Knutson also wrote that it was largely connected to the office of elder, although elders might also be apostles or prophets.[171] Sometimes referred to as an overseer (Greek: *episokopos*), the chief role of an elder (Greek: *presbuteros*) was "to feed the flock of God, and take oversight thereof."[172] Drawing on the scriptural language of a plurality of elders, Knutson affirmed that in most cases, it was best to have multiple elders in leadership over a local church.[173]

In his reflections on church offices, Oscar Knutson emphasized that God's people would discern the divinely given authority of apostles and other leaders in the church, not through human elections or organizational processes, but through attunement and obedience to the Holy Spirit

---

163. Knutson, *Glorious Church*, 31, 32.
164. Knutson, *Glorious Church*, 31.
165. Knutson, *Glorious Church*, 31.
166. Knutson, *Glorious Church*, 31.
167. Knutson, *Glorious Church*, 33.
168. Knutson, *Glorious Church*, 33.
169. Knutson, *Glorious Church*, 33.
170. Knutson, *Glorious Church*, 31, 33.
171. Knutson, *Glorious Church*, 34–35.
172. Knutson, *Glorious Church*, 35.
173. Knutson, *Glorious Church*, 35–36.

speaking through them.[174] In this way, Knutson revealed some of his soteriological convictions, particularly his understanding of human free will. According to Knutson:

> Compliance comes only through the recognizance of the calling of God, and is entirely based on our free will. In everything that pertains to the spiritual things we are free moral agents; that is, we always have our free choice. We can choose to serve God, or choose not to. We can choose to work with, or in fellowship with those whom God has appointed to a special duty, or we can refuse to do so.[175]

Knutson's robust conviction concerning free will and human responsibility not only marked his understanding of the relationship between leaders in the church and the congregations committed to their charge, but it also formed the theological basis for his understanding of how God's people would become the "glorious Church," cleansed of error and division, which Jesus would receive unto himself at his own glorious appearing.[176] In short, God's people must "lay aside" their works, and "yield completely to Him."[177]

---

174. Knutson, *Glorious Church*, 32.
175. Knutson, *Glorious Church*, 32.
176. Knutson, *Glorious Church*, 3, 48.
177. Knutson, *Glorious Church*, 17, 28.

7

"Pilot Me Home"

No storms I fear, the harbor is near,
Pilot me, pilot me home.
The harbor light I can see thru the night
Across the raging foam.
God's loving care, in Jesus I share,
Pilot me, pilot me home.
—O. M. Knutson, "Pilot Me Home"

THE LATE 1940S MARKED the beginning of a major ministry transition for Oscar Knutson and his family, as Knutson prepared to conclude his pastoral ministry in Okanogan, Washington, and pursue gospel publishing full time. Before that transition formally occurred, however, the Knutson family celebrated the wedding of their daughter, Fern, to Alvin John Olson of Buffalo Springs, North Dakota, on October 16, 1948.[1] Officiated by Rev. C. Albert Moseid, the wedding took place at the Full Gospel Christian Assembly in Okanogan.[2] At Fern's request, Oscar wrote a song for the occasion, and while his son, Lloyd, sang it at the wedding ceremony, Oscar provided

---

1. *Okanogan Independent*, "Miss Fern Knutson, Mr. Alvin Olson," 5.
2. *Okanogan Independent*, "Miss Fern Knutson, Mr. Alvin Olson," 5.

accompaniment on the organ.³ Entitled "My Beloved Is Mine," the song was inspired by the First Epistle of John and the Song of Solomon.⁴ Oscar wrote the song just two weeks before the wedding while at the home of Rev. Andrew Teuber—presumably during his time supervising the church building project in Wenatchee, Washington—and composed music for it the evening before the wedding.⁵ According to newspaper accounts, the wedding was a lovely and joyous event with many out of town guests. Afterward, Fern and her husband Alvin made their home near Bowman, North Dakota, a town which the Knutson family had previously visited on multiple occasions while holding Pentecostal revival meetings. As with plenty of other communities between the Pacific Northwest and the Midwest, Bowman had become an important connection for the Knutsons since their initial visit in spring 1934.⁶

Even in late 1948, it was becoming evident to Oscar Knutson that many years of preaching and singing for various evangelistic meetings and church services—especially "without the benefit of any public address system"—had begun to wear down his voice.⁷ "At times it would just fade away to a whisper," Knutson wrote in his personal reflections.⁸ Knutson thus determined that it was nearly time to resign his pastorate and begin pursuing publishing ministry full time. More than just gospel tracts and theological pamphlets, however, Knutson also planned to publish Pentecostal songbooks, following in the footsteps of his old friend and mentor, Rev. A. D. Guth. Guth, tragically, had died in mid February 1948, but seems to have (either formally or informally) left Knutson the rights to his songbook, *Selected Gospel Songs*.

In January 1949, the Knutsons took a trip eastward with the intention of acquiring musical copyright permissions in order to publish Pentecostal

---

3. *Okanogan Independent*, "Miss Fern Knutson, Mr. Alvin Olson," 5; unidentified newspaper clipping, "Okanogan Is Setting for Fall Nuptials," ca. Oct. 1948, Oscar M. Knutson archival collection, in scrapbook, unprocessed box; Knutson, *My Beloved Is Mine*, inside cover.

4. Knutson, *My Beloved Is Mine*, inside cover.

5. Knutson, *My Beloved Is Mine*, inside cover.

6. *Okanogan Independent*, "Miss Fern Knutson, Mr. Alvin Olson," 5. Although there does not appear to be any documentary evidence for how Fern Knutson and Alvin Olson met, it is possible that they met during one of the Knutson family's evangelistic visits to Bowman, North Dakota, and the surrounding area.

7. Knutson, *His Loving Care*, 93.

8. Knutson, *His Loving Care*, 93.

songbooks.⁹ Initial stops did not yield much success, but on January 15, the Knutsons had an encouraging meeting with R. E. Winsett of Dayton, Tennessee.¹⁰ Winsett, who was celebrating his eightieth birthday the very day that the Knutsons visited, was a popular writer and publisher of gospel songs during the Pentecostal movement's early years.¹¹ Winsett heartily granted permission for Oscar to publish any of his music free of charge and then suggested that the Knutsons travel to Eureka Springs, Arkansas, to meet with another popular Pentecostal songwriter, Thoro Harris, and inquire about permissions for publishing his songs. According to Winsett, Harris was interested in selling his many song copyrights but had been waiting for the right opportunity.¹²

Born in Washington, DC, in March 1874, Thoro Dennis Harris was the son of physician Joseph Dennis Harris and his wife Elizabeth (née Worthington).¹³ Thoro Harris was a mixed-race person, as his father was African American and his mother was white.¹⁴ In his early life, Thoro officially identified himself as mixed-race or black, but because he could pass as white, Thoro mostly identified himself as white, probably to avoid racial discrimination.¹⁵ Unfortunately, Thoro's father—who had previously served as a combat doctor for the Union during the Civil War—was largely absent from Thoro's life due to a mental breakdown in 1876 that left him in a psychiatric hospital until his death in 1884.¹⁶ As such, Thoro's mother was essentially a single parent to Thoro and his older sister Worthy.

---

9. Oscar and Marie Knutson, oral history interview with Wayne Warner, Sept. 5, 1983, audio recording, Flower Pentecostal Heritage Center; Knutson, *His Loving Care*, 94.

10. Knutson, *His Loving Care*, 94.

11. Knutson, *His Loving Care*, 94; Wayne E. Warner, "Winsett, Roger Emmet," in Burgess and van der Maas, *New International Dictionary*, 1200.

12. Knutson, *His Loving Care*, 94.

13. E. Alan Long to Glenn Gohr, July 12, 2006, in "Clip file, Personal papers—Thoro Harris," archival record file, Flower Pentecostal Heritage Center; Young, "'Sing On, Pray On.'"

14. Young, "'Sing On, Pray On.'"

15. Young, "'Sing On, Pray On';" 1880 US Federal Census, Ancestry.com; *Evening Star*, "Marriage Licenses," 10; Thomas Harris, "Thirteenth Census of the United States, 1910—Population," Ancestry.com; Thoro Harris, "Fourteenth Census of the United States, 1920—Population," Ancestry.com.

16. Young, "'Sing On, Pray On';" Salmon and *Dictionary of Virginia Biography*, "J. D. Harris (ca. 1833–1884)."

Thoro Harris seems to have been something of a child prodigy with regard to music. He composed his first melody at age four and created his own musical notation system by age eleven.[17] In the 1890s, Harris formally studied music at Howard University, a historically black university in Washington, DC, and then at Battle Creek College in Battle Creek, Michigan.[18] In 1898, Harris married Agnes Hart of Charlestown, West Virginia, and together the couple had three children.[19] In 1902, Thoro compiled a hymnal entitled *Echoes of Paradise* and, after its publication in 1903, accepted an invitation from gospel songwriter Peter Bilhorn to move to Chicago, Illinois, and collaborate in publishing gospel songbooks.[20] For the next three decades, Harris produced many songbooks through his publishing firm, the Windsor Music Company, which were very popular in Pentecostal circles. In addition to Bilhorn, Harris collaborated with George Meyer, James Rowe, and Henry Date, among other important figures in the gospel songbook publishing industry.[21] On June 13, 1913, Thoro Harris received the baptism of the Holy Spirit during a revival meeting conducted by Maria Woodworth-Etter at Stone Church in Chicago. The following day, he wrote "Pentecost in My Soul," which became one of his most famous gospel songs.[22]

Tragically, in March 1922, Thoro Harris's wife Agnes died of smallpox.[23] In October 1927, Harris married German immigrant Freda Walters, and in 1932, they moved to Eureka Springs, Arkansas, where Harris

---

17. Lillenas, *Modern Gospel Song Stories*, 39; biographical sketch of Thoro Harris by R. T. Taylor Jr., July 20, 2000, in "Clip file, Personal papers—Thoro Harris," archival record file, Flower Pentecostal Heritage Center.

18. *Washington Post*, "Howard's Normal Graduates," 4; "Thoro Harris, hymn writer," Oct. 29, 1990, in "Clip file, Personal papers—Thoro Harris," archival record file, Flower Pentecostal Heritage Center.

19. *Evening Star*, "Marriage Licenses," 10; E. Alan Long to Glenn Gohr, July 12, 2006, in "Clip file, Personal papers—Thoro Harris," archival record file, Flower Pentecostal Heritage Center; "Thirteenth Census of the United States, 1910—Population," Ancestry.com.

20. Thoro Harris, typed biographical notes, in "Clip file, Personal papers—Thoro Harris," archival record file, Flower Pentecostal Heritage Center.

21. Everett A. Wilson, "Harris, Thoro," in Burgess and van der Maas, *New International Dictionary*, 691.

22. "Thoro Harris, hymn writer," Oct. 29, 1990, in "Clip file, Personal papers—Thoro Harris," archival record file, Flower Pentecostal Heritage Center.

23. Agnes H. Harris, Certificate of Death, 1922, in "Clip file, Personal papers—Thoro Harris," archival record file, Flower Pentecostal Heritage Center.

continued writing and publishing gospel songs.[24] Sadly, Freda died of heart failure in December 1936, although she left Thoro "a great inheritance"—some twenty-six cats—according to Marie Knutson's reflections in a 1983 oral history interview.[25] Harris remarried soon after Freda's death, marrying Rubye Bryant of Smith County, Mississippi, in February 1937.[26] Harris continued writing and publishing music and also served at various local churches in Eureka Springs in a musical capacity.[27]

Oscar and Marie Knutson met Thoro Harris in January 1949, and with shared backgrounds in the Pentecostal movement and a common love for gospel music, they appear to have connected immediately. They also seem to have gotten to know one another well during their time together in Eureka Springs.[28] When asked about Harris in a 1983 oral history interview, Marie Knutson reflected: "He was full of music, and that's about all he knew, all he could do—to write music, to play it, and sing it."[29] Ultimately, Harris agreed to sell his approximately eighteen hundred song copyrights to Oscar.[30] In later reflections, Knutson noted that in yet another example of God's provision, he received the thousands of dollars it cost to purchase Harris's song copyrights and the other necessary equipment for full-time gospel publishing because the Lord had "laid it on the heart of some of

---

24. In a miscellaneous clippings file pertaining to Thoro Harris, there is a handwritten note referring to a marriage license between Thoro Harris and Isabell Yodell, dated December 12, 1923. However, because the note has been uncorroborated with documentary evidence, this detail is not included in the main text of Harris's abbreviated biography. E. Alan Long to Glenn Gohr, July 12, 2006, in "Clip file, Personal papers—Thoro Harris," archival record file, Flower Pentecostal Heritage Center.

25. *Caroll Courier*, "Mrs. Thoro Harris" (Dec. 31, 1936), in "Clip file, Personal papers—Thoro Harris," archival record file, Flower Pentecostal Heritage Center; Oscar and Marie Knutson, oral history interview with Wayne Warner, Sept. 5, 1983, audio recording, Flower Pentecostal Heritage Center.

26. E. Alan Long to Glenn Gohr, July 12, 2006, in "Clip file, Personal papers—Thoro Harris," archival record file, Flower Pentecostal Heritage Center.

27. E. Alan Long to Glenn Gohr, July 12, 2006, in "Clip file, Personal papers—Thoro Harris," archival record file, Flower Pentecostal Heritage Center; biographical sketch of Thoro Harris by R. T. Taylor Jr., July 20, 2000, in "Clip file, Personal papers—Thoro Harris," archival record file, Flower Pentecostal Heritage Center.

28. Oscar and Marie Knutson, oral history interview with Wayne Warner, Sept. 5, 1983, audio recording, Flower Pentecostal Heritage Center.

29. Oscar and Marie Knutson, oral history interview with Wayne Warner, Sept. 5, 1983, audio recording, Flower Pentecostal Heritage Center.

30. Knutson, *His Loving Care*, 94; Oscar and Marie Knutson, oral history interview with Wayne Warner, Sept. 5, 1983, audio recording, Flower Pentecostal Heritage Center.

the folk at Bowman, N[orth] Dak[ota], to provide much of the necessary finance[s]."[31] Over the next three decades, Oscar remained the owner and custodian of Harris's music and used Harris's music to publish thousands of Pentecostal songbooks.[32]

Having secured the necessary permissions and equipment to begin full-time publishing ministry, Oscar Knutson resigned as pastor of the Full Gospel Christian Assembly in Okanogan at the end of March 1949, nearly six years after planting the church.[33] With a new pastor scheduled to arrive in Okanogan in June—Rev. Edward Logelin of Goodridge, Minnesota—Knutson and his family moved to Seattle and began "preparing for our new work."[34]

In Seattle, Knutson published his first songbook, *Crusade Songs*, for a large, local Pentecostal tent meeting campaign held in summer 1949.[35] Dubbed the United Full Gospel Crusade, it was the second installment of a tent meeting campaign first held in summer 1948.[36] Born out of a collaboration between six different Pentecostal churches in Seattle—Philadelphia Church, Evangel Temple, Bethany Baptist Church, Fremont Tabernacle, Ballard Gospel Tabernacle, and Foursquare Gospel Church—the United Full Gospel Crusade was intended to save souls, facilitate greater unity among local Pentecostal fellowships, and raise the profile of the Pentecostal message in Seattle.[37] Subsequent editions of the songbook included a note reporting the success of the United Full Gospel Crusade each year.[38]

---

31. Knutson, *His Loving Care*, 95–96.

32. Oscar and Marie Knutson, oral history interview with Wayne Warner, Sept. 5, 1983, audio recording, Flower Pentecostal Heritage Center; *Ken Rock Herald*, "Published 20,000 Books!," 1.

33. *Okanogan Independent*, "Knutson Resigns as Full Gospel Pastor," 2; Knutson, *His Loving Care*, 93.

34. *Okanogan Independent*, "Knutson Resigns as Full Gospel Pastor," 2; "Rev. Edward Logelin of Minnesota," 10; Knutson, *His Loving Care*, 94. Rev. Edward Logelin appears to have been associated with the Independent Assemblies of God, which probably explains how he came to succeed Oscar Knutson as pastor of the Full Gospel Christian Assembly in Okanogan. "Fellowship Meeting," 26; Riveness, "Summer Convention in Karlstad," 9.

35. Knutson, *His Loving Care*, 94; Ashworth et al., *Crusade Songs* (Seattle/Estherville), inside cover.

36. Ashworth et al., *Crusade Songs* (Seattle/Estherville), inside cover.

37. Ashworth et al., *Crusade Songs* (Seattle/Estherville), inside cover, back cover.

38. Ashworth et al., *Crusade Songs* (Seattle), inside cover.

Knutson did multiple printings of *Crusade Songs* before eventually revising it and turning it into a regular songbook intended for general use in Pentecostal camp meetings or revival services.[39]

With the initial publication of *Crusade Songs* in 1949, Oscar Knutson adopted a new name for his publishing business—the Christian Book Concern—and established his home office in Seattle at 5339 Ballard Avenue, as well as a branch office in Estherville, Iowa.[40] After *Crusade Songs*, Knutson published a handful of smaller songbooks, featuring some selections from the music of Thoro Harris and some other gospel songwriters. Most significantly, however, these smaller songbooks featured songs that Knutson had written and composed himself, including "Down Came the Fire," "I've Found the Way," "He Will Lead Me," and "My Beloved Is Mine," which he had written for his daughter Fern's wedding.[41] Knutson also included "There's a Drawing From on High," his very first song, written nearly two decades prior while pastoring in Huron, South Dakota, in fall 1931.[42] According to Knutson's recounting, the song came to him as he was singing and playing piano while trying "to keep the devil from trying to discourage us."[43] At the time, "our cupboard was completely bare and we did not have the money for a five cent loaf of bread." The Lord blessed them with a song and also provided food and finances for the Knutson family.[44]

As Oscar Knutson published his first songbooks in Seattle, he also began to work on a new project—a revised and updated edition of Rev. A. D. Guth's *Selected Gospel Songs*. Anticipating its completion, he even advertised the project within one of his smaller songbooks.[45] Published in June 1950, Knutson called the new, 345-page songbook *Selected Gospel Songs, Number Two*.[46] In an introductory note to the songbook, Knutson acknowledged Guth and explained that he kept the best of the original songbook while

---

39. *Crusade Songs*.

40. Advertisement for *Selected Gospel Songs, Number Two*, a new Pentecostal songbook compiled by O. M. Knutson, 15.

41. *Down Came the Fire*; Knutson, *There's a Drawing From on High*; Knutson, *My Beloved Is Mine*, inside cover; *Okanogan Independent*, "Miss Fern Knutson, Mr. Alvin Olson," 5.

42. Knutson, *There's a Drawing From on High*, 2–3; Knutson, *His Loving Care*, 58; Knutson, *Songs of Victory*, 30b.

43. Knutson, *Songs of Victory*, 30b.

44. Knutson, *Songs of Victory*, 30b; Knutson, *His Loving Care*, 58.

45. Knutson, *My Beloved Is Mine*, inside back cover.

46. Advertisement for *Selected Gospel Songs, Number Two*, 15.

also making some adjustments to it. "This song book contains a well[-]rounded selection, carefully chosen after consulting with many ministers and song leaders in several states," Knutson wrote.[47] "Our hope is that this song book may become a rich blessing to many. May we sing to the [p]raise and [g]lory of our Lord and Redeemer."[48]

In the early 1950s, Oscar and Marie Knutson moved the main office of their publishing operation from Seattle to Rockford, Illinois, although they retained their Estherville branch office for at least a year after the move.[49] In Rockford, the Knutsons purchased a large electrically operated printing press and other publishing equipment from a local print shop that had recently closed after the death of its owner.[50] They also made a special agreement with local property owner Richard L. Bates, who offered to finance the construction of a building on a vacant lot next to his house, which the Knutsons could rent for the Christian Book Concern, provided that Oscar supervised its construction.[51] Located at 703 Barnum Road, the new building was completed in about three months, and the Knutsons opened the new office for their publishing business in time to be listed in Rockford's 1952 city directory.[52]

Assisted by their son, Lloyd, Oscar and Marie Knutson operated the Christian Book Concern in Rockford for the next several years, publishing "Song Books and Christian Books and Literature."[53] An August 1952 article in Rockford's local newspaper, *Ken Rock Herald*, specially featured the Knutson family and the Christian Book Concern. The article noted that, in the last three years, the Knutsons had published more than twenty thousand copies of *Selected Gospel Songs, Number Two* and stated that the songbook was "in demand throughout America."[54] In addition to promoting their publishing ministry, the article explained that the Knutsons had been Pentecostal traveling evangelists for twenty years and had "conducted

47. Knutson, *Selected Gospel Songs, Number Two*, front matter.

48. Knutson, *Selected Gospel Songs, Number Two*, front matter.

49. Knutson, *His Loving Care*, 95, 96; Knutson, *Revival Echoes* (Rockford/Estherville), inside cover.

50. Knutson, *His Loving Care*, 96; *Ken Rock Herald*, "Published 20,000 Books!," 1.

51. Knutson, *His Loving Care*, 95–96; R. L. Polk & Co., *Rockford City Directory, 1951*; R. L. Polk & Co., *Rockford City Directory, 1952*.

52. Knutson, *His Loving Care*, 96; R. L. Polk & Co., *Rockford City Directory, 1952*.

53. Christian Book Concern business stationery, ca. 1950s, Rockford, Illinois, Oscar M. Knutson archival collection, unprocessed box.

54. *Ken Rock Herald*, "Published 20,000 Books!," 1.

services in 36 states."⁵⁵ The article also noted that Oscar and Marie were currently holding revival meetings in Cadott, Wisconsin, and had plans to do some evangelistic ministry in the New England states.⁵⁶

While *Selected Gospel Songs, Number Two* was their preeminent publication, the Knutsons also published many other (smaller) Pentecostal songbooks, featuring a diversity of songs from old gospel songwriters such as William J. Kirkpatrick, R. E. Hudson, John R. Sweney, P. P. Bliss, F. A. Graves, Ira D. Sankey, R. E. Winsett, W. H. Doane, R. Kelso Carter, C. P. Jones, and of course Thoro Harris, among others. Oscar's own songs were scattered throughout the songbooks too. Steeped in the Pentecostal theological tradition, major themes throughout the songbooks included the power and presence of the Holy Spirit, forgiveness of sins in the atonement, salvation as deliverance, divine healing, personal relationship with God, and the Second Coming of Jesus and eternal life with God. Upon request, the Knutsons printed customized songbooks for particular churches or special occasions.⁵⁷ In addition to Pentecostal songbooks, the Knutsons published theological pamphlets and gospel tracts, as well as advertisements for various Pentecostal evangelistic campaigns, revival meetings, and/or church conventions. Notably, the Christian Book Concern published advertisements and songbooks for Rev. Andrew Teuber, who, after resigning his pastorate in Wenatchee, Washington, in the early 1950s, held a series of evangelistic campaigns with his "tent cathedral" across several states.⁵⁸

55. *Ken Rock Herald*, "Published 20,000 Books!," 1.

56. *Ken Rock Herald*, "Published 20,000 Books!," 1. Oscar described some of his and Marie's experiences in the New England states in *His Loving Care*. Knutson, *His Loving Care*, 96–98.

57. One copy (courtesy of Bernice M. Fergus) of *Selected Gospel Songs, Number Two* has "First Church Assemblies of God, Oakland, Calif." embossed on cover. Some other representative examples of customized songbooks follow. Knutson, *Revival Echoes, from Illinois District Camp Meeting*, cover; *Sing Unto the Lord: Silver Lake Bible Camp, Souvenir Copy*, cover.

58. Advertisement for "Back to the Bible Revival . . . Salvation-Healing Campaign with the Andrew Teuber Evangelistic Party . . . ," ca. 1952, scrapbook featuring materials printed by Oscar Knutson, courtesy of Phillip W. Knutson; *Songs of Revival* (Rockford/Estherville), cover, opening pages, back cover. This songbook was especially printed for Rev. Andrew Teuber's evangelistic campaigns.

On October 12, 1952, the Knutsons celebrated the wedding of their son, Lloyd, to Lois Esther Krob of Hutchinson, Kansas.[59] Held at the Full Gospel Assembly Church in Hutchinson, the event was surely joyful, but perhaps also an occasion of mixed emotions for Oscar. For nearly two decades, Hutchinson had been the home of his dear friend and mentor, the late Rev. A. D. Guth, to whom Lois Krob was in fact related; Guth's older sister Barbara was Lois's grandmother.[60] Admittedly, further wedding details do not seem to have survived, but sometime after their honeymoon, Lloyd and Lois settled in Rockford to assist Oscar and Marie with the gospel publishing business.[61]

In addition to gospel publishing and some occasional evangelistic ministry, various examples of business cards and office stationery reflect that Oscar and Marie Knutson also pursued some other business ventures in Rockford in the 1950s. Oscar seems to have utilized the print shop for other local printing services, and he also sold automobile insurance.[62] Marie, meanwhile, operated an artificial flower business.[63] Evidently, both Oscar and Marie continued these independent business ventures—selling automobile insurance and artificial flowers, respectively—after they left Rockford and moved back to the Pacific Northwest.[64]

Oscar and Marie Knutson closed their Rockford publishing office in late 1957 and moved back to Seattle, where Oscar returned to the construction

---

59. Invitation to wedding of Lois Krob and Lloyd Knutson, 1952, scrapbook compiled by Oscar Knutson, Oscar M. Knutson archival collection, unprocessed box.

60. R. L. Polk & Co., *Hutchinson City Directory, 1933*; R. L. Polk & Co., *Hutchinson City Directory, 1937*; R. L. Polk & Co., *Hutchinson City Directory, 1947*; genealogical note documenting the connection between the Krob family and the Guth family, courtesy of Bernice M. Fergus.

61. Knutson, *His Loving Care*, 98.

62. Business stationery, O. M. Knutson Insurance, Central Security Mutual Insurance Company, ca. 1950s, Oscar M. Knutson archival collection, unprocessed box; business card, Rockford Printing Service, ca. 1950s, Oscar M. Knutson archival collection, unprocessed box.

63. Business cards, Marvel Artificial Flowers, ca. 1950s–1960s, Oscar M. Knutson archival collection, unprocessed box.

64. Business cards, Marvel Artificial Flowers, ca. 1950s–1960s, Oscar M. Knutson archival collection, unprocessed box; business stationery, O. M. Knutson Insurance, ca. 1950s–1960s, on opposite side of handwritten theological reflections "Pentecost: Yesterday and Today, 1901–1990," Oscar M. Knutson archival collection, box 2, folder 36.

industry, in addition to being active in various local Pentecostal churches and doing occasional ministry work. Mostly building and renovating houses in Everett and Edmonds, Washington, Oscar built at least five fifteen- to sixteen-thousand-dollar houses by the end of 1959 alone.[65] He continued working as a builder during the 1960s, and although the 1969 Edmonds city directory listed Knutson as retired, printed business cards indicate that he formally owned and operated a business called Active Construction Company for multiple years, including into the early 1970s, before ultimately transferring ownership to his son, Lloyd.[66] Some official business stationery indicates that the Knutsons continued operating the Christian Book Concern during 1960s and 1970s, although perhaps just in a minimal capacity as the print shop was not formally listed with Oscar and Marie Knutson in city directories until 1979.[67]

After his retirement from the construction business, Oscar Knutson spent much of the 1980s and early 1990s as something of an armchair Pentecostal theologian, writer, and pastor. No longer traveling for evangelistic meetings, nor even in full-time pastoral ministry, Knutson formally operated the Christian Book Concern until 1985 and spent much of his time reflecting and writing on personal and family history, as well as various theological subjects.[68] In late 1979 or early 1980, Oscar Knutson wrote and published a book of reflections on his life and ministry entitled *His Loving Care*.[69] Just over one hundred pages long, the book was filled with signifi-

---

65. *Daily Herald*, "County building permit" (Jan. 3, 1958), 16; *Daily Herald*, "Seattleite, O. M. Knutson," 28; *Daily Herald*, "County building permit" (Dec. 30, 1958), 13; *Daily Herald*, "County building permit" (Jan. 20, 1959), 17; *Daily Herald*, "O. M. Knutson of Seattle," 31. An inflation calculator indicates that fifteen thousand dollars in the late 1950s was the equivalent of approximately one hundred sixty thousand to one hundred seventy thousand dollars in 2024.

66. *Daily Herald*, "Building Continues at Near Record Pace," 14; R. L. Polk & Co., *Edmonds City Directory, 1969*; business cards, Active Construction Co., ca. 1960s–1970s, Oscar M. Knutson archival collection, unprocessed box; business stationery, Active Construction Co., ca. 1970s, on opposite side of some typed theological reflections, Oscar M. Knutson archival collection, box 2, folder 30.

67. Business stationery for the Christian Book Concern, address at 811 Puget Lane, Edmonds, Washington, ca. 1960s, on opposite side of some typed theological reflections, Oscar M. Knutson archival collection, box 2, folder 25.

68. R. L. Polk & Co., *Seattle City Directory, 1979*; R. L. Polk & Co., *Seattle City Directory, 1985*.

69. Knutson, *His Loving Care*, 30.

cant historical detail and compelling personal anecdotes. In the foreword, Knutson wrote that:

> My main purpose in writing this book is to tell how the Lord has proved to us over and over again that He watches over His own—that He sees every test and trial we may have to endure. If we will but trust in Him, He will sustain and uphold us. He has shown us in such a clear and revealing way that He sees our daily needs and provides a way to supply them.[70]

In 1983, Oscar Knutson compiled and published his last Pentecostal songbook, *Songs of Victory*. Apparently, he and Marie had been getting calls for years "inquiring about old songs that are hard to find."[71] According to Oscar's advertisement for the songbook: "My wife and I spent many evenings searching through our 'old book' library, and very often we would find [the songs]."[72] Knutson thus decided to publish a new songbook, filled with "specials, some new songs, and, some of the old precious and favorit[e] songs."[73] In September of the same year, Oscar and Marie visited the Assemblies of God denominational headquarters in Springfield, Missouri, where they first met with Wayne Warner, director of the Assemblies of God Archives, for an oral history interview to discuss their life and ministry.[74] Then, after the interview, the Knutsons arranged to transfer their Thoro Harris song copyright permissions to the music department of the Assemblies of God, so that the denomination could publish Harris's music in their own songbooks and hymnals. Although Oscar continued to sell the songbooks that he had left in stock, the decision to transfer the copyrights seemed fitting, given his advanced age.[75]

Around the same time that Oscar Knutson was concluding his songbook publishing ministry, he wrote and published a brief theological

---

70. Knutson, *His Loving Care*, 6.

71. Advertisement for *Songs of Victory* songbook, ca. 1980s, Oscar M. Knutson archival collection, unprocessed box.

72. Advertisement for *Songs of Victory* songbook, ca. 1980s, Oscar M. Knutson archival collection, unprocessed box.

73. Advertisement for *Songs of Victory* songbook, ca. 1980s, Oscar M. Knutson archival collection, unprocessed box.

74. Oscar and Marie Knutson, oral history interview with Wayne Warner, Sept. 5, 1983, audio recording, Flower Pentecostal Heritage Center.

75. Oscar and Marie Knutson, oral history interview with Wayne Warner, Sept. 5, 1983, audio recording, Flower Pentecostal Heritage Center; advertisement for the Christian Book Concern, ca. 1980s, Oscar M. Knutson archival collection, unprocessed box.

pamphlet entitled *God's Plan for Marriage and a Happy Home*. Published in 1983 or 1984, the pamphlet sought to offer a clear but concise perspective on marriage and family from a biblical standpoint.[76] Evidently, Knutson believed that a proper teaching on such matters was necessary, given the ubiquity of divorce (and remarriage), promiscuity, cohabitation, and homosexuality among both Christians and the broader culture.[77]

Beginning with some reflections on the goodness of God and of his design for human relationships, Oscar Knutson wrote about the sacredness of marriage and the significance of a husband and wife as being "one flesh."[78] For Knutson, this had deep implications for spousal unity as well as spousal equality. "The Bible nowhere says that the wife is in any way inferior to her husband as a human being. They are *one*. They are equal," he wrote.[79] Knutson affirmed the scriptural exhortation that wives "submit" to their husbands and the scriptural assertion that "the husband is the head of the wife" and interpreted these statements as meaning that husbands were responsible for making "the final decision" on certain matters in the home.[80] "Like in any business, or government, one must make the final decision[;] so also should it be in the home," Knutson wrote.[81] His perspective was not unqualified, however. "Husbands, weigh your wife's opinions on the same scale you weigh your own on. Treat her as an equal because that is what she is."[82] Knutson also offered some scripturally based relational advice for Christian marriages, calling for unselfishness and patience and for spouses to "be considerate, good tempered, kind, [and] loving."[83] He also suggested a posture of preferring to give rather than receive, to "never answer quickly or sharply," and to "never do to your wife or husband what you would not want him or her to do to you."[84] Finally, "add to this a strong love for the Lord, and for your companion."[85]

---

76. Knutson, *God's Plan for Marriage*, 5.
77. Knutson, *God's Plan for Marriage*, 12–13, 16–17.
78. Knutson, *God's Plan for Marriage*, 4.
79. Knutson, *God's Plan for Marriage*, 8.
80. Knutson, *God's Plan for Marriage*, 7.
81. Knutson, *God's Plan for Marriage*, 7.
82. Knutson, *God's Plan for Marriage*, 7.
83. Knutson, *God's Plan for Marriage*, 5.
84. Knutson, *God's Plan for Marriage*, 5.
85. Knutson, *God's Plan for Marriage*, 5.

While Oscar Knutson provided some positive reflections on marriage, much of *God's Plan for Marriage and a Happy Home* offered warnings against compromising on God's word when it came to marriage-related matters.[86] "Satan . . . is on a rampage to wreck all the homes he can . . . . It is his plan to drag as many souls with him to hell as he possibly can," Knutson wrote.[87] Primarily concerned about divorce and remarriage after divorce—including divorces caused by infidelity—Knutson printed within his pamphlet the testimony of J. M. Humphrey, an early twentieth-century Holiness preacher who got a divorce after his wife's infidelity, spent seven years in singleness, and then got remarried, only to end his second marriage because he felt conviction that it was sinful (given that his previous wife was still living).[88] Knutson acknowledged the difficulty and sensitivity of the subject but was nevertheless convinced that such matters should not be trifled with. God is merciful, to be sure, but "the price" of missing God's word on marriage and divorce was "too great . . . . We cannot take any chances," he wrote.[89]

Oscar Knutson's published reflections in *God's Plan for Marriage and a Happy Home* may have inspired another set of theological reflections from around 1985, titled in various draft forms: "The Joy of the Lord," "The Joy of the Lord and the Love of God," "In God's Likeness," "The Fruit of the Spirit," "Spiritual Man vs. Carnal Man," and "The Carnal Man: How Goes the Battle[?]"[90] The papers containing these reflections include various chapter divisions and outlines, editing marks and other annotations, which indicate that this was another book project for Knutson, although he apparently never finished it, and thus it went unpublished. Partial drafts of *The Glorious Church* that are interspersed within these papers may further indicate that, in the mid 1980s, Knutson was returning to some theological reflections that originated in the late 1940s.[91] Largely an exposition of the difference between people who have not obeyed the gospel, but rather follow their own worldly passions—which Knutson dubbed "carnal

---

86. Knutson, *God's Plan for Marriage*, 2, 30.

87. Knutson, *God's Plan for Marriage*, 10.

88. Knutson, *God's Plan for Marriage*, 20–28; Wesley Center Online, "Jerry Miles Humphrey."

89. Knutson, *God's Plan for Marriage*, 2, 29.

90. Typed and handwritten theological reflections, Oscar M. Knutson archival collection, box 2, folders 22–39.

91. Typed and handwritten theological reflections, Oscar M. Knutson archival collection, box 2, folders 22–39.

man"—and people who are born again, washed in the blood of Christ, and walk in accordance with the Holy Spirit—which Knutson dubbed "spiritual man"—these reflections touched on many theological matters including heaven and hell, the Trinity, creation, the resurrection of all things at Jesus' glorious appearing, the image of God, the nature of the soul, the nature of the body, the devil, the difference between materiality and sin, the baptism of the Holy Spirit, and the meaning of true love and joy found in God.[92]

In addition to these theological writings, Oscar Knutson spent some time between the late 1980s and early 1990s drafting some general reflections on the Pentecostal movement, looking back on it after several decades.[93] Titled "Pentecost—Yesterday and Today," Knutson sought to "take stock and see where we are on our heavenward journey," inquiring of the Pentecostal movement "whether we have gained or lost ground? Drawn closer to the Lord? Or have we lost some of the fire and zeal and determination to serve the Lord?"[94] Admittedly, the surviving drafts of these reflections are incomplete, but Knutson's 1983 oral history interview disclosed his perspective on the matter. When asked about the Pentecostal movement and its changes over time, Knutson lamented, "I do think that we have lost something."[95] In the early days of the movement, people received the baptism of the Holy Spirit and were "lost in the Lord for days," according to Knutson.[96] By contrast, in the 1980s, people could (allegedly) receive Holy Spirit baptism and then joke and laugh mere minutes later, as if what had just happened was trivial or unimportant.[97]

Oscar Knutson's reflections on the Pentecostal movement not only raised some important theological questions about experiencing the presence of God (particularly, in the baptism of the Holy Spirit) but also revealed his view of church history. Located within a broadly Protestant

---

92. Typed and handwritten theological reflections, Oscar M. Knutson archival collection, box 2, folders 22–39.

93. Typed and handwritten theological reflections, Oscar M. Knutson archival collection, box 2, folders 35–37.

94. Handwritten theological reflections, "Pentecost—Yesterday and Today," Oscar M. Knutson archival collection, box 2, folder 35.

95. Oscar and Marie Knutson, oral history interview with Wayne Warner, Sept. 5, 1983, audio recording, Flower Pentecostal Heritage Center.

96. Oscar and Marie Knutson, oral history interview with Wayne Warner, Sept. 5, 1983, audio recording, Flower Pentecostal Heritage Center.

97. Oscar and Marie Knutson, oral history interview with Wayne Warner, Sept. 5, 1983, audio recording, Flower Pentecostal Heritage Center.

but still uniquely Pentecostal theological framework, Knutson's view of church history tended to follow major movements of the Holy Spirit but was in many ways bleak. It was also tied to his previous "Spiritual—Carnal" theological contemplations and writings.[98] According to Knutson, the early church had initially been filled with the power and presence of the Holy Spirit, but began to deteriorate "after the Apostles were all gone."[99] For subsequent centuries, most of church history was a "decline into spiritual darkness," until "finally, total spiritual darkness prevailed."[100] God did not abandon his church, however, and "in the time of Martin Luther a ray of light shone through. Then step by step more light shone through . . . . Then one after another revival came, till the fire of the Holy Spirit sprang forth at Azusa Street and elsewhere."[101]

Oscar Knutson's reference to the Azusa Street Mission in Los Angeles, California, followed a larger narrative pattern among his contemporaries in the early Pentecostal movement to laud the Azusa Street Revival as the beginning of North American Pentecostalism. However, unlike his contemporaries, Knutson was also quite critical of the Azusa Street Mission. Observing that multiple splits and schisms occurred at the mission in the years and decades following the 1906 revival, Knutson saw such divisions as evidence that both leadership and congregants were not faithfully listening to the Holy Spirit and were instead relying upon sinful impulses and worldly wisdom.[102] In a personal scrapbook, Knutson went so far as to keep a newspaper clipping reporting that between late 1930 and early 1931,

---

98. Handwritten theological reflections, Oscar M. Knutson archival collection, box 2, folders 35–36.

99. Handwritten theological reflections, Oscar M. Knutson archival collection, box 2, folder 35.

100. Handwritten theological reflections, Oscar M. Knutson archival collection, box 2, folder 35.

101. Handwritten theological reflections, Oscar M. Knutson archival collection, box 2, folder 35. Knutson's upbringing in the Evangelical Free Lutheran Church in Norway likely influenced his attitude toward Luther. His perspective on church history was also certainly informed by the longtime theological dispositions of various Pentecostal ministry partners. For example, a very similar recounting of church history can be found in an article penned by A. D. Guth, published in *The Full Gospel Testimony* in 1925. Guth, "Two Kinds of Unity," 2–3, 6. Interestingly, each issue of *The Full Gospel Testimony* included a section of martyrologies and other testimonies from the early church period, indicating a genuine interest in church history and a sense of continuity with the Christians some two millennia prior.

102. Handwritten theological reflections, Oscar M. Knutson archival collection, box 2, folders 36–37.

"Pilot Me Home"

Los Angeles police had to break up multiple riots at the Azusa Street Mission due to fighting between rival pastors and their constituencies, which had been drawn on lines of race and gender.[103] Police quenched one riot in which rival factions were hurling hymn books at one another and brandishing chairs above their heads. On another occasion, no hymnals nor chairs were thrown, but police were called in because rival factions were causing an enormous ruckus, hurling songs and prayers at one another, trying to drown each other out.[104]

Although Oscar Knutson maintained his critiques of the Azusa Street Mission, he acknowledged that the initial 1906 revival had been a great outpouring of the Holy Spirit, paralleling the experience of the "first" Pentecost in Jerusalem, as recorded in the Acts of the Apostles. Many souls had been saved, and many were strengthened in the faith. The spiritual implications of the Azusa Street Revival were incalculable, and theological implications on church history followed. Reminiscing about the birth of the Pentecostal movement, Knutson's reflections were undeniably eschatological, not to mention steeped in an evangelistic framework:

> I can remember when I was a very young boy in the early days of the present century, how many were looking for the Lord to return to catch away His Bride. But instead of the Lord coming at that time, the Lord sent the Holy Spirit to prepare His bride for His return. So in the very beginning of this century, the Holy Spirit came, and to those who were ready and hungry He would come in.[105]

More traditional expressions of the Christian faith—such as Roman Catholicism, Eastern Orthodoxy, and Anglicanism—hold a particular view of church history that emphasizes tangible continuity with the faith of the apostles and the early church—"the faith which was once delivered," to use the parlance of the apostle Jude.[106] Although the Pentecostal movement largely declined many traditional theological, liturgical, and ecclesial forms, it nevertheless asserted its own continuity with the church of the

---

103. *Great Falls Tribune*, "Hymn Book Throwing Banned"; Robeck, *Azusa Street Mission and Revival*, 320.

104. *Great Falls Tribune*, "Hymn Book Throwing Banned"; Robeck, *Azusa Street Mission and Revival*, 320.

105. Handwritten reflections on Pentecostal history, Oscar M. Knutson archival collection, box 2, folder 22.

106. Jude 1:3, KJV. Jude is known in church tradition as the brother of James of Jerusalem, the "brother of the Lord." Jude was not one of Jesus' twelve apostles, but he is traditionally called an apostle.

New Testament. This is evident, in part, in the names of various early Pentecostal groups, such as the Apostolic Faith Movement, and even the term *Pentecostal* itself. Rather than an apostolic episcopal lineage, or the use of historic liturgical rites, the Pentecostal movement held that its connection to the apostles and the early church was based in its experience of the same Holy Spirit that filled and empowered the New Testament church. God was present among the Pentecostals just as he was present in the early church—actively and powerfully moving in them and through them to heal and to save. Pentecostals' understanding and experience of God's own Spirit with them was further reflected in the names of their fellowships, using terms like *tabernacle, temple*, and the like, to convey that theirs was a place in which people could come to meet with God.

Oscar Knutson's reflections on church history in his later years evidently aligned with this broader Pentecostal conviction and its theological ramifications. These were not simply convictions held later in life. Knutson's sense of connection with the New Testament church also went back to his days of traveling evangelism with his "Big Brown Tent," and likely earlier as well.[107] In an advertisement for one of his Pentecostal tent meetings in Sultan, Washington, from the late 1930s or early 1940s, Knutson invited folks to visit and hear "the *Old Time Gospel*."[108] The advertisement posed a series of questions and answers that reflected Knutson's sense of continuity with the historic Christian faith:

> *Is this something New?* We are not here to bring you something new; some new creed or doctrine. We have no new ideas nor issues that we wish to put over, nor have we any new interpretations of the Bible. *What is it then?* We preach the same Gospel as was preached by the Lord Jesus, and by the Apostles. It is old, and yet it is up to date. It is old fashioned, and yet it is modern. It has been preached by thousands of others since the days of the Apostles.[109]

---

107. Advertisement for Oscar Knutson tent meetings in Sultan, Washington, ca. 1930s–1940s, scrapbook featuring items printed by Oscar Knutson, courtesy of Phillip W. Knutson.

108. Advertisement for Oscar Knutson tent meetings in Sultan, Washington, ca. 1930s–1940s, scrapbook featuring items printed by Oscar Knutson, courtesy of Phillip W. Knutson.

109. Advertisement for Oscar Knutson tent meetings in Sultan, Washington, ca. 1930s–1940s, scrapbook featuring items printed by Oscar Knutson, courtesy of Phillip W. Knutson.

"Pilot Me Home"

In addition to various real estate ventures and writing projects in the final decades of his life, Oscar Knutson traveled to Norway with his wife, Marie, to visit family on at least two occasions in the 1970s. Family members recall these trips, and they also remember Oscar purchasing two separate vehicles in Norway—a station wagon as well as a Volkswagen Jetta—and then arranging to ship them back to America for him and Marie to use.[110] Back home in the Seattle area, Oscar also did some smaller scale, though nevertheless important, ministry work during the final decades of his life. Active in local Pentecostal fellowships such as Westgate Chapel in Edmonds and the Westminster Assembly of God Church and Philadelphia Church in Seattle, Knutson spent time visiting people in the hospital, talking with them, and praying with them.[111] Oscar and Marie also spent time with family, and their grandchildren remember several meaningful overnight visits. In particular, grandchildren remember participating in Oscar and Marie's "evening prayer" routine each night, in which they would sit in their living room together, read from the Bible, and then "turn and kneel at their chairs for prayer."[112]

According to recollections from family members, Oscar Knutson suffered a handful of medical episodes in his latter years. On one occasion, he experienced sudden, intense chest pressure and dizziness while going up some stairs in his home, but miraculously stayed upright, tightly gripping the handrail while the event passed.[113] Knutson subsequently visited the

110. Unpublished family recollections of the final decades of Oscar Knutson's life, compiled by Bernice M. Fergus, 2024, Oscar M. Knutson archival collection, box 1, folder 2.

111. Fiftieth wedding anniversary of Oscar and Marie Knutson invitation, 1974, Oscar M. Knutson archival collection, unprocessed box; sixtieth wedding anniversary of Oscar and Marie Knutson invitation, 1984, Oscar M. Knutson archival collection, unprocessed box; Marie B. Knutson, funeral bulletin, Apr. 17, 1993, Oscar M. Knutson archival collection, box 1, folder 2; Oscar M. Knutson, funeral bulletin, Apr. 26, 1993, Oscar M. Knutson archival collection, box 1, folder 2; unpublished family recollections of the final decades of Oscar Knutson's life, compiled by Bernice M. Fergus, 2024, Oscar M. Knutson archival collection, box 1, folder 2.

112. Unpublished family recollections of the final decades of Oscar Knutson's life, compiled by Bernice M. Fergus, 2024, Oscar M. Knutson archival collection, box 1, folder 2.

113. Unpublished family recollections of the final decades of Oscar Knutson's life, compiled by Bernice M. Fergus, 2024, Oscar M. Knutson archival collection, box 1, folder 2. According to retired internal medicine specialist Samuel Palpant, MD, of Spokane,

hospital, and a medical imaging test revealed a blockage to a heart artery that required non-urgent surgical attention.[114] Oscar and Marie prayed for God's intervention, and on the day of the scheduled operation—much to the surprise of the cardiologist—another medical imaging test revealed that other blood vessels had grown around the blocked artery to form an alternative arterial pathway for blood to flow.[115] Surgery was no longer necessary. Their prayers were answered! Oscar was overjoyed to see this divine healing documented in official medical records.[116]

Tragically, on Saturday, April 10, 1993, Oscar and Marie Knutson were involved in a devastating car accident in Seattle, in which Marie was killed instantly and others were injured, some seriously.[117] Oscar was

---

Washington, "this sounds like a classic example of exercise-induced angina pectoris, which can be a warning sign of a myocardial infarction, known more commonly as a heart attack." Conversation with the author, Spokane, Washington, July 17, 2024.

114. Although Oscar Knutson's medical records are no longer available, Sam Palpant (see chapter 7, n113) speculates that this was "likely a coronary angiogram, a dye-study of the heart arteries. The test evidently revealed some degree of blockage of one of the arteries, either a complete blockage or a significant though stable narrowing of the blood vessel. The cardiologist probably prescribed some heart medications and cautioned against excessive physical exertion. Apparently, a period of watchful waiting with careful observation of further symptoms seemed appropriate or necessary for scheduling the surgery." Conversation with the author, July 17, 2024.

115. According to Sam Palpant, "this procedure was apparently another coronary angiogram, which suggests a significant time interval between the studies. This second test appears to have revealed new blood vessels (medically called 'angiogenesis') or enlargement of smaller blood vessels around the blocked artery to provide another pathway for blood-flow to the heart muscle." Palpant notes that "the circulation of the heart is built with the possibility of enlarging certain pathways when one is gradually blocked. This is not an uncommon experience but is nevertheless significant." Palpant explained that "it takes time for this kind of thing to happen, which is why the cardiologist was apparently surprised. It altered the standard surgical plan that had been in place." Conversation with the author, July 17, 2024.

116. From a theological standpoint, Oscar Knutson's story illustrates that divine healing is not only accomplished through immediate physical intervention by God but also occurs through his own marvelous design in the physiology of his creation to bring restoration and repair. Sam Palpant noted that, in the natural world, parallel examples can be seen in a river delta in which one stream is blocked and other streams enlarge around it, or in a tree in which one branch dies and others enlarge around it to fill in the gap. While perhaps not as flashy as immediate divine interventions, these more organic ways in which healing occurs are no less praiseworthy. They reflect the amazing goodness of God and his incredible design of the human body, not to mention the magnificence of God's whole created order.

117. Jerry Sitser, "One Dead, Four Hurt in Ballard Collision," unidentified newspaper article, Apr. 1993, courtesy of Bernice M. Fergus. On the testimony of multiple witnesses,

promptly taken to the hospital to receive medical attention. Over the next couple days, family members recall him asking, "Where's my Marie?" repeatedly, before his daughter, Fern, son, Lloyd, and a local minister visited Oscar together and broke the news of Marie's death.[118] It was an enormous blow. Oscar and Marie had been married over sixty-eight years. "I'm ready to go to heaven," Oscar told family members who visited him in the hospital.[119]

Oscar Knutson spent a little over a week at the hospital, recovering from the accident. Family members who visited him recall that "he still had a good memory," and one of his grandsons remembers having a conversation with him about an upcoming mission trip.[120] In addition to visits from family, a Norwegian-speaking nurse on staff at the hospital would "come and sit with Oscar at the end of her shift and they would have conversations in Norwegian."[121] These conversations were filled with laughter and were evidently a great encouragement to Oscar. When Oscar was discharged from the hospital, some family members successfully advocated for him to return home with a caretaker, rather than enroll him in a nursing home.[122] On Thursday, April 22, 1993, just twelve days after the accident, Oscar died.[123] His death certificate listed various medical conditions and blunt trauma from the car accident as his cause of death, but

---

the newspaper reports that the Knutson vehicle, driven by Oscar, was responsible for the accident. The precise cause of the accident was unknown, although the most likely explanation given the description in the newspaper report is that Oscar lost control of the vehicle due to a sudden medical episode, probably a temporary loss of consciousness.

118. Unpublished family recollections of the final decades of Oscar Knutson's life, compiled by Bernice M. Fergus, 2024, Oscar M. Knutson archival collection, box 1, folder 2.

119. Unpublished family recollections of the final decades of Oscar Knutson's life, compiled by Bernice M. Fergus, 2024, Oscar M. Knutson archival collection, box 1, folder 2.

120. Unpublished family recollections of the final decades of Oscar Knutson's life, compiled by Bernice M. Fergus, 2024, Oscar M. Knutson archival collection, box 1, folder 2.

121. Unpublished family recollections of the final decades of Oscar Knutson's life, compiled by Bernice M. Fergus, 2024, Oscar M. Knutson archival collection, box 1, folder 2.

122. Unpublished family recollections of the final decades of Oscar Knutson's life, compiled by Bernice M. Fergus, 2024, Oscar M. Knutson archival collection, box 1, folder 2.

123. Oscar M. Knutson, Certificate of Death, 1993, Washington State Digital Archives.

multiple grandchildren hold that Oscar ultimately died of a broken heart, missing his beloved Marie.[124]

---

124. Oscar M. Knutson, Certificate of Death, 1993, Washington State Digital Archives; unpublished family recollections of the final decades of Oscar Knutson's life, compiled by Bernice M. Fergus, 2024, Oscar M. Knutson archival collection, box 1, folder 2. According to Oscar Knutson's death certificate, an autopsy was performed. Sam Palpant stated that the death certificate "shows the immediate cause of death were bilateral pulmonary emboli, that is, blot clots in both lungs. These clots came from clots in the veins, known in medical parlance as deep venous thrombosis, which was caused by the blunt trauma of the car accident and subsequent inactivity." Conversation with the author, July 17, 2024.

Conclusion

SPIRITUAL BIOGRAPHY UTILIZES HISTORY as a means of doing theology and thus illuminates the importance of history for the Christian theological tradition. It also reveals the value of history in working out relationship with the triune God on a personal level and in families and local church communities. In the final decades of his life, Oscar Knutson became very interested in history. In 1983, he wrote and compiled an unpublished booklet of family history called "The Knutson Family Tree: 1766–1983."[1] Featuring some detailed anecdotes from his early life as well as extensive genealogical information, Knutson printed a copy for each of his grandchildren. Knutson believed it important to document family history and to pass this heritage along to his descendants.

Oscar Knutson's interest in history preceded his work on "The Knutson Family Tree." As mentioned in the concluding chapter, Knutson published a book in 1979 or 1980 entitled *His Loving Care*, which contained significant recollections and reflections on his life and ministry. More than just an autobiographical work, Knutson intended the book to be a testimony to the goodness and faithfulness of God, who "watches over His own."[2] Although the stories shared were indeed the Knutsons', a closer examination of the whole book reveals that it was not Oscar or Marie but God himself, who was the primary character. Oscar's view of history was, in this way, evangelical and even hagiographical in nature.[3] Oscar understood the

---

1. Oscar Knutson, "Knutson Family Tree, 1766–1983," 1–2, Oscar M. Knutson archival collection, box 2, folder 7.

2. Knutson, *His Loving Care*, 6.

3. Here the term *evangelical* is used exclusively in a theological manner. It designates the centrality of the gospel and evangelistic focus. There is no political disposition or affiliation implied. The term *hagiographical*, meanwhile, is used to reference the theological conviction of early Christian literature on saints—literature that has since been dubbed *hagiography*—which understands the saints as sharing in the divine life of the

main purpose of history to be a means by which to tell the story of God's redemptive mission in and through his children and to invite others into that redemption which is found in Jesus. For Oscar, *His Loving Care* was service rendered to God for the furthering of his kingdom. More than that, Oscar's telling of his own life as a participation in the life and mission of God was also an act of worship.

Oscar Knutson's perspective on history—illustrated in *His Loving Care* and buttressed by "The Knutson Family Tree"—reflects a profound spiritual truth: doing history can be a highly theological, and even liturgical, venture. By extension, doing history—along with the related subjects of autobiography and biography—is a means of doing theology. From an academic standpoint, history and theology are different disciplines, with different methodological processes, different elements, and different end results. Yet Knutson, who was not a historian nor a theologian in the classical sense, identified that there is an important intersection between history and theology, with important ramifications for the church presently, not just in the past.

Within the field of theology, spiritual biography is a genre largely filled with opportunity for further academic engagement. Even so, two contemporary scholars—Stephen J. Plant and John D. Barbour—have explored the connection between history and theology. Although they do not say so expressly, their conclusions invite further scholarly conversation about spiritual biography. In his article "The Theological Role of Biography," theologian Stephen Plant outlines the historical use of biography within the Christian theological tradition, acknowledges its decline during the twentieth century, and offers suggestions as to how biography may continue to be of theological value to Christians presently.[4] Plant notes that the early centuries of church history are filled with examples of writings about the saints—for example, St. Gregory of Nyssa's *Life of Moses* and St. Athanasius of Alexandria's *Life of St. Antony*.[5] Plant observed that such writings were often composed to provide an example of holiness for the church, not

---

Father, the Son, and the Holy Spirit, thus making the triune God the "main character" of the story, rather than the saint themselves. No derogatory meaning is intended by the term *hagiographical*.

4. Plant, "Theological Role of Biography," 164.

5. Plant, "Theological Role of Biography," 165.

to mention to serve an apologetic purpose.[6] Most significantly, the saints featured in such writings were understood to be holy and faithful people because their lives shared in the life of the triune God.[7]

By the medieval period of church history, literature concerning the saints was ubiquitously used in a devotional manner and contributed to the practice of saints on earth seeking the intercessions of saints in heaven.[8] The devotional and intercessory utilization of the "life of saints" literature became highly disputed during the Protestant Reformation, however, and even more so during the Enlightenment period which succeeded it.[9] Plant notes that in 1631, the term *hagiography* was coined in England as a pejorative term, challenging long-held confidence in the classical method of sacred biography.[10] Protestants like John Foxe—who published *Foxe's Book of Martyrs* in 1663—went so far as to begin using biographical sketches of the saints as a rallying cry to resist the Roman Catholic Church and even as "a weapon for the Protestant cause."[11] Plant argues that by the twentieth century, the influence of Marxism, Freudianism, and Feminism, along with other similar philosophical-social movements, threw the genre of biography into "an identity crisis," which had ramifications for the church.[12] Since the twentieth century, there has been less formal emphasis on the theological role of biography, though Plant suggests that biography nevertheless maintains theological value for the church. Plant affirms biography's contribution to church history, as well as its emphasis on lived experience within the context of faith.[13] Plant also holds that biography holds devotional and theological value, although he suggests that "the earlier tendency of using saints' lives to describe a life lived towards perfection is being replaced with biography that focuses on what it is like to remain faithful in the midst of the intrinsic messiness of human life."[14]

6. Plant, "Theological Role of Biography," 166.

7. Plant, "Theological Role of Biography," 165.

8. Plant, "Theological Role of Biography," 167. Here it should be noted that Plant is speaking primarily, if not entirely, of Western church history.

9. Plant, "Theological Role of Biography," 167.

10. Plant, "Theological Role of Biography," 167. Lacking a better term, I follow Thomas Heffernan's use of the term *sacred biography* to describe the medieval literature concerning the saints. Heffernan, *Sacred Biography*, 16.

11. Plant, "Theological Role of Biography," 167.

12. Plant, "Theological Role of Biography," 168.

13. Plant, "Theological Role of Biography," 169–70, 172–73.

14. Plant, "Theological Role of Biography," 171.

In his article "Autobiography, Biography, and Theological Questioning," John Barbour analyzes the genres of autobiography and biography—which he calls *life writing*—as a means of doing theology.[15] Focused on unpacking the theological content found in life writing, Barbour observes that autobiography and biography tell stories rather than present systematic theology.[16] As a result, life writing dramatizes dynamic theological themes such as searching for God and navigating between assurance and doubt, affirmation and questioning.[17] Barbour notes that because life writing captures people's religious convictions and spiritual experiences, it often presents theological questions and convictions that do not always conform neatly to established doctrinal norms or ecclesial structures, even if the author or subject desires conformity.[18] This common tension raises questions of authority. Do personal experiences hold more authority than official ecclesiastical dogma? Does the former inform or nuance the latter? Should the latter always override the former?[19]

In addition to noting the tension regarding authority, Barbour observes that life writing often features a tension between a desire to write one's story in accordance with accepted theological and literary norms—say, following the traditional elements of Christian conversion narrative—and an equally powerful desire to tell one's own unique experiences.[20] After all, if writing one's life is simply a rehashing of someone else's story, why do it? But then, if one's life differs enough from others' stories, is it even worth telling?[21] Barbour notes that, traditionally, life writing justifies itself by claiming to offer benefits to readers, generally didactically.[22] However, twentieth-century cultural developments have offered life writing a more personal justification, that is, the benefit of "defining a unique personal

---

15. Barbour, "Autobiography, Biography, and Theological Questioning," 2. Barbour mostly focuses on the Christian theological tradition, but not exclusively. Even so, his analysis of theological content within biographical and autobiographical literature is helpful for considering the content of expressly Christian spiritual biography and its engagement with elements of related literature.

16. Barbour, "Autobiography, Biography, and Theological Questioning," 2–3.

17. Barbour, "Autobiography, Biography, and Theological Questioning," 2–3, 6.

18. Barbour, "Autobiography, Biography, and Theological Questioning," 9–11.

19. Barbour, "Autobiography, Biography, and Theological Questioning," 11–12.

20. Barbour, "Autobiography, Biography, and Theological Questioning," 10.

21. Barbour, "Autobiography, Biography, and Theological Questioning," 10.

22. Barbour, "Autobiography, Biography, and Theological Questioning," 9–10, 14.

Conclusion

identity," including spiritual experiences and religious convictions.[23] Regardless, Barbour asserts that life writing features theological content for a theological purpose, even if that purpose may vary depending on the work.[24] According to Barbour, the common theme among theological life writing is that it seeks to enact one spiritual journey in literary form for the purpose of encouraging readers to take action and do some spiritual journeying of their own.[25]

Like Stephen Plant, Oscar Knutson clearly understood biography to hold tremendous theological value, especially from a devotional, and even apologetic, standpoint. In *His Loving Care*, Knutson shared his own story because he hoped it would serve as a testimony to the grace and goodness of God. The title itself discloses this perspective. Knutson's theological commentary within the text of *His Loving Care*, however, indicates expansion beyond Plant's suggestions as to the value of biography to theology. Knutson expressly wrote *His Loving Care* to call others to deeper faith in Christ, but he also wrote his story as an act of worship. Following the scriptural pattern found in various psalms which recount the history of God's people for the purpose of offering praise to God for his redeeming activities in and through them, Knutson also narrated his own life to give glory to God.[26]

Oscar Knutson's own use of autobiography in *His Loving Care* aligns with multiple points articulated by John Barbour. Knutson wrote his own life story for a particular theological purpose—to call others to trust in Jesus and follow him faithfully, and to bring glory to God. Furthermore, Knutson's theology—both that of the classical Pentecostal theological tradition and that which was more particularly his own—reflected something of an interplay between conformity to, and departure from, the broader Christian theological tradition. Knutson believed in the Holy Trinity, the centrality of Jesus, the authority of Scripture, the importance of the church, and other fundamental Christian tenets. Yet some of his convictions on ecclesiology, sacramentality, liturgical form, and the use of creeds, among other matters, were innovative in comparison to traditional interpretations and norms. In accordance with Barbour's observations, Knutson's life story, as presented in *His Loving Care*, is dynamic and compelling. It also features significant influence of other people within Knutson's own story. Contrary

---

23. Barbour, "Autobiography, Biography, and Theological Questioning," 10.
24. Barbour, "Autobiography, Biography, and Theological Questioning," 6–7.
25. Barbour, "Autobiography, Biography, and Theological Questioning," 8–9, 16–18.
26. See Pss 105, 106, 135, and 136.

to many examples of life writing that Barbour discusses, however, *His Loving Care* is not filled with theological wavering or concern.²⁷ It features robust spiritual conviction, but not necessarily spiritual vulnerability, at least not in the way of narrating much personal doubt or questioning. Finally, while Barbour notes that other examples of life writing include tension between personal experience and a larger story, Knutson resolves any such conflict by narrating his own experiences in such a way that theologically contextualizes them squarely within God's greater story.

Among other contributions, Oscar Knutson's spiritual biography makes a significant contribution to Pentecostal church history. Knutson's story is, of course, located within the broader historical and theological context of North American Pentecostalism, which has in the last two decades alone received tremendous scholarship by historians and theologians such as Grant Wacker, Douglas Jacobsen, Allan Heaton Anderson, Stanley M. Burgess, Adam Stewart, Peter Althouse, Cecil M. Robeck Jr., Roger G. Robins, Wolfgang Vondey, and many others.²⁸ The significance of Knutson's story, however, is that it focuses on the incarnational ministry done on the local level by Pentecostals like Knutson and his various ministry companions— Joseph Lantz, Jack Nelson, Annie Applegate, A. D. Guth, Lee Henson, and so on. Much scholarship has been devoted to major Pentecostal centers such as Los Angeles and Chicago, and yet the Holy Spirit is also present and active in comparatively smaller communities, such as Okanogan, Washington; Estherville, Iowa; and Huron, South Dakota.

In addition to the various local communities within which Oscar Knutson's ministry took place, the list of people with whom Knutson collaborated is another important contribution to Pentecostal church history. It is an extensive list, though only a handful of these ministry partners were portrayed in this spiritual biography. Following the pattern of the New Testament, Knutson clearly believed that ministry was done best in collaboration with others, and he held his coworkers in the gospel in high regard. In

---

27. One brief, although not unimportant exception, is Knutson's narration of seeking, and eventually receiving, the baptism of the Holy Spirit.

28. See Wacker, *Heaven Below*; Jacobsen, *Thinking in the Spirit*; Anderson, *To the Ends of the Earth*; Burgess and van der Maas, *New International Dictionary*; Stewart, *Handbook of Pentecostal Christianity*; Althouse and Waddell, *Perspectives in Pentecostal Eschatologies*; Robeck, *Azusa Street Mission and Revival*; Robins, *Pentecostalism in America*; Vondey, *Pentecostal Theology*.

Conclusion

The Glorious Church, a late 1940s pamphlet which outlined Knutson's ecclesiological convictions, Knutson wrote of one ministry coworker whom he deemed to be of particular importance. Although he did not identify the man by name, Knutson's comments are striking:

> For years I labored for the Lord in a field where another man had laid the foundation. He was a spiritual man, and of sound judgment, and I felt a deep respect for him. I gladly received his advice and admonition. I obeyed what he might suggest, not blindly, but because I felt it was sound. To me this man served as an apostle although that title was never used, nor any other title, nor was ever a word mentioned in regards to it, but it was there just the same. Possibly he does not recognize it himself, but I recognized his calling of God.[29]

Oscar Knutson's reflections on the man whom he recognized to be an apostle, in addition to other comments throughout *The Glorious Church* and other writings about the necessity of ministers being sound in doctrine and character, indicate that Knutson was thoughtful and intentional about those with whom he did ministry. He cared that it was the Lord who called them to ministry and the Lord who equipped and empowered them for it. Anyone who tried to set themselves up as a pastor or evangelist without God was missing the mark. Although only God knows people's hearts, Knutson sought to be a good discerner of doctrine and character with regard to potential ministry partners, both for the sake of honoring God and for the success of his own ministry work.

Oscar Knutson's high degree of collaboration in ministry is significant, both for its contribution to Pentecostal church history and for illustrating yet another important element about spiritual biography as a genre, that one person's life-story illuminates not simply their own story but also the stories of those with whom they came in contact. This in mind, it seems fitting to include some brief biographical sketches to conclude the stories of some of Knutson's most significant ministry partners.

Rev. Joseph Lantz, who had planted the first Pentecostal church in Great Falls, Montana, pastored the congregation until September 1928, when he turned over pastoral leadership to his son-in-law, Rev. William Paul Jones.[30] Having resigned to pursue other ministry work, Reverend Lantz kept permanent residence in Great Falls and did significant preaching

---

29. Knutson, *Glorious Church*, 33.
30. Roset et al., *Assemblies of God in Montana*, 40.

and teaching in various local contexts.[31] He also established the Mission Covenant Church in Cook, Minnesota, and an Assembly of God church in Grand Junction, Colorado.[32] In 1937, Reverend Lantz formally affiliated with the Assemblies of God as an evangelist.[33] After his wife died in 1939, Reverend Lantz continued pursuing ministry, although poor health often inhibited his ministry activities.[34] Toward the end of his life, Reverend Lantz published a handful of small theological pamphlets, including *The Baptism of the Holy Spirit: Is It Scriptural?*[35] He died in his home in November 1952, at age eighty-three, after a short illness.[36]

After getting married, Brother Jack Nelson—who later became known as Rev. J. C. Nelson—continued doing evangelistic ministry in the Seattle vicinity in the 1920s. In 1926 or 1927, Nelson became the pastor of the Pentecostal Mission at 1215 Jackson Street in Seattle, although for a few years he also continued traveling locally for Pentecostal revival meetings.[37] Some of Nelson's evangelistic work led to the establishment of an Assembly of God church in Enumclaw, Washington, in 1929.[38] Unfortunately, Nelson and his wife Jessie seem to have separated in the early 1930s, but

---

31. "Pioneer Montana Minister Passes," unidentified obituary clipping for Joseph Lantz, 1952, in "Deceased Ministers—Lantz, Joseph," archival record file, Flower Pentecostal Heritage Center.

32. "Pioneer Montana Minister Passes," unidentified obituary clipping for Joseph Lantz, 1952, in "Deceased Ministers—Lantz, Joseph," archival record file, Flower Pentecostal Heritage Center.

33. Joseph Lantz, ordination papers, in "Deceased Ministers—Lantz, Joseph," archival record file, Flower Pentecostal Heritage Center.

34. *Great Falls Leader*, "Funeral Pending," 10; "Pioneer Montana Minister Passes," unidentified obituary clipping for Joseph Lantz, 1952, in "Deceased Ministers—Lantz, Joseph," archival record file, Flower Pentecostal Heritage Center.

35. *Great Falls Leader*, "Funeral Pending," 10; "Pioneer Montana Minister Passes," unidentified obituary clipping for Joseph Lantz, 1952, in "Deceased Ministers—Lantz, Joseph," archival record file, Flower Pentecostal Heritage Center; Lantz, *Is the Baptism of the Holy Spirit Scriptural?*

36. Joseph Lantz, State of Montana, Certificate of Death, 1952, Ancestry.com; William Paul Jones to J. Roswell Flower, Nov. 26, 1952, in "Deceased Ministers—Lantz, Joseph," archival record file, Flower Pentecostal Heritage Center.

37. *News Tribune*, "Pentecostal Christian Assembly" (Dec. 13, 1924), 5; *News Tribune*, "Pentecostal Christian Assembly" (Feb. 7, 1925), 9; *Daily Herald*, "Evangelist Jack Nelson," 6; R. L. Polk & Co., *Seattle City Directory, 1926*; R. L. Polk & Co., *Seattle City Directory, 1927*.

38. Tannenberg, *Let Light Shine Out*, 65.

Conclusion

Jack nevertheless continued his pastoral ministry in Seattle.[39] In the mid to late 1930s, Reverend Nelson's Pentecostal mission moved from its Jackson Street location to 416½ 12th Street South.[40] It also expanded its ministry scope to be not simply a church but also a home for the elderly. It ultimately changed its name to "Calvary Pentecostal Mission and Faith Home," and later, "Calvary Pentecostal Mission and Old Peoples Home."[41] Reverend Nelson held pastoral leadership until around 1962, when poor health forced his resignation.[42] He died in November 1963, at the age of seventy-six.[43]

Rev. Annie Applegate maintained her Assemblies of God ordination credentials as an evangelist for the rest of her life. She also continued pastoring the Pentecostal mission in Billings, Montana.[44] Throughout her ministry, Reverend Applegate was driven by an acute eschatological urgency.[45] Jesus was coming soon, and there were souls to save! Reverend Applegate also seems to have been rather attuned to spiritual matters—perhaps more than most. Evidently, she often viewed her ministry work as spiritual warfare and may have been something of a Pentecostal mystic.[46] After three decades of ministry, she died of a heart attack in June 1935, at age sixty-three.[47]

---

39. Jack Nelson's wife Jessie is not listed with him in the 1930 Federal Census, although Jack is noted as having marital status. Jessie is not listed with Jack in the 1932 Seattle city directory, is back in 1933, and is absent again in 1934. Although Jack is listed as married in the 1940 Federal Census, his status changes to "separated" in the 1950 Federal Census.

40. R. L. Polk & Co., *Seattle City Directory, 1935*; R. L. Polk & Co., *Seattle City Directory, 1937*.

41. R. L. Polk & Co., *Seattle City Directory, 1937*; Jacob Charley Nelson, World War II Draft Registration Card, 1942, Ancestry.com.

42. R. L. Polk & Co., *Seattle City Directory, 1960*; R. L. Polk & Co., *Seattle City Directory, 1961–62*.

43. Jack C. Nelson, Certificate of Death, 1963, Washington State Digital Archives.

44. Ordination documents, in "Deceased Minsters—Applegate, Annie Belle," archival record file, Flower Pentecostal Heritage Center.

45. Applegate, "Reports from the Field: Billings, Mont.," 12; Applegate, "New Work in Wyoming," 12; "Fighting the Good Fight," 12.

46. Applegate, "Billings, Mon.," 14; Applegate and Applegate, "Reports," 8; Applegate, "Jesus Is Coming Soon," 8. In this latter article, Reverend Applegate described a mystical experience that she had on November 30, 1920, in which she had a vision of "a fleecy, white cloud" with drops of blood on the outer edges and the words *Coming Soon* in gold letters at the center of the cloud. In addition to the vision, various eschatological passages of Scripture were brought to mind, both during the event and afterward.

47. *Billings Gazette*, "Local Woman Dies of Heart Attack," 5.

In late 1931, Rev. Henry G. Schmid became the pastor of the German-speaking Pentecostal church in Huron, South Dakota. Although formerly an Assemblies of God church, the congregation existed as an independent Pentecostal church under Reverend Schmid's pastoral leadership. "We are independent, preaching the full gospel in all its original purity," a local newspaper advertisement for church services declared.[48] In addition to regular prayer meetings and Sunday services—held in both English and German—the church participated in a local jail ministry as well as a local radio ministry. In February 1932, Reverend Schmid welcomed an evangelistic visit from Rev. A. D. Guth, who appears to have stayed and held revival meetings for a time.[49] Although beloved by his Huron congregation, Reverend Schmid served as pastor for less than a year. He died in August 1932, at age sixty-three.[50]

After assisting the Knutsons with the establishment of the Full Gospel Mission in Estherville, Iowa, in January 1932, Rev. A. D. Guth, who had based himself near family in Hutchinson, Kansas, spent the next two decades ministering in many communities across various states, mostly in the Midwest.[51] When he was not traveling, Reverend Guth also did ministry in his own Hutchinson community.[52] In May 1934, Reverend Guth held revival meetings at Pleasant Valley Church in O'Neill, Nebraska.[53] In March 1935, he held services at Wells Gospel Tabernacle in Wells, Minnesota, pastored by Rev. Sanford Carlsen, a former member of the Pentecostal community in Estherville, Iowa.[54] In August 1937, Reverend Guth visited Estherville itself, about six months after Rev. Linus Heidt's resignation to pursue ministry in nearby Spirit Lake, Iowa.[55] In late 1938, Reverend Guth

---

48. *Daily Plainsman*, "Pentecostal Mission," 8; *Daily Plainsman*, "Pentescotal Mission [sic]," 3.

49. *Daily Plainsman*, "Pentescotal Mission [sic]," 3.

50. Find a Grave, "Henry G. Schmid."

51. R. L. Polk & Co., *Hutchinson City Directory, 1933*; R. L. Polk & Co., *Hutchinson City Directory, 1937*; R. L. Polk & Co., *Hutchinson City Directory, 1947*.

52. *Hutchinson News*, "Full Gospel Mission (Pentecostal)," 7; *Hutchinson News*, "Full Gospel Mission," 7.

53. *Frontier and Holt County Independent*, "Revival Meetings," 1.

54. *Wells Mirror*, "Wells Gospel Tabernacle" (Mar. 14, 1935), 4; *Wells Mirror*, "Wells Gospel Tabernacle" (Mar. 21, 1935), 6. When Rev. A. D. Guth and the Knutson family were delayed by inclement weather conditions, Sanford Carlsen led the very first formal church service for the Estherville church, on January 2, 1932. *Calvary Gospel Assembly*, 7.

55. *Estherville Daily News*, "Gospel Mission," 2; *Estherville Enterprise*, "Gospel

Conclusion

and Reverend Heidt returned to Estherville to co-officiate the ordination service of Lawrence Guge, who subsequently pastored the Full Gospel Mission until 1954.[56] In the late 1930s, Reverend Guth also collaborated with the Estherville community to plant a Pentecostal fellowship in Dry Run, Indiana.[57] In 1941, Reverend Guth visited Sunny Side Church in Sioux Falls, South Dakota, and in 1942, he visited Salem Heights Community Church in Salem, Oregon.[58] Reverend Guth appears to have made at least two evangelistic visits to Addielee, Oklahoma, between 1946 and 1947.[59] Tragically, in February 1948, Reverend Guth fell down some stairs at the church building of a Pentecostal fellowship in Indianapolis, Indiana, and died as a result of his injuries. He was sixty-six years old.[60]

Having received pastoral leadership of the Pentecostal community in Windom, Minnesota, from Oscar Knutson in 1932, Rev. Clarence W. Hart and his wife Annie apparently continued their ministry work in Minnesota for a couple years, before returning to the Pacific Northwest in 1934.[61] In July 1934, Reverend Hart formalized his ministry credentials by affiliating with the Assemblies of God denomination, and although he had returned to pastor in Washington State, he kept his ministerial address in Mountain Lake, Minnesota, a town located about twelve miles northeast of Windom.[62] For about a year, Reverend Hart pastored Grace Full Gospel Church in Coulee City, Washington, and reportedly left in August 1935 to pastor Grace Gospel Church in Cashmere, Washington.[63] In 1937, Reverend Hart moved back to the Midwest to become the pastor of the Full Gospel Tabernacle in St. James, Minnesota, and he held this pastorate until around 1941.[64] Between 1942 and 1943, Reverend Hart continued doing ministry

---

Mission," 2; *Calvary Gospel Assembly*, 10.

56. *Calvary Gospel Assembly*, 11.

57. *Calvary Gospel Assembly*, 10.

58. *Argus-Leader*, "Sunny Side," 5; *Statesman Journal*, "Salem Heights Community," 7.

59. *Stilwell Democrat-Journal*, "Bro. A. D. Guth," 7; *Westville Record*, "Bro. A. D. Guth," 6.

60. Find a Grave, "Rev Aaron D. Guth," obituary; Aaron D. Guth, Montana State Board of Health, Certificate of Death, 1948, Ancestry.com.

61. *Coulee City Dispatch*, "Rev. Hart Leaves Today for Cashmere," 7.

62. Assemblies of God General Council Ministers Directories, 1934–35, Consortium of Pentecostal Archives.

63. *Coulee City Dispatch*, "Rev. Hart Leaves Today for Cashmere," 7; *Spokane Chronicle*, "C. W. Hart," 7.

64. Assemblies of God General Council Ministers Directories, 1937–41, Consortium

work in Minnesota as an Assemblies of God pastor.[65] He subsequently moved to Seattle and apparently discontinued his formal affiliation with the Assemblies of God. In Seattle, Reverend Hart assisted his old friend, Rev. Jack C. Nelson, with pastoring the Calvary Pentecostal Faith Mission from 1944 until his death in March 1947 at age fifty-three.[66]

Rev. Frank Edgemon continued pastoring in Bridgeport, Washington, from 1933 until 1935, when he left to plant a Pentecostal church in Oroville, Washington.[67] Reverend Edgemon formally affiliated with the Assemblies of God in 1936 and continued pastoring in Oroville until 1941.[68] Notably, in 1939, Reverend Edgemon's daughter Lois married Pentecostal evangelist Cecil E. Grice of Orting, Washington.[69] Tragically, she died in May 1943, but her husband Cecil's active evangelistic ministry over the next several decades eventually became known on the national level.[70] In 1941, Rev. Frank Edgemon and his wife Mildred briefly returned to Bridgeport before moving to Spanaway, Washington in 1942.[71] There, Reverend Edgemon pastored the Full Gospel Tabernacle for about a year. Reverend Edgemon pastored the Assembly of God church in Pomeroy, Washington, from 1943 to 1945, the Assembly of God church in Cashmere, Washington, from 1948 to 1950, and the Pomeroy Assembly of God again, from 1951

---

of Pentecostal Archives.

65. Assemblies of God General Council Ministers Directories, 1942–43, Consortium of Pentecostal Archives; Clarence W. Hart, World War II Draft Registration Card, 1942, Ancestry.com.

66. *Seattle Star*, "Rev. Clarence W. Hart," 15; Clarence W. Hart, Washington State Department of Health, Certificate of Death, 1947, Ancestry.com.

67. "Fifteenth Census of the United States, 1940," Ancestry.com; Tannenberg, *Let Light Shine Out*, 95.

68. Assemblies of God General Council Ministers Directories, 1936–41, Consortium of Pentecostal Archives.

69. *News Tribune*, "Marriage Licenses," 6; Tannenberg, *Let Light Shine Out*, 59.

70. Lois Irene Edgemon Grice, Certificate of Death, 1943, Washington State Digital Archives; *Santa Rosa Republican*, "Evangelistic Meetings," 9; *Toronto Star*, advertisement for Pentecostal meetings held by evangelist Cecil Grice, 8; *Kitsap Sun*, "Revival Singer Slates Series," 2; *San Bernardino County Sun*, "Singer-Evangelist to Hold 5 Meetings," 12; *Woodward County Republican*, "Church Holds Services Here," 3; *News Tribune*, "Rev. Cecil Grice Will Speak," 4; *Tri-City Herald*, advertisement for visit by evangelist Cecil Grice, 10; Cecil Eugene Grice, Certificate of Death, 1993, Washington State Digital Archives.

71. Assemblies of God General Council Ministers Directories, 1941–42, Consortium of Pentecostal Archives.

Conclusion

to 1952.[72] In 1953, Reverend Edgemon moved to Ellensburg, Washington, where he continued doing ministry work until his death in March 1954, at age sixty-one.[73]

After planting what became the Assembly of God church in Kittitas, Washington, in fall 1934, Tom Overland turned over pastoral leadership to Rev. Ralph Baker, preferring to raise his family and continue his profession as a baker in Ellensburg rather than pursue Pentecostal ministry work exclusively.[74] In October 1937, Overland collaborated with Pentecostal pastor Rev. Leslie Davis to hold three weeks of evangelistic meetings in Othello, Washington.[75] Shortly thereafter, Overland and his family moved to Othello and spent the next two years trying to plant a church, although these efforts did not come to fruition.[76] In mid 1940 the family moved to Yakima, Washington, where Tom again took up the baking profession. The Overlands lived in Yakima for about a year before the death of Tressie, Tom's wife, in July 1941.[77] A single dad, Tom remained in Yakima with his children for the next few years. Notably, on his World War II Draft Registration Card from 1942, Tom listed Rev. R. F. Ashworth as the person who would always know his address.[78] Reverend Ashworth was also listed as a witness on some additional naturalization paperwork which Overland submitted in 1943.[79] Reverend Ashworth, who later moved to Seattle and in the late 1940s served as pastor of Evangel Temple and one of the main

---

72. Assemblies of God General Council Ministers Directories, 1943–45, 1948–52, Consortium of Pentecostal Archives.

73. Assemblies of God General Council Ministers Directories, 1953–54, Consortium of Pentecostal Archives; Franklin Ross Edgemon, Certificate of Death, 1954, Washington State Digital Archives.

74. *Kittitas Assembly of God Church History: 50th Anniversary, 1937–1987*, compiled by Church History Committee and Pastor Gary R. Fountain, n.p., in "*Churches*—General II" archival file, Ellensburg Public Library.

75. Tannenberg, *Let Light Shine Out*, 115.

76. Tannenberg, *Let Light Shine Out*, 115.

77. *Courier-Herald*, "Word reached the valley," 4; Tressie Gladys Overland, Certificate of Death, 1941, Washington State Digital Archives.

78. Thomas Overland, World War II Draft Registration Card, 1942, Ancestry.com. Admittedly, the registration card says "Rev. R. S. Ashworth," but other sources indicate this was a typist error and that the pastor was in fact Rev. R. F. Ashworth. Assemblies of God General Council Ministers Directories, 1941–43, Consortium of Pentecostal Archives; Tannenberg, *Let Light Shine Out*, 196.

79. Thomas Overland, "Petition for Naturalization," US naturalization paperwork, 1942–1943, Ancestry.com.

coordinators of the United Full Gospel Crusade—for which Oscar Knutson published his first songbook—pastored in Yakima in the early 1940s and served on the Board of Presbytery for the Northwest District of the Assemblies of God between 1941 and 1944.[80] In 1944, Tom Overland remarried.[81] In 1945, he lived in Goldendale, Washington, with his children and new wife Mildred (née Record) and served as pastor of the local Assembly of God church.[82] By 1947, the Overlands returned to Yakima, with Tom again working as a baker.[83] Except for another brief period in Othello in 1955, Overland spent the next three decades in Yakima, working as a baker and likely participating in the local Pentecostal community.[84] He died in May 1981, at age eighty-three.[85]

After assisting Oscar Knutson in Kettle Falls, Washington, in 1938, Rev. Lee Henson returned to Seattle to pastor the Full Gospel Mission on Ballard Avenue. Although he is missing from the next few Seattle city directories, his presence in the 1943–1944 city directory as pastor of the Ballard Avenue mission—then called the "Full Gospel Mission House of Prayer"—suggests that he had been serving in this pastoral capacity for the last several years.[86] Significantly, on his 1942 World War II Draft Registration Card, Reverend Henson listed Oscar Knutson as the person who would always know his address.[87] Knutson always held Reverend Henson in high regard, and the feelings were mutual. Unfortunately, references to Reverend Henson in city directories and other historical records seem to be scarce for the next few decades.[88] In early 1962, Reverend Henson moved to

80. Ashworth et al., *Crusade Songs* (Seattle), inside cover; Ashworth et al., *Crusade Songs* (Seattle/Estherville), inside cover, back cover; Tannenberg, *Let Light Shine Out*, 196.

81. Thomas Overland and Mildred Record, State of Washington, Certificate of Marriage, 1944, Ancestry.com.

82. *Goldendale Sentinel*, "Assembly of God Church" (Mar. 1, 1945), 2; *Goldendale Sentinel*, "Assembly of God Church" (Apr. 26, 1945), 9.

83. *Spokesman-Review*, "Retail bakery for sale," 28.

84. *Spokane Chronicle*, "Bakery in fast growing Columbia basin town," 22; *Spokesman-Review*, "All around baker," 33; *Longview Daily News*, "They're Engaged," 5; Thomas Overland, Certificate of Death, 1981, Washington State Digital Archives.

85. Thomas Overland, Certificate of Death, 1981, Washington State Digital Archives.

86. R. L. Polk & Co., *Seattle City Directory, 1938*; R. L. Polk & Co., *Seattle City Directory*, 1943–44.

87. Lee Elliot Henson, World War II Draft Registration Card, 1942, Ancestry.com.

88. Although there may be another explanation for the lack of available historical records concerning Reverend Henson between the 1940s and the 1960s, racism should not be ruled out as a possibility. Reverend Henson was a black man, and racism—especially

Conclusion

Walla Walla, Washington, where he served as pastor of the local Full Gospel Mission for about four months. He died in May 1962 at age eighty-one, probably of a heart attack.[89]

Rev. C. Albert Moseid continued pastoring the Ballard Pentecostal Tabernacle in Seattle until June 1947, when he resigned to pursue other ministry work.[90] In September 1948, Reverend Moseid accepted a call to pastor Bethel Temple in Ferndale, Washington.[91] As aforementioned, Reverend Moseid continued to collaborate in ministry with Oscar Knutson during the 1940s and even officiated the wedding of Knutson's daughter, Fern, in October 1948.[92] In addition to his pastoral leadership of Bethel Temple in Ferndale, which he held until mid 1951, Reverend Moseid remained an active member of the Independent Assemblies of God. Along with his older brother, Rev. John Moseid, colleague Oscar Knutson, and several other Pentecostal ministers, Rev. Albert Moseid attended a fellowship convention in Los Angeles in February 1950.[93] In mid 1951, Reverend Moseid left Ferndale to pursue evangelistic ministry.[94] He moved to Minnesota and remained a Pentecostal evangelist until his death in April 1958, at age sixty-five.[95]

Rev. John W. Moseid, the older brother of Rev. Albert Moseid, pastored Bethel Pentecostal Assembly in Tacoma, Washington, for about ten years, having initially accepted the pastorate in 1940.[96] Rev. John Moseid's second wife, Mabel, died in December 1945.[97] Reverend Moseid appears

during that time period—often excluded people of color from city directories and other such historical records.

89. Lee Henson, Certificate of Death, 1962, Washington State Digital Archives. The precise cause of death was not determined, as no autopsy was performed.

90. "Rec. C. A. Moseid Resigns [sic]," 8.

91. "Rev. C. A. Moseid," 15.

92. *Okanogan Independent*, "Miss Fern Knutson, Mr. Alvin Olson," 5.

93. *Bellingham Herald*, "Bethel Temple Handmaidens," 6; *Chippewa Herald-Telegram*, "At Cadott Service," 3; Johnson and Johnson, "Convention in Los Angeles," 6.

94. *Chippewa Herald-Telegram*, "At Cadott Service," 3.

95. *Chippewa Herald-Telegram*, "Cadott Gospel Tabernacle," 3; *Minneapolis Star*, "Glad Tidings Church," 4; Find a Grave, "Rev Charles Albert Moseid."

96. *Daily Herald*, "Rev. John W. Moseid," 19; *News Tribune*, "Bethel Assembly" (July 31, 1950), 2; *News Tribune*, "Bethel Assembly" (Sept. 18, 1950), 8.

97. *News Tribune*, "Mrs. John W. Moseid," 12; Mable Florence Moseid, Certificate of Death, 1945, Washington State Digital Archives. Admittedly, the death certificate for Mabel Moseid spells her name "Mable," but census records and her obituary in the newspaper spell her name as "Mabel."

to have married again in 1946 or 1947 and continued pursuing ministry with his third wife, Cora.[98] In addition to his pastoral leadership in Tacoma, Reverend Moseid remained active in the Independent Assemblies of God and, like his younger brother Albert, attended its Los Angeles convention in February 1950, along with other ministry associates, including Oscar Knutson.[99] Unfortunately, in 1948, Rev. John Moseid suffered a debilitating stroke, which largely impacted his ability to speak and preach for his final few years of formal ministry.[100] In late 1950 or early 1951, he resigned from his pastorate, and he and his wife seem to have left Tacoma around 1952.[101] By 1959, they moved to Lake Stevens, Washington, and were active in a local Assembly of God church. After a brief illness, Rev. John Moseid died in May 1965, at age seventy-four.[102]

In 1951, Rev. Andrew Teuber resigned his pastorate at the Assembly of God church in Wenatchee, Washington, and began pursuing full-time evangelistic work.[103] Basing himself in Springfield, Missouri, the headquarters of the Assemblies of God denomination, Reverend Teuber spent the rest of the 1950s holding a series of Pentecostal evangelistic campaigns in his "big tent cathedral."[104] Oscar Knutson printed songbooks and advertisements for Reverend Teuber's tent campaigns, including the "Back to the Bible Revival," a "Salvation-Healing Campaign."[105] Campaign advertisements stated that tent meetings were "For All People" and "For All Churches," and noted hundreds in attendance in various locations in Pennsylvania,

98. R. L. Polk & Co., *Tacoma City Directory, 1947*.

99. Johnson and Johnson, "Convention in Los Angeles," 6.

100. Johnson and Johnson, "Convention in Los Angeles," 6; Moseid, "Tacoma, Wash.," 11.

101. R. L. Polk & Co., *Tacoma City Directory, 1951*; R. L. Polk & Co., *Tacoma City Directory, 1953*.

102. *Daily Herald*, "Rev. John W. Moseid," 19; John W. Moseid, Certificate of Death, 1965, Washington State Digital Archives.

103. Andrew S. Teuber, ordination record cards, in "Deceased Ministers—Teuber, Andrew S.," archival record file, Flower Pentecostal Heritage Center.

104. Andrew S. Teuber, ordination record cards, in "Deceased Ministers—Teuber, Andrew S.," archival record file, Flower Pentecostal Heritage Center; various advertisements for Rev. Andrew Teuber's tent campaigns, ca. 1950s, in "Clip file, Personal papers—Teuber, Andrew S.," archival record file, Flower Pentecostal Heritage Center; advertisements for Rev. Andrew Teuber's evangelistic tent campaigns, scrapbook featuring materials printed by Oscar Knutson, courtesy of Phillip W. Knutson.

105. Advertisements for Teuber tent campaigns, scrapbook featuring materials printed by Oscar Knutson, courtesy of Phillip W. Knutson.

CONCLUSION

Nebraska, Montana, South Dakota, Washington, and other states.[106] In addition to Pentecostal preaching, the tent campaigns emphasized praying for the sick and reported many "Instant Miracles and Healings" because of "God's Miracle Working Power in Every Service."[107] In 1960, Reverend Teuber and his wife Freda moved to Sioux Falls, South Dakota, where they pastored the Assembly of God Gospel Tabernacle for nearly a decade.[108] Reverend Teuber also served briefly as assistant district superintendent for the South Dakota District of the Assemblies of God.[109] In 1969, Reverend Teuber resigned his pastorate in Sioux Falls and pursued Pentecostal evangelistic ministry throughout the 1970s.[110] He retired from formal ministry work in 1981, although he maintained his ordination status with the Assemblies of God until his death in September 1994, at age eighty-three.[111]

Rev. Andrew Teuber's older sister Letta and her husband, Rev. Harold E. Hansen, remained in Omak through the late 1940s and into the early 1950s, assisting in local ministry as needed. In late 1951, they moved to Okanogan, where Reverend Hansen accepted the pastorate of the Full Gospel Christian Assembly, which Oscar Knutson had planted in 1943. Rev. Edward Logelin, who had succeeded Knutson as pastor, had resigned to pursue evangelistic work. Reverend Hansen pastored in Okanogan until June 1956, when his declining health necessitated a move.[112] In a letter writ-

---

106. Various advertisements for Rev. Andrew Teuber's tent campaigns, ca. 1950s, in "Clip file, Personal papers—Teuber, Andrew S.," archival record file, Flower Pentecostal Heritage Center.

107. Advertisements for Teuber tent campaigns, scrapbook featuring materials printed by Oscar Knutson, courtesy of Phillip W. Knutson.

108. Andrew S. Teuber, ordination record cards, in "Deceased Ministers—Teuber, Andrew S.," archival record file, Flower Pentecostal Heritage Center; Assemblies of God General Council Church Directories, 1960–69, Consortium of Pentecostal Archives.

109. *Sioux City Journal*, "Assembly of God Church to Host Fellowship Event," 7.

110. Andrew S. Teuber, ordination record cards, in "Deceased Ministers—Teuber, Andrew S.," archival record file, Flower Pentecostal Heritage Center; Gutierrez, "Faith Is Forever Growing at First Assembly," 15.

111. Andrew S. Teuber, ordination record cards, in "Deceased Ministers—Teuber, Andrew S.," archival record file, Flower Pentecostal Heritage Center; *News-Leader*, "Andrew S. Teuber, 83," 4.

112. *Okanogan Independent*, "Full Gospel Christian Assembly" (Dec. 20, 1951); H. E. Hansen to Rev. J. Roswell Flower, June 29, 1953, in "Deceased Ministers—Hansen, H. E. (Harold E.)," archival record file, Flower Pentecostal Heritage Center; Assemblies of God General Council Ministers Directories, 1951, 1953–55, Consortium of Pentecostal Archives; *Okanogan Independent*, "H. E. Hokenson [sic] Starts Pastorate at Local Church"; Ong, *Letta in China*, 161. The first newspaper clipping listed here indicates that Rev.

ten while pastoring in Okanogan in 1953, Reverend Hansen asserted that: "[I] am still a missionary in my heart and while I cannot be an active one on the foreign field, I do all I can at home in every way."[113] After resigning the pastorate in Okanogan, the Hansens moved to Lomita, California, where they became involved with the Harbor City Foursquare Church and assisted in local ministry until Reverend Hansen's death in late December 1958.[114] He was seventy-seven years old.[115] After the death of her husband, Letta remained active in local ministry until May 1961, when she moved to Hawaii with her son Harold Jr. and his family. Harold Jr. was himself an Assemblies of God minister and had accepted a pastorate in Hawaii.[116] In October 1962, Letta moved to Singapore, where she did ministry work with her daughter Margaret and her family—Assemblies of God missionaries. Letta often counseled, preached, and taught at two Pentecostal churches which were pastored by Margaret and her husband, Rev. Frederick O. Seaward.[117] In Singapore, Letta experienced several health crises, although she

---

Harold E. Hansen became pastor of the Okanogan church in December 1951. The other primary sources listed corroborate this timeline. However, *Letta in China*, a biography of Reverend Hansen's wife Letta, indicates that she and her husband moved to pastor the church in Okanogan in late 1949 or early 1950. Ong, *Letta in China*, 152–53. Ong's timeline is difficult to reconcile, given other available historical evidence. A newspaper clipping from mid September 1950 indicates that Rev. Edward Logelin was still the main pastor of the Okanogan church. *Okanogan Independent*, "Full Gospel Christian Assembly" (Sept. 14, 1950). Additionally, Reverend Logelin is listed in the August 1951 Okanogan telephone directory. It is possible that Rev. Harold Hansen served as an assistant pastor in Okanogan from late 1949 until late 1951 when, it is surmisable, he became the main pastor. However, the Full Gospel Christian Assembly did not print regular advertisements for church services between mid September 1950 and late December 1951, so such details are apparently unavailable. Ong, whose book does not contain citations, does not frame 1949–1950 as an assistant pastorate. As an additional note, it was Rev. A. Ephraim Hokanson, an ordained Assembly of God minister, who succeeded Reverend Hansen as pastor of the Okanogan church in 1956. The newspaper article that details this pastoral transition, cited above, includes a misspelling of the new pastor's name in the article title ("Hokenson" instead of "Hokanson"). Assemblies of God General Council Ministers Directory, 1956, Consortium of Pentecostal Archives; "New Addresses," 28.

113. H. E. Hansen to Rev. J. Roswell Flower, June 29, 1953, in "Deceased Ministers—Hansen, H. E. (Harold E.)," archival record file, Flower Pentecostal Heritage Center.

114. Ong, *Letta in China*, 161–64.

115. *News-Pilot*, "Rev. H. E. Hansen Services Slated," 2.

116. Ong, *Letta in China*, 169.

117. Ong, *Letta in China*, 171, 173; Assemblies of God General Council Ministers Directories, 1956–58, Consortium of Pentecostal Archives.

Conclusion

also experienced many instances of divine healing.[118] Herself something of a Pentecostal mystic, Letta died in October 1965 while back in America, visiting family in Omak. She was sixty-seven years old.[119]

Thoro Harris, the gospel songwriter who sold some eighteen hundred song copyrights to Oscar Knutson in 1949, remained in Eureka Springs, Arkansas, until his death in March 1955, just before his eighty-first birthday.[120] Active in the Eureka Springs community during his latter years, Harris often served in various local churches in a musical capacity.[121] Although he wrote hundreds of songs during his lifetime, some of his most popular include "More Abundantly" (1914), "All That Thrills My Soul Is Jesus" (1931), and "He's Coming Soon" (1944).[122] Harris also wrote alternative versions of "Jesus Loves the Little Children" and "Give Me Oil in My Lamp" in 1921 and 1926, respectively.[123]

Oscar Knutson's connection to the people listed above, not to mention many others, reveals that history is never disconnected from biography. History is about people and their lives. Impersonal forces that operate within history mean nothing apart from the concrete actions of real people. In the words of historian Charles F. Mullett, referencing sixteenth-century English religious history: "Queen Mary did not burn Protestantism at the stake, she burnt Hugh Latimer."[124] Just as history is always connected to biography, theology is always connected to history (and thus biography), even when this connection is unapparent. Theology is always worked out

---

118. Ong, *Letta in China*, 174–82.

119. Ong, *Letta in China*, 186–87; *News Tribune*, "Missionary Dies in Omak," 2.

120. *Chicago Tribune*, "Thoro Harris," 26.

121. Various biographical sketches of Thoro Harris, in "Clip file, Personal papers—Thoro Harris," archival record file, Flower Pentecostal Heritage Center.

122. Everett A. Wilson, "Harris, Thoro," in Burgess and van der Maas, *New International Dictionary*, 691; various biographical sketches of Thoro Harris, in "Clip file, Personal papers—Thoro Harris," archival record file, Flower Pentecostal Heritage Center.

123. Everett A. Wilson, "Harris, Thoro," in Burgess and van der Maas, *New International Dictionary*, 691; various biographical sketches of Thoro Harris, in "Clip file, Personal papers—Thoro Harris," archival record file, Flower Pentecostal Heritage Center; unpublished gospel songbook featuring "Oil" by Thoro Harris, 12, courtesy of Bernice M. Fergus.

124. Mullett, *Biography as History*, 5.

in people's minds, wills, and actions as they seek to make sense of God and their encounters with him, and as they seek to relate to him.

Spiritual biography is central to that theological endeavor. Through spiritual biography, we consider—and even wrestle with—our own hopes and dreams, not to mention our own sufferings and failures. How does God see these things? How does God see us? Furthermore, how do we see God? How are we relating to him in the everyday stuff of life, both good and bad? Do we trust him? Do we believe in the forgiveness of sins? Do we believe God hears us? Do we believe he answers prayer? Do we believe he works miracles? Do we believe he is in our midst, renewing and restoring all things?

The enduring value of spiritual biography for the church is that it provides an important context for the kind of theological reflection and spiritual engagement that is central to the Christian faith. Spiritual biography provides a historical record of God's own life-giving activities in and through his people and, especially, specific persons like Oscar Knutson who set forth a faithful example of what it means to love, trust, and serve the Lord. Far from simply a collection of old facts, however, the historical record found within spiritual biography functions as a testimony and inherently offers present connection to God himself. Once relationship with God is established, the life and experiences of real people featured in spiritual biography turns to provide a reliable roadmap for others to follow. In this way, spiritual biography invites further theological exploration and calls people to an ongoing act of faith and worship—the orientation of all of life around relationship with the triune God, trusting in his loving care.

Appendix

Photographs[1]

Oscar Marius Knutson (1900–1993), ca. 1920s

1. Unless otherwise noted, all photographs are courtesy of Bernice Fergus, granddaughter of Oscar M. Knutson.

Marie Bell Baldwin (1905–1993), ca. 1920s

Oscar Knutson (top row, third from left, with glasses), with his parents, Andrew and Elvina Knutson, and siblings, ca. 1920s

Photographs

Marie Baldwin (top row, second from right), with her parents—Jay and Cora May Baldwin—siblings, and brother-in-law, ca. 1920s

Oscar Knutson and Marie Baldwin, married September 17, 1924

PHOTOGRAPHS

Oscar and Marie Knutson, with children, Fern (b. 1926) and Lloyd (b. 1929), early 1930s

Oscar and Marie Knutson, with children, Fern and Lloyd, early 1930s

Photographs

Oscar and Marie Knutson, mid-1930s

Oscar and Marie Knutson, with children, Fern and Lloyd, ca. late 1930s

PHOTOGRAPHS

Oscar Knutson (left) and Jack Nelson (right)

Brother Jack Nelson (left), with ministry coworkers
Mary Sanders (right) and "Sister Holla[n]d" (middle)

PHOTOGRAPHS

Knutson family automobile and trailer, ca. 1930s,
used for traveling evangelism during the Great Depression

Knutson family with trailer used for traveling evangelism, ca. 1930s

Knutson family with another trailer, used for traveling evangelism, ca. 1930s

Photographs

Unidentified Pentecostal street meetings, ca. 1930s or 1940s

PHOTOGRAPHS

Unidentified photographs, likely water baptism(s), ca. 1940s.
Oscar, Lloyd, Fern, and unidentified friend

Photographs

Rev. Lee Henson, ministry associate of Oscar Knutson

Knutson family with Rev. Lee Henson, "Food Shower—Kettle Falls," ca. 1938–1939

Oscar Knutson's tent for Pentecostal "Gospel Meetings," ca. late 1930s to early 1940s

Oscar and Marie Knutson, ca. 1930s

Unidentified photograph, probably a picnic held after a tent meeting or church service, ca. 1940s. Oscar is sitting next to the "Rice Krispies" box, and Marie is standing.

PHOTOGRAPHS

Knutson family with musical instruments, ca. late 1940s. Oscar with an accordion, Fern with a banjo, Marie with a guitar, and Lloyd with an octofone.

Photographs

Knutson family with musical instruments, ca. late 1940s

Knutson family, ca. 1940s, Lloyd, Oscar, Fern, Marie (left to right)

PHOTOGRAPHS

Former bowling alley, Okanogan, Washington, 1944

Full Gospel Christian Assembly, Okanogan, 1944, former bowling alley

Full Gospel Christian Assembly, Okanogan congregation, ca. 1944

Photographs

Former bowling alley building, Okanogan, Washington. Presently a Spanish-speaking church, August 3, 2022. Image courtesy of Barry I. George.

Full Gospel Christian Assembly, Okanogan, Washington, 4th Avenue and Tyee Street, ca. 1947–1948. Oscar Knutson oversaw the construction of this church building.

Photographs

Former building of the Full Gospel Christian Assembly, Okanogan, Washington.
Present-day location of New Life Church, August 1, 2022.
Image courtesy of Barry I. George.

Rev. A. D. Guth, ministry associate of Oscar Knutson[2]

---

2. *Calvary Gospel Assembly*, 7.

Photographs

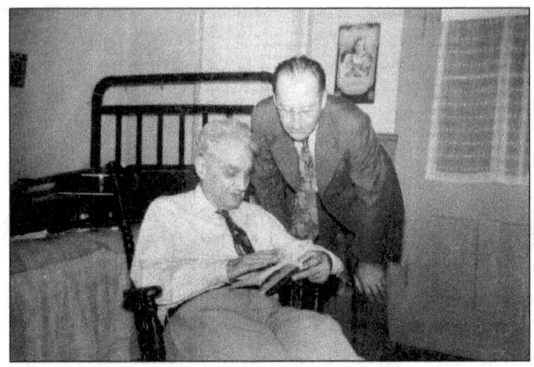

Thoro Harris, gospel songwriter (left) and Oscar Knutson (right), 1949

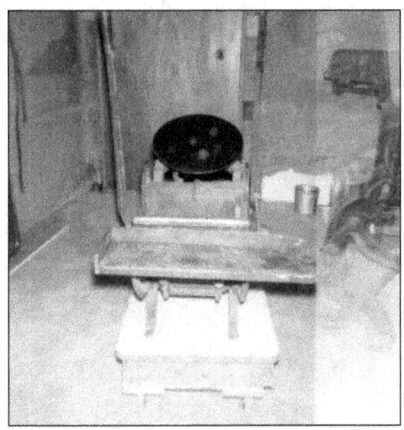

Oscar Knutson's first printing press, "10 by 15 C," hand powered. Purchased in Michigan in 1934 for $35. Photographs in scrapbook, courtesy of Phillip Knutson.

Photographs

"Part of our Typesetting Dept." Photograph in scrapbook, courtesy of Phillip Knutson.

Oscar Knutson's "11–17 Multi" printing press.
Photograph in scrapbook, courtesy of Phillip Knutson.

"Paper Cutter." Photograph in scrapbook, courtesy of Phillip Knutson.

Oscar Knutson's printing equipment.
Photographs in scrapbook, courtesy of Phillip Knutson.

PHOTOGRAPHS

Oscar Knutson's printing equipment.
Photographs in scrapbook, courtesy of Phillip Knutson.

Oscar Knutson's printing equipment.
Photographs in scrapbook, courtesy of Phillip Knutson.

Cover of *Crusade Songs*, the first songbook published by Oscar Knutson. It was printed to support the United Full Gospel Crusade in Seattle in summer 1949.

Cover of *Selected Gospel Songs, Number Two*, compiled and published by Oscar Knutson in June 1950. Inspired by Rev. A. D. Guth's *Selected Gospel Songs* (ca. 1918), more than 20,000 copies of this 345-page songbook were published in the first few years of printing.

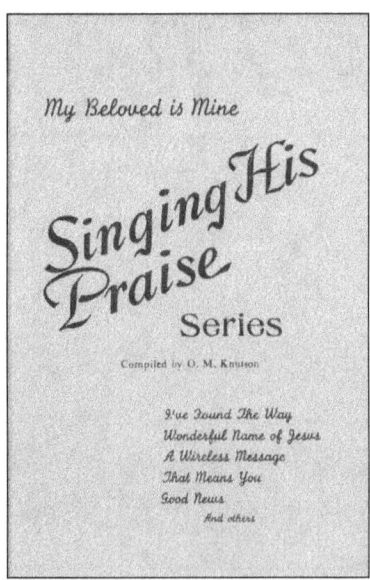

Cover of *My Beloved Is Mine: Singing His Praise Series*, compiled and published by Oscar Knutson, ca. 1949. Featured on the next page is the title song, "My Beloved Is Mine," which was written and composed by Knutson for his daughter Fern's wedding in fall 1948.

Photographs

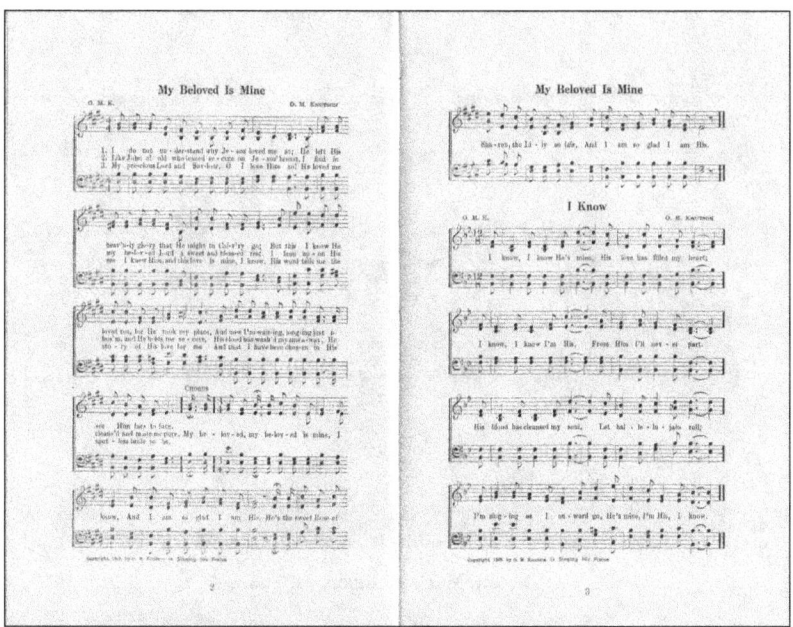

Unpublished song, "Praise the Lord," written and composed by Oscar Knutson, 1965

Oscar and Marie Knutson, ca. 1960s

Oscar and Marie Knutson, ca. early 1990s

Photographs

Oscar and Marie Knutson, 1992

Bibliography

ARCHIVES

Ancestry.com. https://www.ancestry.com/.
Billings Public Library. Montana Room. Billings, Montana.
Consortium of Pentecostal Archives. https://pentecostalarchives.org.
Ellensburg Public Library. Northwest Collection. Ellensburg, Washington.
Eureka Springs Historical Museum. Eureka Springs, Arkansas.
Flower Pentecostal Heritage Center. Archives of the Assemblies of God, General Council. Springfield, Missouri.
Great Falls History Museum. Great Falls, Montana.
Historical Society of Marshall County. Marshalltown, Iowa.
Northwest University Archives. Kirkland, Washington.
Okanogan County Auditor's Office. Okanogan, Washington.
Okanogan County Historical Society. Okanogan, Washington.
Oscar M. Knutson Archival Collection. Whitworth University Archives. Spokane, Washington.
Seattle Public Library. Seattle, Washington.
Shiloh Museum of Ozark History. Springdale, Arkansas.
Washington State Archives, Digital Archives. Cheney, Washington. https://digitalarchives.wa.gov/.
Western Heritage Center. Billings, Montana.

NEWSPAPER ARTICLES

Argus-Leader. "Evangelist O. M. Knutson . . ." Sioux Falls, SD, June 27, 1942, 4.
———. "Independant Pentecostal [*sic*]." Sioux Falls, SD, June 27, 1942, 4.
———. "Independent Pentecostal." Sioux Falls, SD, July 11, 1942, 5.
———. "Sunny Side." Sioux Falls, SD, Oct. 4, 1941, 5.
Augusta News. "Church News." Augusta, MT, June 26, 1930, 8.
Bellingham Herald. "The Bethel Temple Handmaidens . . ." Bellingham, WA, Jan. 12, 1951, 6.
Billings Gazette. "Assembly of God." Billings, MT, May 17, 1925, 14.
———. "Assembly of God." Billings, MT, Jan. 3, 1926, 14.

BIBLIOGRAPHY

———. "Assembly of God." Billings, MT, Mar. 21, 1926, 16.
———. "Assembly of God." Billings, MT, Aug. 21, 1927, 26.
———. "Assembly of God Mission." Billings, MT, Aug. 22, 1931, 4.
———. "Assembly of God Mission." Billings, MT, Dec. 30, 1933, 5.
———. "Local Woman Dies of Heart Attack." Billings, MT, June 30, 1935, 5.
———. "Pentecostal Assembly of God." Billings, MT, May 9, 1926, 16.
———. "Pentecostal Assembly of God." Billings, MT, Feb. 5, 1928, 18.
Butte Gazette. "Revival Meetings." Butte, NE, June 18, 1931, 5.
Butte Miner. "Evangelistic." Butte, MT, May 3, 1925, 11.
Capital Journal. "Glad Tidings Mission." Salem, OR, Aug. 1, 1925, 6.
———. "Hear Evangelist A. D. Guth . . ." Salem, OR, July 29, 1925, 5.
Chicago Tribune. "Retired Villa Park Cleric Dies of Train Injuries." Chicago, IL, July 14, 1943, 12.
———. "Thoro Harris." Chicago, IL, Mar. 29, 1955, 26.
Chippewa Herald-Telegram. "At Cadott Service." Chippewa Falls, WI, July 27, 1951, 3.
———. "Cadott Gospel Tabernacle." Chippewa Falls, WI, June 13, 1952, 3.
Coulee City Dispatch. "Rev. Hart Leaves Today for Cashmere." Coulee City, WA, Aug. 22, 1935, 7.
Courier-Herald. "Word reached the valley . . ." Kennewick, WA, July 17, 1941, 4.
Cut Bank Pioneer Press. "At the Churches: Full Gospel Tabernacle (Assembly of God)." Cut Bank, MT, Aug. 7, 1936, 1.
Daily Herald. "Building Continues at Near Record Pace." Everett, WA, July 16, 1962, 14.
———. "Church News." Everett, WA, May 16, 1917, 9.
———. "Church News." Everett, WA, May 12, 1922, 13.
———. "Church News." Everett, WA, Oct. 13, 1922, 13.
———. "Church News." Everett, WA, Jan. 23, 1923, 10.
———. "City Charge Against Minister Dismissed: Mission Meeting Noises Occasion Complaint by Neighbors." Everett, WA, Feb. 20, 1920.
———. "A county building permit . . ." Everett, WA, Jan. 3, 1958, 16.
———. "A county building permit . . ." Everett, WA, Dec. 30, 1958, 13.
———. "A county building permit . . ." Everett, WA, Jan. 20, 1959, 17.
———. "Evangelist Jack Nelson . . ." Everett, WA, June 7, 1926, 6.
———. "Jay Neil Baldwin." Everett, WA, Feb. 28, 1928, 14.
———. "Lloyd O. Knutson." Everett, WA, Apr. 24, 2007, 12.
———. "Ministers Elect Officers at First Meeting of the Year." Everett, WA, Sept. 14, 1925, 4.
———. "Missions." Everett, WA, Sept. 14, 1918, 11.
———. "Missions." Everett, WA, Dec. 3, 1921, 11.
———. "Missions: Consolidated Pentecostal Mission." Everett, WA, Feb. 25, 1922, 11.
———. "O. M. Knutson of Seattle . . ." Everett, WA, Apr. 15, 1959, 31.
———. "Pentecostal Mission." Everett, WA, Feb. 16, 1918, 12.
———. "Pentecostal Mission." Everett, WA, Sept. 14, 1918, 11.
———. "Pentecostal Mission." Everett, WA, July 5, 1924, 12.
———. "Pentecostal Mission." Everett, WA, Aug. 23, 1924, 12.
———. "Postal Aid Sought in Locating Family." Everett, WA, Apr. 5, 1932, 8.
———. "Rev. John W. Moseid." Everett, WA, May 10, 1965, 19.
———. "A Seattleite, O. M. Knutson . . ." Everett, WA. June 11, 1958, 28.
———. "Stanwood." Everett, WA, Sept. 15, 1931, 11.
———. "Startup." Everett, WA, July 19, 1929, 9.

Bibliography

———. "Startup." Everett, WA, Aug. 19, 1929, 8.
———. "Startup." Everett, WA, Mar. 12, 1930, 4.
———. "Startup." Everett, WA, May 2, 1930, 10.
———. "Startup." Everett, WA, Nov. 9, 1930, 10.
Daily Inter Lake. "Pentecostal Mission." Kalispell, MT, Jan. 2, 1920, 2.
Daily Plainsman. "Evangelists to Hold Meetings Next Week." Huron, SD, Sept. 12, 1931, 3.
———. "Full Gospel Assembly." Huron, SD, Oct. 14, 1927, 14.
———. "Full Gospel Assembly." Huron, SD, June 1, 1928, 5.
———. "Full Gospel Tabernacle." Huron, SD, Jan. 18, 1929, 6.
———. "Full Gospel Tabernacle." Huron, SD, Feb. 8, 1929, 12.
———. "Huron Gospel Tabernacle." Huron, SD, May 31, 1929, 7.
———. "Huron Gospel Tabernacle." Huron, SD, Dec. 27, 1929, 6.
———. "Huron Gospel Tabernacle." Huron, SD, Jan. 10, 1930, 5.
———. "Huron Gospel Tabernacle." Huron, SD, May 1, 1930, 3.
———. "Huron Gospel Tabernacle." Huron, SD, May 1, 1931, 12.
———. "Pentecostal Mission." Huron, SD, Dec. 4, 1931, 8.
———. "Pentescotal Mission [*sic*]." Huron, SD, Feb. 19, 1932, 3.
———. "Revival Service Continues Here." Huron, SD, Oct. 18, 1929, 12.
———. "Tomorrow on Your Radio . . . WOWO Ft. Wayne . . . 9:00—Gospel Tabernacle." Huron, SD, June 22, 1929, 4.
Dunn County News. "Albert Moseid . . ." Menomonie, WI, Apr. 19, 1923, 13.
———. "Albert Moseid . . ." Menomonie, WI, Aug. 2, 1923, 10.
———. "Applications for marriage licenses . . ." Menomonie, WI, Aug. 22, 1918, 5.
———. "Colfax." Menomonie, WI, Mar. 15, 1923, 11.
———. "Mr. and Mrs. Albert Moseid . . ." Menomonie, WI, Apr. 21, 1921, 11.
———. "Mr. and Mrs. Albert Moseid . . ." Menomonie, WI, Dec. 22, 1921, 9.
———. "Mrs. E. C. Erickson, who had been a guest at the home of her sister, Mrs. Albert Moseid . . ." Menomonie, WI, June 10, 1920, 14.
———. "Pentecostal meetings . . ." Menomonie, WI, Nov. 20, 1924, 10.
Ellendale Eagle. "Mrs. John Moseid Buried Here Thursday." Ellendale, MN, Aug. 19, 1925, 1.
Estherville Daily News. "Gospel Mission." Estherville, IA, Aug. 12, 1937, 2.
———. "The Rev. O. M. Knutson . . ." Estherville, IA, May 14, 1942, 1.
———. Untitled article noting the wedding of Martin Guge and Harda Knutson. Estherville, IA, Feb. 21, 1933, 2.
Estherville Enterprise. "Gospel Mission." Estherville, IA, Aug. 19, 1937, 2.
Evening Star. "Marriage Licenses . . . Colored." Washington, DC, Oct. 22, 1898, 10.
Friend Tribune. "The Rev. John Moseid . . ." Friend, NE, Nov. 5, 1937, 1.
Frontier and Holt County Independent. "Revival Meetings." O'Neill, NE, May 11, 1934, 1.
Goldendale Sentinel. "Assembly of God Church." Goldendale, WA, Mar. 1, 1945, 2.
———. "Assembly of God Church." Goldendale, WA, Apr. 26, 1945, 9.
Great Bend Tribune. "Local Happenings." Great Bend, KS, Feb. 23, 1915, 8.
Great Falls Leader. "City Gospel Mission." Great Falls, MT, Aug. 12, 1923, 6.
———. "Funeral Pending for Mrs. Lantz, Minister's Wife." Great Falls, MT, Oct. 19, 1939, 10.
———. "Glad Tidings Rescue Mission." Great Falls, MT, Mar. 2, 1929, 4.
———. "In the Churches." Great Falls, MT, June 30, 1921, 5.
———. "In the Churches: Pentecostal Mission." Great Falls, MT, Jan. 22, 1922, 6.

BIBLIOGRAPHY

———. "In the Churches: Pentecostal Mission." Great Falls, MT, Feb. 5, 1922, 7.
———. "In the Churches: Pentecostal Mission." Great Falls, MT, May 28, 1922, 6.
———. "Pentecostal Assembly." Great Falls, MT, Feb. 24, 1917, 7.
———. "Pentecostal Mission." Great Falls, MT, Dec. 4, 1920, 7.
———. "Pentecostal Tent Meetings." Great Falls, MT, Aug. 16, 1919, 5.
———. "The Petition of O. M. Knutson . . ." Great Falls, MT, June 1, 1927, 3.
———. "Rites Friday for Rev. Lantz." Great Falls, MT, Nov. 4, 1952, 15.
———. "South Side S. S. Chapel." Great Falls, MT, Mar. 13, 1920, 13.
Great Falls Tribune. "Church Services Today: Pentecostal Mission." Great Falls, MT, Mar. 18, 1922, 5.
———. "Denounces Her 'Healer' Spouse as 'Bad Actor.'" Great Falls, MT, Aug. 21, 1923, 10.
———. "Evangelist to 'Purge Self of Sin' by Pleading Guilty." Great Falls, MT, Apr. 1, 1926, 5.
———. "The Glad Tidings Rescue Mission." Great Falls, MT, Feb. 24, 1929, 7.
———. "Glad Tidings Mission Will Resume Soon." Great Falls, MT, Aug. 24, 1931, 3.
———. "Glad Tidings Rescue Home Opens Again." Great Falls, MT, Nov. 2, 1930, 10.
———. "Hold 'Healer' on Complaint in Check Chase." Great Falls, MT, Aug. 25, 1923, 6.
———. "Hymn Book Throwing Banned So Songs and Prayers Hurled." Great Falls, MT, Jan. 5, 1931, 2.
———. "Interdenominational Gospel Station." Great Falls, MT, May 22, 1927, 18.
———. "Johnson-Knudson." Great Falls, MT, May 4, 1920, 9.
———. "Marriage Licenses." Great Falls, MT, May 4, 1920, 13.
———. "Mrs. Inga Johnson Dies in Seattle." Great Falls, MT, July 6, 1945, 9.
———. "O. M. Knutson requested . . ." Great Falls, MT, May 24, 1927, 3.
———. "Pentecostal Assembly." Great Falls, MT, Jan. 30, 1921, 21.
———. "Pentecostal Mission." Great Falls, MT, Dec. 15, 1918, 21.
———. "Pentecostal Mission Holds Its Services." Great Falls, MT, June 27, 1921, 9.
———. "The request of O. M. Knutson . . ." Great Falls, MT, June 1, 1927, 3.
———. "Rescue Mission." Great Falls, MT, Dec. 28, 1930, 24.
———. "Rev. Lantz, Local Church Founder, Dies." Great Falls, MT, Nov. 5, 1952, 9.
———. "South Side Sunday School Chapel." Great Falls, MT, Mar. 14, 1920, 29.
———. "Will Open a Two Weeks' Mission." Great Falls, MT, July 28, 1916, 7.
Gutierrez, Lisa. "Faith Is Forever Growing at First Assembly." *Argus-Leader* (Sioux Falls, SD), Apr. 7, 1987, 15.
Hardin Tribune. "Mrs. M. A. Bartells . . ." Hardin, MT, Aug. 19, 1921, A6.
Hutchinson News. "Full Gospel Mission." Hutchinson, KS, Mar. 3, 1934, 7.
———. "Full Gospel Mission (Pentecostal)." Hutchinson, KS, June 17, 1933, 7.
———. "Peter Guth, an aged Mennonite farmer, died . . ." Hutchinson, KS, Aug. 9, 1913, 12.
Independent-Record. "'Evangelist' Held at Great Falls on Charge of Larceny." Helena, MT, Apr. 1, 1926, 12.
Ken Rock Herald. "Published 20,000 Books! Local Man Is Known Over America." Rockford, IL, Aug. 7, 1952, 1.
Kitsap Sun. "Revival Singer Slates Series." Bremerton, WA, Oct. 14, 1950, 2.
Knutson, O. M. "3-Day Fellowship Bible Conference." *Okanogan Independent* (Okanogan, WA), Apr. 12, 1945, 12.
Longview Daily News. "They're Engaged." Longview, WA, Mar. 11, 1967, 5.
Los Angeles Times. "Real Estate Record: Recent Transfers." Los Angeles, CA, Mar. 9, 1907, 27.
———. Untitled article indicating transfer of property to A. D. Guth. Los Angeles, CA, Apr. 8, 1906, 80.

Bibliography

Louisiana Press-Journal. "Special Meetings." Louisiana, MO, Dec. 21, 1916.
Melstone Messenger. "Peter Larson Retires." Melstone, MT, Aug. 21, 1930, A1.
Milford Review. "Pentecostal Assembly." Milford, NE, Sept. 7, 1916, 1.
———. "Rev. G. H. Rake New Pastor Here." Milford, NE, Apr. 30, 1931, 1.
Minneapolis Journal. "Full Gospel Assembly Pentecostal." Minneapolis, MN, Aug. 13, 1927, 5.
Minneapolis Star. "Bloomington Gets Pastor: Former Evangelist Succeeds Rev. Moseid." Minneapolis, MN, June 4, 1938, 7.
———. "Glad Tidings Church." Minneapolis, MN, Oct. 6, 1956, 4.
———. "Marriage Licenses." Minneapolis, MN, Mar. 2, 1928, 19.
———. "Pastor of Gospel Church Resigns." Minneapolis, MN, Nov. 14, 1936, 5.
———. "Smith Brothers Revival Meetings . . ." Minneapolis, MN, Jan. 16, 1937, 8.
Montana Record-Herald. "Pentecostal Tent Meetings." Helena, MT, Aug. 9, 1921, 9.
Morning Call. "Butler." Patterson, NJ, Feb. 20, 1918, 7.
News-Leader. "Andrew S. Teuber, 83." Springfield, MO, Sept. 20, 1994, 4.
News-Pilot. "Rev. H. E. Hansen Services Slated." San Pedro, CA, Dec. 30, 1958, 2.
News Tribune. "Bethel Assembly." Tacoma, WA, July 31, 1950, 2.
———. "Bethel Assembly." Tacoma, WA, Sept. 18, 1950, 8.
———. "Marriage Licenses." Tacoma, WA, Sept. 1, 1939, 6.
———. "Missionary Dies in Omak." Tacoma, WA, Oct. 16, 1965, 2.
———. "Mrs. John W. Moseid." Tacoma, WA, Dec. 18, 1945, 12.
———. "Pentecostal Christian Assembly." Tacoma, WA, Dec. 13, 1924, 5.
———. "Pentecostal Christian Assembly." Tacoma, WA, Feb. 7, 1925, 9.
———. "Rev. Cecil Grice Will Speak." Tacoma, WA, Oct. 24, 1970, 4.
———. "Rev. John W. Moseid." Tacoma, WA, May 13, 1965, 37.
Okanogan Independent. "$14,000 Church Building Begun." Okanogan, WA, Aug. 21, 1947.
———. "Church Application Gets Another Hearing." Okanogan, WA, Aug. 7, 1947.
———. "Congregation Buys Second Ave. Building." Okanogan, WA, Feb. 24, 1944, 1.
———. "Dedicate New Gospel Edifice, Monday, July 19." Okanogan, WA, July 8, 1948, 1.
———. "Full Gospel Christian Assembly." Okanogan, WA, Jan. 6, 1944.
———. "Full Gospel Christian Assembly." Okanogan, WA, Dec. 18, 1947.
———. "Full Gospel Christian Assembly." Okanogan, WA, Sept. 14, 1950.
———. "Full Gospel Christian Assembly." Okanogan, WA, Dec. 20, 1951.
———. "Full Gospel Christian Assembly Church Dedication." Okanogan, WA, July 22, 1948, 14.
———. "Gospel Assembly to Build at 4th-Tyee." Okanogan, WA, Aug. 14, 1947.
———. "H. E. Hokenson [sic] Starts Pastorate at Local Church." Okanogan, WA, June 21, 1956.
———. "Heavy Building Program Seen." Okanogan, WA, July 10, 1947.
———. "Knutson Resigns as Full Gospel Pastor." Okanogan, WA, Mar. 31, 1949, 2.
———. "Local Pastor and Family Home from Trip South." Okanogan, WA, June 19, 1947, 3.
———. "Local Pastor and Family to Take Trip." Okanogan, WA, Dec. 12, 1946, 8.
———. "Miss Fern Knutson, Mr. Alvin Olson." Okanogan, WA, Oct. 21, 1948, 5.
———. "Missionaries to Hold Meetings." Okanogan, WA, Jan. 4, 1945.
———. "Old Fashioned Gospel Meetings at the Big Brown Tent." Okanogan, WA, Aug. 12, 1943.
———. "Outdoor Skating Rink Is Recreation Center." Okanogan, WA, Dec. 30, 1943.

Bibliography

———. "Public Hearing on Proposed Church Site Draws Record Crowd." Okanogan, WA, July 24, 1947.

———. "Robert G. Smyth, Pastor of Bethel Church, Bridgeport will preach Thursday Nite, Aug. 19, at the Big Brown Tent . . ." Okanogan, WA, ca. Aug. 1943.

———. "Work Goes Ahead on Skating Rink." Okanogan, WA, Dec. 14, 1940.

Omak Chronicle. "Large Attendance at Full Gospel Daily Bible School." Omak, WA, Aug. 5, 1943.

People's Press. Untitled article noting the wedding of John W. Moseid and Mabel J. Anderson. Owatonna, MN, July 30, 1915, 12.

San Bernardino County Sun. "Singer-Evangelist to Hold 5 Meetings." San Bernardino, CA, May 7, 1955, 12.

Santa Rosa Republican. "Evangelistic Meetings." Santa Rosa, CA, Mar. 14, 1944, 9.

Sault Star. "Penticostal Tabernacle [sic]." Sault St. Marie, ON, Canada, Aug. 30, 1930, 9.

Seattle Star. "Crowd Again Attends Evangelistic Service." Seattle, WA, Jan. 27, 1921, 13.

———. "Canadian Evangelist Service Draws Crowds." Seattle, WA, Jan. 26, 1921, 11.

———. "Pine Street Pentecostal Mission." Seattle, WA, Sept. 13, 1919, 8.

———. "Rev. Clarence W. Hart." Seattle, WA, Mar. 18, 1947, 15.

———. "Strange Tongues Spoken by Cult; Men Shake and Woman Grovels on the Floor." Seattle, WA, Aug. 13, 1919, 7.

Seattle Union Record. "Building Permits: Tent . . . Green Lake way . . . Pentecostal Mission, 121 Pine." Seattle, WA, June 30, 1919, 17.

———. "Building Permits: Tent . . . Green Lake way . . . Pentecostal Mission, 121 Pine." Seattle, WA, July 1, 1919, 7.

———. "Healing Services Held at North Green Lake Tent." Seattle, WA, Aug. 12, 1921, 9.

Silver Blade. "German Divine Quits: Rev. Schmid Leaves Rathdrum After Hearing." Rathdrum, ID, July 26, 1918, 1.

Sioux City Journal. "Assembly of God Church to Host Fellowship Event." Sioux City, IA, Oct. 16, 1969, 7.

Spokane Chronicle. "Bakery in fast growing Columbia basin town . . ." Spokane, WA, Jan. 6, 1955, 22.

———. "C. W. Hart." Spokane, WA, Mar. 22, 1947, 7.

Spokesman-Review. "All around baker . . ." Spokane, WA, June 19, 1955, 33.

———. "Church Members of White Bluffs Work Week in Pastor's Orchard." Spokane, WA, Feb. 28, 1912, 9.

———. "Coulee City." Spokane, WA, Mar. 12, 1903, 6.

———. "Retail bakery for sale . . ." Spokane, WA, May 23, 1947, 28.

———. "Revival Meetings Opened." Spokane, WA, Dec. 9, 1931, 8.

———. "White Bluffs." Spokane, WA, Aug. 11, 1911, 8.

Star Tribune. "Evangelist Services." Minneapolis, MN, Dec. 5, 1936, 14.

———. "Full Gospel Mission, Pentecostal." Minneapolis, MN, Mar. 26, 1927, 10.

Statesman Journal. "Glad Tidings Mission." Salem, OR, Sept. 7, 1929, 6.

———. "Salem Heights Community." Salem, OR, June 6, 1942, 7.

Sterling Kansas Bulletin. "Enterprise." Sterling, KS, Oct. 22, 1897, 4.

———. "Obituary of Peter Guth." Sterling, KS, Aug. 14, 1913, 4.

Stilwell Democrat-Journal. "Bro. A. D. Guth . . ." Stilwell, OK, Sept. 5, 1946, 7.

Tacoma Daily Ledger. "Olaf Solberg." Tacoma, WA, July 24, 1929, 12.

———. "Pentecostal Christian Assembly." Tacoma, WA, Jan. 8, 1922, 13.

———. "Pentecostal Christian Assembly." Tacoma, WA, Feb. 19, 1922, 38.

BIBLIOGRAPHY

———. "The Pentecostal Christian Assembly." Tacoma, WA, Apr. 2, 1922, 43.
Tacoma Times. "Rev. J. W. Moseid Will Preach Here." Tacoma, WA, Mar. 29, 1940, 19.
Times. "Calumet City Church of Christ." Munster, IN, Mar. 21, 1936.
Times Leader. "Charles Simmonett." Wilkes-Barre, PA, Feb. 5, 1957, 6.
Toronto Star. Newspaper advertisement for Pentecostal meetings held by evangelist Cecil Grice. Toronto, ON, Canada, Apr. 1, 1944, 8.
Tri-City Herald. Newspaper advertisement for visit by evangelist Cecil Grice. Pasco, WA, Sept. 6, 1985, 10.
Twice-A-Week Times. "Pentecostal Revival . . . ." Louisiana, MO, Oct. 26, 1915, 6.
———. "The Pentecost Church . . . [sic]." Louisiana, MO, Nov. 7, 1916, 2.
———. "Revival Meeting." Louisiana, MO, Dec. 12, 1916, 3.
Washington Post. "Howard's Normal Graduates." Washington, DC, May 29, 1895, 4.
Waterloo Region Record. "Faith Mission." Kitchener, ON, Canada, Nov. 8, 1924, 3.
Wells Mirror. "Wells Gospel Tabernacle." Wells, MN, Mar. 14, 1935, 4.
———. "Wells Gospel Tabernacle." Wells, MN, Mar. 21, 1935, 6.
Westville Record. "Bro. A. D. Guth . . ." Westville, OK, Nov. 14, 1947, 6.
White Bluffs Spokesman. "Gospel Services." White Bluffs, WA, Dec. 17, 1915, 4.
———. "Gospel Services." White Bluffs, WA, May 5, 1916, 4.
———. "Jay Baldwin moved his family . . ." White Bluffs, WA, May 25, 1917, 4.
———. "Town and Valley News." White Bluffs, WA, Aug. 18, 1916, 4.
———. "Town and Valley News." White Bluffs, WA, Apr. 20, 1917, 4.
———. "Wesley Baldwin." White Bluffs, WA, Mar. 16, 1917, 1.
———. "Word has been received . . ." White Bluffs, WA, Mar. 30, 1917, 4.
Woodward County Republican. "Church Holds Services Here." Woodward, OK, Jan. 19, 1962, 3.

OTHER SOURCES

Advertisement for *Selected Gospel Songs, Number Two. Herald of Faith* 15.6 (June 1950) 15.
Althouse, Peter, and Robby Waddell, eds. *Perspectives in Pentecostal Eschatologies: World Without End.* Eugene, OR: Pickwick, 2010.
Anderson, Allan Heaton. *An Introduction to Pentecostalism: Global Charismatic Christianity.* Cambridge: Cambridge University Press, 2004.
———. *To the Ends of the Earth: Pentecostalism and the Transformation of World Christianity.* New York: Oxford University Press, 2013.
Applegate, Annie. "Jesus Is Coming Soon." *Full Gospel Testimony* 3.1 (Jan. 1927) 8.
———. "New Work in Wyoming." *Pentecostal Evangel* no. 691 (Apr. 2, 1927) 12.
———. "Reports from the Field: Billings, Mon." *Pentecostal Evangel* no. 496 (May 12, 1923) 14.
———. "Reports from the Field: Billings, Mont." *Pentecostal Evangel* no. 572 (Nov. 15, 1924) 12.
Applegate, John, and Annie Applegate. "Reports." *Full Gospel Testimony* 2.4 (Oct. 1925) 8.
Argue, Zelma. *Contending for the Faith.* Winnipeg: Messenger of God, 1928.
Ashworth, R. F., et al., comps. *Crusade Songs.* Seattle: The Christian Book Concern, ca. 1949.
———. *Crusade Songs.* Seattle/Estherville, IA: The Christian Book Concern, ca. 1949.

Bibliography

Barbour, John D. "Autobiography, Biography, and Theological Questioning." *Oxford Research Encyclopedias: Religion*, Aug. 5, 2016. https://doi.org/10.1093/acrefore/9780199340378.013.207.

Berardino, Angelo D., et al., eds. *Encyclopedia of Ancient Christianity*. Vol. 2: *F-O*. Downers Grove, IL: IVP Academic, 2014.

Berglund, Nils J. "Resebrev." *Sanningens Vittne* 25.212 (Feb. 1935) 6.

Boze, Joseph Mattsson. "Denominational Organization." *Herald of Faith* 15.12 (Feb. 1950) 5–6, 14.

Burgess, Stanley M., ed. *Encyclopedia of Pentecostal and Charismatic Christianity*. New York: Routledge, 2006.

Burgess, Stanley M., and Eduard M. van der Maas, eds. *The New International Dictionary of Pentecostal and Charismatic Movements*. Grand Rapids: Zondervan, 2002.

Burgess, Stanley M., and Gary B. McGee, eds. *Dictionary of Pentecostal and Charismatic Movements*. Grand Rapids: Regency Reference Library, 1988.

Calvary Gospel Assembly, Estherville, Iowa: 50th Anniversary, 1932–1982. Lake Mills, IA: Graphic Publishing Company, 1982.

Camp Meeting Songs. Rockford, IL: The Christian Book Concern, ca. 1950s.

Campbell, Ted A. "Spiritual Biography and Autobiography." In *The Cambridge Companion to American Methodism*, edited by Jason E. Vickers, 243–60. New York: Cambridge University Press, 2013.

Central Assembly of God, 1923–1998: Celebrating 75 Years, Yesterday, Today, and Tomorrow. N.p.: N.p., 1998.

Clark, Elmer T. *The Small Sects in America*. New York: Abingdon-Cokesbury, 1949.

Crusade Songs. Rockford, IL/Estherville, IA: The Christian Book Concern, ca. 1950s.

Day, Peter. *A Dictionary of Christian Denominations*. London: Continuum, 2003.

Down Came the Fire, and, My Heart Leaps with Rapture Divine. Seattle: The Christian Book Concern, ca. 1950s.

Echoes of Victory. Rockford, IL: The Christian Book Concern, ca. 1950s.

Elderkin, Geo. D., ed. *The Finest of Wheat: Hymns New and Old, for Missionary and Revival Meetings, and Sabbath-Schools*. Chicago: R. R. McCabe, 1890.

Evangel Songs. Springfield, MO: Gospel Publishing House, 1931.

Ewart, F. J., and Harry Van Loon. "Special Notice." *Pentecostal Testimony* 2.3 (Aug. 1912) 16.

Fahlbusch, Erwin, et al., eds. *The Encyclopedia of Christianity*. Vol. 1: *A-D*. Translated by Geoffrey W. Bromiley. Grand Rapids: Eerdmans, 1999.

———. *The Encyclopedia of Christianity*. Vol. 2: *E-I*. Translated by Geoffrey W. Bromiley. Grand Rapids: Eerdmans, 1999.

———. *The Encyclopedia of Christianity*. Vol. 3: *J-O*. Translated by Geoffrey W. Bromiley. Grand Rapids: Eerdmans, 1999.

Fairfield Heritage Committee. *Boots and Shovels: A History of the Greenfield Irrigation District, Division of the Sun River Project, Fairfield, Montana*. Fairfield, MT: Fairfield Times, 1978.

"Fellowship Meeting." *Herald of Faith* 10.7 (July 1945) 26.

Ferguson, Sinclair B., et al., eds. *New Dictionary of Theology*. Downers Grove, IL: InterVarsity, 1988.

"Fighting the Good Fight." *Pentecostal Evangel* no. 721 (Nov. 5, 1927) 12.

Find a Grave. "Henry G. Schmid." https://www.findagrave.com/memorial/84812807/henry-g-schmid.

Bibliography

———. "Rev Aaron D. Guth." https://www.findagrave.com/memorial/37319058/aaron_d_guth.

———. "Rev Charles Albert Moseid." https://www.findagrave.com/memorial/30415928/charles-albert-moseid.

Flower, J. Roswell. "God Honors Faith." *The Pentecost* 2.3 (Feb. 1, 1910) 1.

Fold3 Military Records. "US, WWII Draft Registration Cards, 1940." Last modified 2024. https://www.fold3.com/publication/816/us-wwii-draft-registration-cards-1940/description.

French, Talmadge Leon. "Early Oneness Pentecostalism, Garfield Thomas Haywood, and the Interracial Pentecostal Assemblies of the World (1906–1931)." PhD diss., University of Birmingham, England, 2011.

Frodsham, Stanley H. "A Wonderful Life Ended: The Home-Call of Sister Lilian Garr." *Confidence* 4.5 (May 1916) 1–2.

Full Gospel Songs. Springfield, MO: Gospel Publishing House, ca. 1940s.

Garraty, John A. *The Great Depression*. Garden City, NY: Anchor, 1987.

Garrett, Harry S. "A History of the Montana District Council of the Assemblies of God." BD diss., Western Evangelical Seminary, Portland, Oregon, 1960.

Gerla, R. J. "To Omak, Wash." *Herald of Faith* 10.2 (Feb. 1945) 28.

Goldberg, Michael. *Theology and Narrative: A Critical Introduction*. Philadelphia: Trinity Press International, 1991.

Gospel Songs of Praise. Rockford, IL: The Christian Book Concern, ca. 1950s.

Gross, H. A. "Marvelous Revival in West Coast Convention." *Herald of Faith* 6.12 (Dec. 1941) 19–20.

Gupta, Nijay K. *Tell Her Story: How Women Led, Taught, and Ministered in the Early Church*. Downers Grove, IL: InterVarsity, 2023.

Guth, A. D., comp. *Selected Gospel Songs*. Belknap, IL: Full Gospel Assemblies, ca. 1918.

———. "The Two Kinds of Unity." *Full Gospel Testimony* 2.2 (Mar. 1925) 2–3, 6.

Halt, E. V., et al., comps. *Songs of the Christian Faith*. Louisville: Pentecostal Publishing Company, 1936.

Hansen, Harold E. "Bro. and Sister Hansen Arrive in Peking, North China." *Pentecostal Evangel* no. 342/343 (May 29, 1920) 13.

———. "Peking, North China." *Weekly Evangel* no. 175 (Feb. 3, 1917) 12, 16.

———. "Returning to Rest." *Bridegroom's Messenger* no. 212 (Apr. 1919) 3.

———. "The Work in Peking, China." *Bridegroom's Messenger* 15.238 (June/July 1922) 3.

Hardman, Keith. *Seasons of Refreshing: Evangelism and Revivals in America*. Grand Rapids: Baker, 1994.

Harris, Thoro. *Sing His Praise: The Jesus Name Series*. Eureka Springs, AR: Neal Walters Poster Corp., 1948.

———. *Songs of Redemption*. Eureka Springs, AR: N.p., 1937.

Hedeen, Carl. "Tacoma, Washington." *Sanningens Vittne* 30.272 (July 1940) 5.

Heffernan, Thomas J. *Sacred Biography: Saints and Their Biographers in the Middle Ages*. New York: Oxford University Press, 1988.

Hiscox, Edward T. *The Star Book for Ministers*. Philadelphia: Judson, 1946.

Hoffman, Elisha A., ed. *Best Hymns*. Chicago: The Evangelical Publishing Co., 1894.

Hollenweger, Walter J. *The Pentecostals*. Peabody, MA: Hendrickson, 1988.

Hoy, Frances P. "The Renewal of the Spirit." *Paraclete* 14.4 (Fall 1980) 27–30.

"Ice and Snow No Barrier." *Pentecostal Evangel* no. 990 (Mar. 18, 1933) 12.

Bibliography

Jacobsen, Douglas, ed. *A Reader in Pentecostal Theology: Voices from the First Generation.* Bloomington: Indiana University Press, 2006.

———. *Thinking in the Spirit: Theologies of the Early Pentecostal Movement.* Bloomington: Indiana University Press, 2003.

Johnson, Arthur, and Beatrice F. Johnson. "Convention in Los Angeles." *Herald of Faith* 15.4 (Apr. 1950) 6–7.

Jones, Charles Edwin. *A Guide to the Study of the Pentecostal Movement.* Vol. 1: *Parts I and II.* Metuchen, NJ: Scarecrow and the American Theological Library Association, 1983.

Kay, William K. *Pentecostalism: A Very Short Introduction.* New York: Oxford University Press, 2011.

Kerr, Phil. *Music in Evangelism, and Stories of Famous Christian Songs.* 3rd ed. Glendale, CA: Gospel Music Publishers, 1950.

Knight, Timothy. *Panic, Prosperity, and Progress: Five Centuries of History and the Markets.* Hoboken, NJ: Wiley, 2014.

Knutson, O. M. *The Christian and War.* Seattle: The Full Gospel Press, ca. 1941.

———. *The Glorious Church.* Okanogan: The Full Gospel Press, ca. 1948–49.

———. *God's Plan for Marriage and a Happy Home.* Seattle: The Christian Book Concern, ca. 1983.

———, comp. *Harbor Lights: Pilot Me, Book I.* Seattle: The Christian Book Concern, ca. 1955.

———. *His Loving Care.* Seattle: The Christian Book Concern, ca. 1979–80.

———. *The Life of Jesus: Sunday School Lessons, Direct from the Bible, Part One.* Seattle: The Full Gospel Press, ca. 1941.

———. *The Life of Jesus: Sunday School Lessons, Direct from the Bible, Part One and Two.* Seattle: The Full Gospel Press, ca. 1941.

———, comp. *My Beloved Is Mine: Singing His Praise Series.* Seattle: The Christian Book Concern, ca. 1949.

———. "Okanogan, Wash." *Herald of Faith* 9.5 (May 1944) 27–28.

———, comp. *Old Fashioned Camp Meeting Songs.* Rockford, IL: The Christian Book Concern, ca. 1950s.

———, comp. *Revival Echoes.* Rockford, IL: The Christian Book Concern, ca. 1950s.

———, comp. *Revival Echoes.* Rockford, IL/Estherville, IA: The Christian Book Concern, ca. 1952.

———, comp. *Revival Echoes, From Illinois District Camp Meeting, Assemblies of God Camp Grounds, Petersburg, Illinois.* Rockford, IL/Estherville, IA: The Christian Book Concern, ca. 1952.

———, comp. *Sacred Specials.* Rockford, IL: The Christian Book Concern, ca. 1950s.

———, comp. *Selected Gospel Songs, Number Two.* Rockford, IL: The Christian Book Concern, 1950.

———, comp. *Songs of Victory.* Seattle: The Christian Book Concern, 1983.

———, comp. *There's a Drawing From on High: Singing His Praise Series.* Seattle: The Christian Book Concern, 1949.

Kurian, George Thomas, and James D. Smith III, eds. *The Encyclopedia of Christian Literature.* Vol. 1: *Genres and Types/Biographies A-G.* Lanham, MD: Scarecrow, 2010.

Kurian, George Thomas, and Mark A. Lamport, eds. *Encyclopedia of Christianity in the United States.* Vol. 3: *H-M.* Lanham, MD: Rowman & Littlefield, 2016.

Bibliography

Lantz, Joseph. *Is the Baptism of the Holy Spirit Scriptural?* Great Falls, MT: The Tribune Printing Co., n.d.

Lantz, Mrs. Joseph. "Reports from the Field: Great Falls, Mont." *Weekly Evangel* no. 238/239 (May 4, 1918) 14.

Laughery, Mrs. C. B. "Healed of Cancer and Tuberculosis." *Pentecostal Evangel* no. 736 (Feb. 25, 1928) 7.

Lee, Robert Lloyd. *A New Springtime: Centennial Reflections on the Revival in the Nineties Among Norwegian-Americans.* Minneapolis: Heirloom, 1997.

Lillenas, Haldor. *Modern Gospel Song Stories.* Kansas City: Lillenas, 1952.

Louth, Andrew, ed. *The Oxford Dictionary of the Christian Church.* Vol. 1: A-J. New York: Oxford University Press, 2022.

McClendon, James W., Jr. *Biography as Theology: How Life Stories Can Remake Today's Theology.* Philadelphia: Trinity Press International, 1990.

McGee, Gary B. "Early Pentecostal Missionaries—They Went Everywhere Preaching the Gospel." In *Azusa Street and Beyond: Pentecostal Missions and Church Growth in the Twentieth Century*, edited by L. Grant McClung, 32–36. South Plainfield, NJ: Bridge, 1987.

———. *"This Gospel . . . Shall Be Preached": A History and Theology of Assemblies of God Foreign Missions to 1959.* Springfield, MO: Gospel Publishing House, 1986.

McKnight, Stephen Charles. *Empowering Spirit, Empowering Structures: The Contributions of Noel Perkin to Assemblies of God World Missions.* Eugene, OR: Pickwick, 2023.

Mead, Frank S., and Samuel S. Hill. *Handbook of Denominations in the United States, 11th Edition.* Revised by Craig D. Atwood. Nashville: Abingdon, 2001.

Menzies, William W. *Anointed to Serve: The Story of the Assemblies of God.* Springfield, MO: Gospel Publishing House, 1971.

"Missionary Gleanings." *Pentecostal Evangel* no. 334/335 (Apr. 3, 1920) 12.

"Montana Assembly Sponsors Jail Ministry." *Pentecostal Evangel* no. 2494 (Feb. 25, 1962) 15.

Moseid, John. "A Greeting from Pastor John Moseid." *Herald of Faith* 4.11 (Nov. 1939) 10–11.

Moseid, Mrs. John W. "Tacoma, Wash." *Herald of Faith* 15.5 (May 1950) 11.

Mullett, Charles F. *Biography as History: Men and Movements in Europe Since 1500.* New York: Macmillan, 1963.

"Need a Pastor." *Weekly Evangel* no. 136 (Apr. 22, 1916) 15.

"New Addresses." *Pentecostal Evangel* no. 2208 (Sept. 2, 1956) 28.

Nilson, Sverre. "Utländska Missionen: Lourenco, Marques, Portuguese, East Africa." *Sanningens Vittne* 20.163 (Sept. 1930) 6.

Olivebring, Carl E., comp. *Songs I Love to Sing: Gospel Solos and Duets.* Rockford, IL: The Christian Book Concern, 1955.

Olmstead, William B., et al., eds. *Light and Life Songs, Adapted Especially to Sunday Schools, Prayer Meetings and Other Social Services.* Chicago: S. K. J. Chesbro, 1904.

Ong, Connie Seaward. *Letta in China: Great Is Thy Faithfulness.* Renton, WA: Seaward, 2020.

Parker, Martha Berry. *Tales of Richland, White Bluffs and Hanford: 1805–1943, Before the Atomic Reserve.* Fairfield, MT: Ye Galleon, 1979.

Pelikan, Jaroslav, and Valerie Hotchkiss, eds. "The Westminster Shorter Catechism, 1648." In *Creeds and Confessions of the Reformation Era*, 650–62. Vol. 2, pt. 4 of *Creeds and*

Bibliography

Confessions of Faith in the Christian Tradition. New Haven, CT: Yale University Press, 2003.

Peterson, Dan. "Bethel Temple Heritage Part 2." Sept. 2, 2011. https://danwpeterson.wordpress.com/2011/09/02/bethel-temple-heritage-part-2/.

Plant, Stephen J. "The Theological Role of Biography." *Theology* 126.3 (2023) 164–73. https://doi.org/10.1177/0040571X231171278.

"Rec. C. A. Moseid Resigns [sic]." *Herald of Faith* 12.6 (June 1947) 8.

Reed, David A. "From Bethel Temple, Seattle to Bethel Church, Indonesia: The Missionary Legacy of an Independent Church." In *Global Pentecostal Movements: Migration, Mission, and Public Religion*, edited by Michael Wilkinson, 93–116. Leiden: Brill, 2012.

"Rev. C. A. Moseid." *Herald of Faith* 13.9 (Sept. 1948) 15.

"Rev. Edward Logelin of Minnesota . . . ," *Herald of Faith* 14.6 (June 1949) 10.

Riss, Richard M. *A Survey of 20th-Century Revival Movements in North America.* Peabody, MA: Hendrickson, 1997.

Riveness, J. A. "The Summer Convention in Karlstad." *Herald of Faith* 12.8 (Aug. 1947) 9.

R. L. Polk & Co. *Edmonds City Directory, 1968.* Edmonds, WA: R. L. Polk, 1968.

———. *Edmonds City Directory, 1969.* Edmonds, WA: R. L. Polk, 1969.

———. *Edmonds City Directory, 1970.* Edmonds, WA: R. L. Polk, 1970.

———. *Edmonds City Directory, 1971.* Edmonds, WA: R. L. Polk, 1971.

———. *Edmonds City Directory, 1973.* Edmonds, WA: R. L. Polk, 1973.

———. *Everett (Snohomish County, Wash.) City Directory, 1914.* Everett: R. L. Polk, 1914.

———. *Everett (Snohomish County, Wash.) City Directory, 1915.* Everett: R. L. Polk, 1915.

———. *Everett (Snohomish County, Wash.) City Directory, 1917.* Everett: R. L. Polk, 1917.

———. *Everett (Snohomish County, Wash.) City Directory, 1918.* Everett: R. L. Polk, 1918.

———. *Everett (Snohomish County, Wash.) City Directory, 1919–20.* Everett: R. L. Polk, 1920.

———. *Everett (Snohomish County, Wash.) City Directory, 1922.* Everett: R. L. Polk, 1922.

———. *Everett (Snohomish County, Wash.) City Directory, 1923.* Everett: R. L. Polk, 1923.

———. *Everett (Snohomish County, Wash.) City Directory, 1925.* Everett: R. L. Polk, 1925.

———. *Everett (Snohomish County, Wash.) City Directory, 1926–27.* Everett: R. L. Polk, 1927.

———. *Everett (Snohomish County, Wash.) City Directory, 1928–29.* Everett: R. L. Polk, 1929.

———. *Honolulu City Directory, 1912.* Honolulu: R. L. Polk, 1912.

———. *Hutchinson City Directory, 1933.* Hutchinson, KS: R. L. Polk, 1933.

———. *Hutchinson City Directory, 1937.* Hutchinson, KS: R. L. Polk, 1937.

———. *Hutchinson City Directory, 1947.* Hutchinson, KS: R. L. Polk, 1947.

———. *Rockford City Directory, 1951.* Rockford, IL: R. L. Polk, 1951.

———. *Rockford City Directory, 1952.* Rockford, IL: R. L. Polk, 1952.

———. *Seattle City Directory, 1920.* Seattle: R. L. Polk, 1920.

———. *Seattle City Directory, 1921.* Seattle: R. L. Polk, 1921.

———. *Seattle City Directory, 1923.* Seattle: R. L. Polk, 1923.

———. *Seattle City Directory, 1925.* Seattle: R. L. Polk, 1925.

———. *Seattle City Directory, 1926.* Seattle: R. L. Polk, 1926.

———. *Seattle City Directory, 1927.* Seattle: R. L. Polk, 1927.

———. *Seattle City Directory, 1928.* Seattle: R. L. Polk, 1928.

———. *Seattle City Directory, 1929.* Seattle: R. L. Polk, 1929.

———. *Seattle City Directory, 1930.* Seattle: R. L. Polk, 1930.

———. *Seattle City Directory, 1931.* Seattle: R. L. Polk, 1931.

———. *Seattle City Directory, 1932.* Seattle: R. L. Polk, 1932.

Bibliography

———. *Seattle City Directory, 1933*. Seattle: R. L. Polk, 1933.
———. *Seattle City Directory, 1934*. Seattle: R. L. Polk, 1934.
———. *Seattle City Directory, 1935*. Seattle: R. L. Polk, 1935.
———. *Seattle City Directory, 1936*. Seattle: R. L. Polk, 1936.
———. *Seattle City Directory, 1937*. Seattle: R. L. Polk, 1937.
———. *Seattle City Directory, 1938*. Seattle: R. L. Polk, 1938.
———. *Seattle City Directory, 1939*. Seattle: R. L. Polk, 1939.
———. *Seattle City Directory, 1940*. Seattle: R. L. Polk, 1940.
———. *Seattle City Directory, 1941*. Seattle: R. L. Polk, 1941.
———. *Seattle City Directory, 1942*. Seattle: R. L. Polk, 1942.
———. *Seattle City Directory, 1943-44*. Seattle: R. L. Polk, 1944.
———. *Seattle City Directory, 1948-49*. Seattle: R. L. Polk, 1949.
———. *Seattle City Directory, 1951*. Seattle: R. L. Polk, 1951.
———. *Seattle City Directory, 1953*. Seattle: R. L. Polk, 1953.
———. *Seattle City Directory, 1954*. Seattle: R. L. Polk, 1954.
———. *Seattle City Directory, 1955*. Seattle: R. L. Polk, 1955.
———. *Seattle City Directory, 1959*. Seattle: R. L. Polk, 1959.
———. *Seattle City Directory, 1960*. Seattle: R. L. Polk, 1960.
———. *Seattle City Directory, 1961-62*. Seattle: R. L. Polk, 1962.
———. *Seattle City Directory, 1963*. Seattle: R. L. Polk, 1963.
———. *Seattle City Directory, 1964*. Seattle: R. L. Polk, 1964.
———. *Seattle City Directory, 1965*. Seattle: R. L. Polk, 1965.
———. *Seattle City Directory, 1966*. Seattle: R. L. Polk, 1966.
———. *Seattle City Directory, 1967*. Seattle: R. L. Polk, 1967.
———. *Seattle City Directory, 1968*. Seattle: R. L. Polk, 1968.
———. *Seattle City Directory, 1969*. Seattle: R. L. Polk, 1969.
———. *Seattle City Directory, 1970*. Seattle: R. L. Polk, 1970.
———. *Seattle City Directory, 1971-72*. Seattle: R. L. Polk, 1972.
———. *Seattle City Directory, 1973*. Seattle: R. L. Polk, 1973.
———. *Seattle City Directory, 1974*. Seattle: R. L. Polk, 1974.
———. *Seattle City Directory, 1975*. Seattle: R. L. Polk, 1975.
———. *Seattle City Directory, 1976*. Seattle: R. L. Polk, 1976.
———. *Seattle City Directory, 1977*. Seattle: R. L. Polk, 1977.
———. *Seattle City Directory, 1978*. Seattle: R. L. Polk, 1978.
———. *Seattle City Directory, 1979*. Seattle: R. L. Polk, 1979.
———. *Seattle City Directory, 1980*. Seattle: R. L. Polk, 1980.
———. *Seattle City Directory, 1981*. Seattle: R. L. Polk, 1981.
———. *Seattle City Directory, 1983*. Seattle: R. L. Polk, 1983.
———. *Seattle City Directory, 1985*. Seattle: R. L. Polk, 1985.
———. *Seattle City Directory, 1986*. Seattle: R. L. Polk, 1986.
———. *Seattle City Directory, 1987-88*. Seattle: R. L. Polk, 1988.
———. *Seattle City Directory, 1989-90*. Seattle: R. L. Polk, 1990.
———. *Superior (Douglas County, Wisconsin) City Directory, 1935*. Superior: R. L. Polk, 1935.
———. *Tacoma City Directory, 1947*. Tacoma: R. L. Polk, 1947.
———. *Tacoma City Directory, 1951*. Tacoma: R. L. Polk, 1951.
———. *Tacoma City Directory, 1953*. Tacoma: R. L. Polk, 1953.

Bibliography

———. *Wenatchee (Chelan County, Wash.) City Directory, 1946.* Wenatchee: R. L. Polk, 1946.
———. *Wenatchee (Chelan County, Wash.) City Directory, 1948.* Wenatchee: R. L. Polk, 1948.
———. *Wenatchee (Chelan County, Wash.) City Directory, 1949–50.* Wenatchee: R. L. Polk, 1950.
Robeck, Cecil M., Jr. *The Azusa Street Mission and Revival: The Birth of the Global Pentecostal Movement.* Nashville: Thomas Nelson, 2006.
Robeck, Cecil M., Jr., and Amos Yong, eds. *The Cambridge Companion to Pentecostalism.* New York: Cambridge University Press, 2014.
Robins, R. G. *Pentecostalism in America.* Santa Barbara, CA: Praeger, 2010.
Rodgers, Darrin J. *Northern Harvest: Pentecostalism in North Dakota.* Bismarck: North Dakota District Council of the Assemblies of God, 2003.
Roset, W. L., et al. *The Assemblies of God in Montana.* Butte, MT: Crown Communications, 1976.
Salmon, Emily, and *Dictionary of Virginia Biography*. "J. D. Harris (ca. 1833–1884)." *Encyclopedia Virginia*, Dec. 7, 2020. https://encyclopediavirginia.org/entries/harris-j-d-ca-1833-1884/.
Sing Unto the Lord: Silver Lake Bible Camp. Rockford, IL: The Christian Book Concern, ca. 1955.
Sing Unto the Lord: Silver Lake Bible Camp, Souvenir Copy: 1955, Tabernacle Dedication Year. Rockford, IL: The Christian Book Concern, 1955.
"Sister Florence Bush and mother . . ." *Bridegroom's Messenger* 11.205 (Sept. 1918) 3.
Sittser, Gerald L. *Resilient Faith: How the Early Christian "Third Way" Changed the World.* Grand Rapids: Brazos, 2019.
Soden, Dale E. *Outsiders in a Promised Land: Religious Activists in Pacific Northwest History.* Corvallis: Oregon State University Press, 2015.
Songs of Revival. Rockford, IL/Estherville, IA: The Christian Book Concern, ca. 1952.
Stewart, Adam, ed. *Handbook of Pentecostal Christianity.* DeKalb: Northern Illinois University Press, 2012.
Synan, Vinson, ed. *The Century of the Holy Spirit: 100 Years of Pentecostal and Charismatic Renewal, 1901–2001.* Nashville: Thomas Nelson, 2001.
———. *An Eyewitness Remembers the Century of the Holy Spirit.* Grand Rapids: Chosen, 2010.
———. *The Holiness-Pentecostal Tradition: Charismatic Movements in the Twentieth Century.* Grand Rapids: Eerdmans, 1997.
Tannenberg, Ward. *Let Light Shine Out: The Story of the Assemblies of God in the Pacific Northwest.* N.p.: N.p., 1977.
"Testing Days." *Latter Rain Evangel* 13.9 (June 1921) 15–16.
Teuber, Andrew S. *Tongues of Fire.* Springfield, MO: N.p., ca. 1950s.
Tyson, James L. *The Early Pentecostal Revival: History of Twentieth-Century Pentecostals and the Pentecostal Assemblies of the World, 1901–30.* Hazelwood, MO: Word Aflame, 1992.
Vondey, Wolfgang. *Pentecostal Theology: Living the Full Gospel.* London: Bloomsbury T & T Clark, 2018.
———, ed. *The Routledge Handbook of Pentecostal Theology.* Abingdon: Routledge, 2020.
Wacker, Grant. *Heaven Below: Early Pentecostals and American Culture.* Cambridge, MA: Harvard University Press, 2001.

Bibliography

Wesley Center Online. "Jerry Miles Humphrey." https://wesley.nnu.edu/other-theologians/jerry-miles-humphrey/.

Wilkinson, Michael, ed. *Brill's Encyclopedia of Global Pentecostalism*. Boston: Brill, 2021.

Wilson, B. P., comp. *Early Pentecostal and Assemblies of God Missionaries of the Northwest District*. N.p.: N.p., 1983.

Winsett, Robert E., ed. *Christ Exalted in Song*. Dayton: R. E. Winsett, 1924.

Yeager, Jonathan, ed. *The Oxford Handbook of Early Evangelicalism*. New York: Oxford University Press, 2022.

Young, Susan. "'Sing On, Pray On': The Life of Gospel Songwriter Thoro Harris." Shiloh Museum of Ozark History, YouTube, Nov. 17, 2021. https://youtu.be/9LsQoSR6C74?si=ku_aCEk4pWp_hcSJ.

Index

Aberdeen, WA, 38
Addielee, OK, 153
Africa, 101
African American Pentecostalism, 33
    see also Harris, Thoro D.
    see also Henson, Lee
    see also racism
    see also Sanders, Mary
Algona, WA, 31
Allard, L. B., 106
altar calls, 14, 39, 57
Anglicanism, 137
apostles,
    in the Bible, xv, 10–11, 25n34, 28–30, 32–33, 43, 50, 50n49, 53, 54, 68, 71, 72, 89, 105, 114–15, 136, 137–38, 137n106
    modern-day, 113, 118–19, 149
Apostolic Faith, The, 19
Apostolic Faith Mission (Portland, OR), 18–19
Apostolic Faith Movement, 138
Apostolic Faith Rescue Mission (Honolulu, HI), 111
Applegate, Annie Belle, 52–53, 56–57, 58, 66, 148, 151, 151n46
Argue, A. H., 13–14, 27 n 50, 39, 39n113
Argue, Watson, Sr., 13–14
Argue, Zelma, 13
Ashworth, R. F., 155–56, 155n78
    see also United Full Gospel Crusade (Seattle, WA)
Assemblies of God, General Council (denomination), 20, 21, 36, 48, 52, 56, 65 n 49, 81–82n30, 132, 153, 158
Assembly of God church,
    Enumclaw, WA, 150
    Goldendale, WA, 156
    Grand Junction, CO, 150
    Kittitas, WA, 80–81, 155
    Lake Stevens, WA, 158
    Omak, WA, 110, 111n110
    Pomeroy, WA, 154
    Tonasket, WA, 110
    Wenatchee, WA, 109–11, 110–11n108, 113, 122, 129, 158
Assembly of God Gospel Tabernacle (Sioux Falls, SD), 159
atonement, 24, 87, 115–16, 129, 135
Auburn, WA, 27, 31
Augusta, MT, 47, 59, 83, 85
awakening, spiritual, 11, 35–36
Azusa Street Mission (Los Angeles, CA), 18–19, 22, 34, 35, 64, 65n49, 104, 136–37
Azusa Street Revival, 15, 33, 38, 55, 104, 136–37

Baker, Ralph, 155
Baldwin, Cora May, 35, 45, 55, 109, *165*
Baldwin, Jay, 35, 37–38, 40, 45, 55, *165*
Baldwin, Marie, *see* Knutson, Marie
Baldwin, Vera, *see* Blair, Vera May
Baldwin, Wesley, 36–37
Ballard Gospel Tabernacle (Seattle, WA), 126

207

Index

Ballard Pentecostal Tabernacle (Jones Avenue, Seattle, WA), 99–100, 157
baptism of the Holy Spirit, 9–13, 16, 66, 71, 105, 114, 115, 135
    connection to Acts 2 (Pentecost), 10, 11, 16–17, 17 n 67, 56, 57, 95n7, 105n71, 113
    experiences/testimonies of, 14–15, 36, 39, 57, 64, 65n49, 69, 100, 135
    in the Bible, 10, 11
    instances of, 13, 19, 20, 22, 24, 27, 31, 38, 57, 64, 70, 94, 110, 124 (*see also* baptism of the Holy Spirit, experiences/testimonies of)
    refilling with the Holy Spirit, 94, 94–95n7
    relationship to Wesleyan-Holiness theology, 11–13, 18–19, 23
    relationship to water baptism, 9–11
    tongues, 10, 11, 15, 16–17, 39, 56, 95n7
baptism, water, 2–3, 37, 58, 65 n 49, 71, 78, 115, *171*
    in Jesus' name only, *see* Oneness Pentecostalism
    in the Bible, 9–11
    relationship to Holy Spirit baptism, 9–11
    trinitarian formula, 9, 65n49, 66
Beardsley, Carl A., 48
Belknap, IL, 64, 69
Bethany Baptist Church (Seattle, WA), 126
Bethel Pentecostal Assembly (Tacoma, WA), 102, 157
Bethel Temple,
    Ferndale, WA, 157
    Seattle, WA, 7–9, 13–14, 18, 19, 26, 27 (*see also* Pine Street Mission)
Beulah Heights Bible and Missionary Training School (North Bergen, NJ), 36n101
Bible, *see* Scriptures, holy (authority and significance of)
Bilhorn, Peter, 124
Billings, MT, 47, 51, 52–53, 57, 58, 66, 151
Black Diamond, WA, 31, 33–34, 51, 74–75, 85
Blair, Vera May, 36, 86, *165*

blood of Jesus, *see* atonement
Bloomington Temple (Minneapolis, MN), 102
    see also Full Gospel Pentecostal Assembly (Minneapolis, MN)
    see also Full Gospel Temple (Minneapolis, MN)
Bonhoeffer, Dietrich, 90
"born again," *see* conversion
Bowman, ND, 79, 122, 126
Bridgeport, WA, 75, 77–79, 82, 154
Brun, Ella M., 98
Brun, Elma O., 98n28
Buckingham, Arthur, 104
Butte, MT, 51, 66n55

Cadott, WI, 129
Calvary Pentecostal Faith Mission, 151, 154
Calvary Temple (Winnipeg, Canada), 13
Canada, 13, 20–21, 40, 66, 74, 94, 113–14
Catholicism, *see* Roman Catholicism
Carlsen, Sanford, 152, 152n54
Carlson, Carl G., 34, 38–39, 38n111, 111n108
Carlson, Reuben J., 38n111, 111n108
Cashmere, WA, 110, 153, 154
charismatic gifts
    see baptism of the Holy Spirit, tongues
    see healing, divine
    see miracles
charity, *see* rescue missions
China, 111–12
Christian and Missionary Alliance, 20, 23n24
Christian Book Concern, The, 127–29, 131
Christmas, 49, 64, 79
church polity, 16, 73n87, 118
church planting, 8n34, 19, 20–21, 20n7, 26n46, 40n116, 52, 65n49, 67, 69, 77, 80–81, 84, 110, 126, 149, 153–55, 159
City Church (Kirkland, WA), 9
City Gospel Mission (Great Falls, MT), 42
    see also Full Gospel Assembly (Great Falls, MT)

Index

Civil War (American), 123
conversion, 2–3, 3n11, 12, 24, 35, 47, 52, 65, 70, 75, 94, 135, 146
Coulee City, WA, 75, 78, 153
Crawford, Florence, 18–19
Custer, MT, 51–52, 58, 59

Date, Henry, 124
Davenport, WA, 77
Davis, Leslie, 155
Dearborn, MI, 70
demons (evil spirits), *see* spiritual warfare
Devil, *see* spiritual warfare
Disciples of Christ (denomination), 37n101
Dry Run, IN, 153
Duluth Gospel Tabernacle (Duluth, MN), 98n28
Durham, William Howard, 64–65n49
   see also Finished Work theology
Dust Bowl (North Dakota), 79

Eastern Orthodoxy, 8n31, 137
ecclesiology, 71–72
   see also Knutson, Oscar M., ecclesiology
Edgemon, Frank R., 78–79, 154–55
Edmonds, WA, 131, 139
Ellensburg, WA, 80, 155
Ellis Island, NY, 4
Erickson, Elmer C., 98, 99, 102
eschatology, 3n10, 17, 66, 72, 104, 129, 137, 151
   see also Fourfold Gospel
Estherville, IA, 69–73, 75–76, 82, 96, 127–28, 148, 152–53
ethnic diversity, 33–34
Eureka Springs, AR, 123, 124–25, 161
Evangel Temple (Seattle, WA), 126
Evangelical Free Lutheran Church (Norway), 2, 136n101
evangelism, *see* traveling evangelism
Everett, WA, 31, 34, 37–40, 45, 80–81, 131
Ewart, Frank J., 64–65n49

Fairfield Community Church (Fairfield, MT), 5–6
Fairfield Gospel Tabernacle (Fairfield, MT), 48
   see also Beardsley, Carl. A.
Fairfield, MT, 5–6, 19, 25, 26, 47–48
"false teachers," *see* scandal
Faux, William M., 35–37, 36–37n101
female ordination, *see* women
Ferguson, IA, 69
Feuk, John, 22, 102
Finished Work theology, 64–65n49
   see also Durham, William Howard
First Norwegian Methodist Church (Seattle, WA), 6–7
   see also Vereide, Abraham
foreign missions, 17, 37n101, 100, 101, 111–12, 160
Fort Benton, MT, 103
Fourfold Gospel, 23, 28
   see also Full Gospel
   see also Wesleyan-Holiness tradition
Foursquare Gospel Church (Seattle, WA), 126
free will (human responsibility), 120
Fremont Tabernacle (Seattle, WA), 126
Full Gospel, 23, 23n25, 72, 152
   see also Fourfold Gospel
Full Gospel Assembly
   Great Falls, MT, 21–24 (*see also* City Gospel Mission (Great Falls, MT))
   Huron, SD, 61 (*see also* Huron Gospel Tabernacle (Huron, SD))
Full Gospel Assembly Church (Hutchinson, KS), 130
Full Gospel Assembly of God (Muskegon, MI), 81–82n30
Full Gospel Christian Assembly (Okanogan, WA), 96–98, 100–101, 104, 105–107, 108–110, 113, 121, 126, 159, 159–160n112, *177–79*
   Bowling alley building (521 2nd Ave South), 97–98, 97n23, 100–101, 105–106, *177–78*
   New church building (4th and Tyee), 106–107, 109, *178–79*

Index

Full Gospel Church (Cashmere, WA), 110
Full Gospel Mission
   Estherville, IA, 69–73, 75–76, 96, 152–53
   Walla Walla, WA, 157
Full Gospel Mission House of Prayer (Ballard Avenue, Seattle, WA), 86, 156
Full Gospel Pentecostal Assembly (Minneapolis, MN), 102
   see also Bloomington Temple (Minneapolis, MN)
   see also Full Gospel Temple (Minneapolis, MN)
Full Gospel Press, 87, 100
Full Gospel Tabernacle
   Cut Bank, MT, 84
   Spanaway, WA, 154
   St. James, MN, 153
Full Gospel Temple (Minneapolis, MN), 102
   see also Bloomington Temple (Minneapolis, MN)
   see also Full Gospel Pentecostal Assembly (Minneapolis, MN)
Full Gospel Testimony, The, 66, 98n28, 136n101

Gerla, R. J., 110–111n108
German Baptist Church (Startup, WA), 63
German Methodist Episcopal congregations, 63
Glad Tidings Rescue Mission (Great Falls, MT), 48–50
global evangelization, see foreign missions
glossolalia, see baptism of the Holy Spirit, tongues
Good News, The, 83
Gospel Church, The, 52
gospel publishing
   see Guth, A. D., printing ministry
   see Knutson, Oscar M., printing ministry
Grace Full Gospel Church (Coulee City, WA), 153
Grace Gospel Church (Cashmere, WA), 153
Great Commission, 9, 33
Great Depression, 45–46, 48
Great Falls, MT, 4–5, 20–25, 40n116, 42–44, 47–49, 64–66, 82, 105n71, 149
Green Lake Camp Meeting (Seattle, WA), 27, 27n50
Grice, Cecil E., 154
Grice, Lois Edgemon, 154
Guge, Effie, 70
Guge, Lawrence F., 96, 153
Guge, Martin, 76
Guge, William, 70–71
Guth, A. D., 22, 70–71, 73, 122, 127, 130, 136n101, 148, 179
   biographical sketch, 64–69, 152–53
   printing ministry, 22, 98n28, 136n101, 186

hagiography, xi, 143, 143–44n3, 45
Hansen, Hans, 39
Hansen, Harold E., 109, 111–13, 159–161, 159–160n112
Hansen, Letta Teuber, 112–13, 159–61, 160n112
Hansen, Margaret, 111–12
Harbor City Foursquare Church (Lomita, CA), 160
Harris, Thoro D., 123–26, 127, 129, 132, 161, *180*
Hart, Clarence W., 31, 74–75, 78, 153–54
Hauge, Hans Nielsen, 3n11
Hays, D. R., 52
healing, divine, 14, 23–24, 28–31, 51, 52, 55, 129, 138, 140n116, 158–59, 161
heaven, xv–xvi, 9, 12, 23, 29, 33, 90, 104, 115, 117, 135, 141, 145
Heidt, Linus, 75–76, 96, 152–53
hell, 23, 89, 134, 135
Henson, Lee, 34, 59, 84–86, 109, 148, 156–57, 172–73
Herald of Faith, 94
His Loving Care, 60, 82, 108, 129n56, 131–32, 143–44, 147–48

Index

history (in the Christian tradition), xi–xiv, xvi, 143–45, 147
Hokanson, A. Ephraim, 160n112
Horness, Marcus, 81n30
Humphrey, J. M., 134
Huron, SD, 61–64, 67, 75, 82, 127, 148, 152
Huron Gospel Tabernacle (Huron, SD), 61
Hutchinson, KS, 130, 152

immigration, 4, 63, 80, 111
Independent Assemblies of God, 93–94, 98–99, 102, 126n34, 157–58
Independent Pentecostal church,
  Huron, SD, 152
  Sioux Falls, SD, 96
Interdenominational Gospel Station (Great Falls, MT), 44

jail ministry, 21, 38, 152
Japan, 88, 111–12
"Jesus Only" doctrine
  see Oneness Pentecostalism
Johnson, Everett A., 103
Johnson, Inga K., 42, 44, 48–50, 53, 56–57, 84, 103
Johnson, John A., 42
Johnson, John A., Jr., 103
Jones, William Paul, 149
justification, see Wesleyan-Holiness tradition, justification

Kettle Falls, WA, 84, 86, 156, *173*
Kibsgaard, Elvina
  see Knutson, Elvina
Knutson, Andrew O., 1–2, 4–6, 47, 95, 107–8, *164*
Knutson, Elvina, 1–2, 4, 4 n 14, 6, 47, 107, *164*
Knutson, Fern, see Olson, Fern
Knutson, Harda, 76
Knutson, Inga
  see Johnson, Inga K.
Knutson, Lloyd, x, 45, 85, 121, 128, 130–31, 141, *166–67, 169, 171, 173, 175–76*

Knutson, Lois, 130
Knutson, Marie, 27n50, 55, 77, 80–81, 109, 125, 143
  business ventures, 130
  early life, 34–41
  later years, 139–42
  ministry with Oscar, 42, 44–48, 57, 58–62, 64, 70, 128–32
  photographs of, *164–67, 169, 173–76, 188–89*
Knutson, Oscar M.,
  baptism of the Holy Spirit, 9, 13–15
  call to ministry, 25–27
  church history, view of, 135–37, 136n101
  ecclesiology, 113–18
  marriage/divorce, view on, 133–34
  Pentecostal movement, view of, 104, 135–38
  physical appearance, 95, *163–69, 171, 173, 174–77, 180, 188–89*
  printing/publishing ministry, 68–69, 83, 87, 100, 126–29, 130–31, 132–34, 143, 156, 158, *180–87*
  trust in God's provision, 26, 46, 59–60, 69, 125
  war, theology of, 87–92
Knutson, Ragna, 4
Kristensen, Karl, 101
Krob, Lois, see Knutson, Lois

Lantz, Joseph, 20–24, 40n116, 42, 44, 65, 105n71, 148, 149–50
Larson, Peter, 51
latter rain theology (Pentecostal), 104–5, 105n71
Latter Rain Movement, 113–15, 118
Laughery, Mrs. C. B., 51
Lethbridge, AB, Canada, 21, 40n116, 74
lives of saints, see hagiography
Livingston, MT, 47
Logelin, Edward, 126, 159, 160n112
Luther, Martin, 136
Lutheranism, 1–2, 3n11, 70, 136n101

Mennonites, 20, 62, 64
Menzies, William E., 61

211

Index

Methodism, 6–7, 18, 35n95, 63, 70, 74
Meyer, George, 124
Midwest, xvii, 35, 37n101, 45, 63, 67, 75, 79, 81, 122, 152–53
Milford, NE, 62
miracles, 29–30, 55, 59–60, 85, 108, 139–40, 159
   see also healing, divine
Mission Covenant Church (Cook, MN), 150
missionaries, *see* foreign missions
Missionary Church Association, 20
Mitchell, SD, 60, 64, 67, 69
Moor, Alfred, 79–80
Moseid, C. Albert, 95, 98–100, 101, 109, 121, 157
Moseid, John W., 94–95, 99, 100, 101–2, 109, 157–58
Mountain Lake, MN, 153
Muskegon Heights, MI, 81–83, 81–82n30
Music, xvii, 7–8n31, 13, 31, 68–69, 122, 123, 124–27, 132, 161, 175–76
   gospel songs (testimony songs), 7, 7–8n31, 123–25,
   hymns, 5, 8n31
   songbooks and hymnals, 22, 65–66, 68–69, 122–23, 124, 126–29, 129n57–58, 132, 137, 156, 158, 161n123, *185–87*

Naper Pentecostal Church (Naper, NE), 75
National Prayer Breakfast, 6n24
Nelson, Jack C., 27–28, 27n50, 31–32, 34, 40, 51, 56, 68, 74, 85, 94, 148, 150–51, 154, *168*
New England, 129, 129n56
"New Issue, The"
   see Oneness Pentecostalism
New Order of the Latter Rain, *see* Latter Rain Movement
Norway, 1–4, 7, 80, 111, 136, 139

Offiler, William H., 8
Olson, Alvin, 121–22

Olson, Fern, 41, 44, 121–22, 127, 141, 157, *166–67, 169, 171, 173, 175–76,* 186
Okanogan, WA, 96–98, 100–101, 103–107, 109–11, 113–14, 121–22, 126, 148, 159–60, 159–60n112
Omak, WA, 100, 109, 110–11, 113, 159, 161
Oneness Pentecostalism, 65n49, 66n58
Oroville, WA, 154
Othello, WA, 155–56
Overland, Tom, 80–81, 155–56

Pacific Northwest, ix, xvii, 6n24, 9, 38n111, 45, 63, 67, 75, 77, 79–80, 122, 130, 153
pacificism, 88
Palmer, Beulah M., 38, 39
Palmer, Phoebe, 55
Panic of 1907, 4
patriotism, 63, 87
Pendleton, OR, 80
Pentecost (great outpouring of the Holy Spirit/Acts 2), 10–11, 16, 17n67, 29, 33, 54, 56, 72, 95n7, 104–5, 105n71, 113, 137
Pentecostal Assemblies of the World, 98
Pentecostal Christian Assembly (Tacoma, WA), 28
Pentecostal Mission (Jackson Street, Seattle, WA), 150–51
   see also Calvary Pentecostal Faith Mission
Pfitzer, Alexander, 106
Philadelphia Church (Seattle, WA), 126, 139
Pine Street Mission (Seattle, WA), 8, 27, 39n113
   see also Bethel Temple (Seattle, WA)
"pioneering a new work," *see* church planting
Pleasant Valley Church (O'Neill, NE), 152
Pontiac, MI, 45, 58, 64, 70, 79
Powell, WY, 57
prayer, x, xii, 5, 6n24, 7–8, 8n31, 13, 14, 15, 21, 24, 28, 30, 34–36, 38–39, 51, 57, 70–71, 74, 85, 91, 94,

Index

94n7, 97, 100, 116, 137, 139–40, 152, 159, 162
preaching, 3, 3n11, 12, 13–14, 25, 26, 29, 31, 36, 38, 42–44, 45, 52, 54, 55, 59, 62, 66–67, 69, 79, 84–85, 94, 95n7, 100, 101, 104, 109, 113, 122, 134, 138, 149, 152, 158, 159, 160
Presbyterianism, 35n95, 70, 74
prison ministry, *see* jail ministry
prophets,
    in the Bible, 43, 54, 56, 104, 105n71, 107, 113
    modern-day, 118–19
Prosperity Gospel, 90n87
provision, divine, *see* Knutson, Oscar M., trust in God's provision

racism, 32–34, 85, 156n88
    see also ethnic diversity
radio ministry, 61, 152
Rake, G. H., 61–62
Ramseyer, J. E., 20n9
Rapid City, SD, 60
Rasmussen, A. W., 102
Rasmussen, Harry, 97–98, 106
Rathdrum, ID, 63
refilling with the Holy Spirit,
    see baptism of the Holy Spirit, refilling with the Holy Spirit
repentance, xiv, 8n31, 29, 31, 62, 71, 74–75, 87, 88, 91
    see also conversion
rescue missions, 26, 26n46, 42, 44–45, 48–50, 111
revival, 3n11, 10–11, 15, 30, 33, 38, 55, 73, 75, 87, 95n7, 101, 136–37
Richfield, WA, 63
Rockford, IL, 128, 130
Roman Catholicism, 8n31, 24, 84, 137, 145
Roth, Erma, 100
Rowe, James, 124

Salem Full Gospel Church (Brooklyn, NY), 102
Salem Heights Community Church (Salem, OR), 153

sanctification, *see* Wesleyan-Holiness tradition, sanctification
Sanders, Mary, 34, 39, 56, *168*
Sanningens Vittne, 99
scandal, 36–37n101, 42–43, 60–61, 81–83, 82n30
Scandinavian Assemblies of God, 94, 99, 102
schism, 65n49, 66n58, 136
Schmid, Henry G., 62–64, 152
Scriptures, holy (authority and significance of), xii–xiii, xvii, 3, 3n10, 9–11, 9n35, 20, 23–24, 29, 30, 36, 42, 43, 46, 50, 53–55, 58, 71–72, 87–88, 90–91, 94–95, 95n7, 101, 105n71, 107, 113–14, 118–19, 133, 138, 139, 147, 150, 151n46, 158
Seaward, Frederick, 160
Seaward, Margaret, 160
Seattle, WA, *passim.*
Second Coming of Christ, *see* eschatology
Second Sino-Japanese War, 112
Selected Gospel Songs, 22, 65, 122, 127, 186
Selected Gospel Songs, Number Two, 127–29, 129n57, *186*
Sermon on the Mount, 43, 46, 60, 71, 72
Seymour, William J., 18–19
    see also Azusa Street Mission (Los Angeles, CA)
    see also Azusa Street Revival
Silverton, OR, 85
Simmonett, Charles, 21, 40n116
Simpson, A. B., 23n24
Singapore, 160
Sioux City, IA, 69, 75
Sortland Evangelical Church (Sortland, Norway), 2
Spirit Lake, IA, 152
spiritual biography, xi–xvii, 143–44, 146n15, 148–49, 162
spiritual warfare, 16, 31–34, 43, 57, 89, 127, 134, 135, 151
Springfield, MO, 37n101, 132, 158
Stanwood, WA, 63
Sterling, KS, 22, 65
street meetings, 73, 75, *170*

Index

Sunny Side Church (Sioux Falls, SD), 153
Superior Gospel Tabernacle (Superior, WI), 99
Superior, IA, 73

Tacoma, WA, 28, 45, 63, 94, 100, 102, 109, 110, 157–58
tent meetings, 66, 84, 85, 96, 110, 126, 129, 138, 158–59, *173*
Teuber, Adolph C., 109, 110
Teuber, Andrew S., 100, 105, 109–11, 112, 113, 122, 129, 158–59
Teuber, Letta, *see* Hansen, Letta Teuber
Tollefsen, Margaret Singe, *see* Hansen, Margaret
tongues, speaking in, *see* baptism of the Holy Spirit, tongues
traveling evangelism, 52, 64, 66–68, 82, 84, 98, 102, 128, 138, *169*
Trinity, xv, 65n49, 66, 66n58, 98, 116, 135, 147
　see also baptism, water, trinitarian formula

Union church (White Bluffs, WA), 35, 35n95
United Full Gospel Crusade (Seattle, WA), 126, 156, 185

Valdez, A. C., 99, 102
Van Loon, Harry, 64–65n49
Vereide, Abraham, 6

Warner, Wayne, 132
Wells Gospel Tabernacle (Wells, MN), 152

Wesleyan-Holiness tradition, 8n31, 11–12, 16, 19, 23, 28, 65n49, 134
　justification, 11–12
　sanctification, 12, 18, 19, 23n25, 65n49, 101
　see also Fourfold Gospel
Westgate Chapel (Edmonds, WA), 139
Westminster Assembly of God Church (Seattle, WA), 139
White Bluffs, WA, 35–37, 39, 81
Windom, MN, 73, 75, 153
Winsett, R. E., 123, 129
women
　in Pentecostal tradition, 55–57
　in the Bible, 53–54
　see also Applegate, Annie
　see also Baldwin, Cora May
　see also Johnson, Inga K.
　see also Palmer, Beulah M.
　see also Palmer, Phoebe
　see also Roth, Erma
　see also Sanders, Mary
　see also Woodworth-Etter, Maria
Word of Faith Movement, 90n87
World War I, 63
World War II, 86–87, 90, 93, 95, 97, 112
Wood, Idell H., 40
Woodworth-Etter, Maria, 55, 124
Wyoming, 52, 57

xenolalia, *see* baptism of the Holy Spirit, tongues

Yacolt, WA, 35–36, 39
Yakima, WA, 155–56

www.ingramcontent.com/pod-product-compliance
Lightning Source LLC
Chambersburg PA
CBHW070250230426
43664CB00014B/2477